D1562788

American Crime Fiction

Peter Swirski

American Crime Fiction

A Cultural History of Nobrow Literature as Art

palgrave
macmillan

Peter Swirski
Hong Kong

ISBN 978-3-319-30107-5   ISBN 978-3-319-30108-2   (eBook)
DOI 10.1007/978-3-319-30108-2

Library of Congress Control Number: 2016943196

Cover illustration © Trigger Image / Alamy Stock Photo

Printed on acid-free paper

This Palgrave Macmillan imprint is published by Springer Nature
The registered company is Springer International Publishing AG Switzerland

This book is dedicated to all my students, past and present

CONTENTS

LIST OF IMAGES

CHAPTER 1

Nobrow: Contents and Discontents

THE MOST OSSIFIED POPULAR GENRE OF ALL

Almost half of all the books ever printed and almost half of all the word-smiths who have ever put pen to paper have come onto the scene after the death of Raymond Chandler.

Despite perennial announcements of the death of the book, in the second decade of the third millennium the volume of the printed word virtually defies understanding. The number of new books published each year around the world exceeds three million. In 2013 more than a million and a quarter titles, old and new, were published in the USA alone—about five times more than a little over a decade before. A cross-check of publishers' lists suggests that between 400 and 500 genre paperbacks land every month on America's bookstands.

By now Google has digitized approximately 15 million of the conservative estimates of 150 million books published in the world since the invention of the Gutenberg press. The actual number could be as high as 250 million: a quarter billion individual titles, plus millions more added year in, year out. In 2011 the British Library teamed up with Google to put another quarter million of uncopyrighted books, some forty million pages in total, online. With the Internet colossus footing the bill, other libraries are lining up to get in on the action.

© The Editor(s) (if applicable) and The Author(s) 2016
P. Swirski, *American Crime Fiction*,
DOI 10.1007/978-3-319-30108-2_1

Any way you count it, this explosion of the printed word adds up to the fact that almost half of all the books ever printed and almost half of all the wordsmiths who have ever put pen to paper have come onto the scene after the death of Raymond Chandler. Put differently, almost half of all the writers who have ever lived are living still. Factor in the population growth and the lengthening of the average lifespan and this fraction is bound to grow asymptotically until the day when nearly all writers in history will be creating in the eternal present.[1]

Like it or not, we live in the age of infoglut and infogluttony. The problem with that for the literary tastemakers and gatekeepers is that, although the proportion of what is culturally valuable to the total may not have changed over the ages (and how would you know?), multiplying both a millionfold has the effect of obscuring the former as effectively as if it was not there at all. It may take a long time, but you can be sure to find a proverbial good book in a thousand. But you will never find a million good books in a billion.

These days, with ever more titles in circulation and buyers spoiled for choice, it takes a lot more than a knack for telling a story to stand out as a storyteller. Even established names in the business, from John Grisham to the Bone-Farm forensic anthropologist Jefferson Bass, who previously relied on public relations departments of their publishing houses, now hire their own promo teams to help them and their brand stand out from the crowd. The only thing that has not changed is that big name endorsements still work as authordisiacs, just like they have done since the beginning of time.

When Barack Obama bought an armful of books on his holidays at Martha's Vineyard in 2011, they included a selection of country noirs by Daniel Woodrell, which have been flying off the shelves since. Obama's Democratic predecessor, that consummate populist *and* intellectual Bill Clinton, also enjoyed his mysteries, even as he curried presidential gravitas by joking about his cheap-thrills addiction. Still, two thumbs up from a fan in the Oval Office turned Walter Mosley and his Negro private investigator, Easy Rawlins, into instant celebrities.

Another symptom of the infoglut is that branding now trumps the actual contents of a book or a book review. For recognized authors the system still works, after a fashion. Plaudits in the *New York Times Book Review* or the *Los Angeles Times Book Review* still tend to pump up sales, whereas pans tend to bring them down. For everyone else it is pure *Alice in Wonderland*. Two thumbs up or two thumbs down? Both will give you legs. And while there is nothing new in the old saw that any publicity is good publicity, the extent to which the literary system fights a rearguard battle against the inundation of print is.[2]

Though it does not make the headlines, this state of affairs has dramatic repercussions for publishers, critics, and readers at large. Data I have collected on all continents save Africa and Antarctica suggest that even avid bookworms rarely average reading more than a book a week. Erring on the side of caution and assuming double that plus optimal conditions—no rest, no re-reads, no memory loss—you still end up with only about 100 books a year, or 7000 in a lifetime. This is the upper value on the literary database on which tastemakers can base their judgments. In reality, it is of course much smaller.

A few thousand against a quarter billion sounds pretty pathetic, even when you factor in that a sizeable portion of the total is nonfiction (not that nonfiction cannot be acclaimed as artsy—witness the Nobel Prizes for Literature in 1950, 1953, and 2015). And it is at this point that cultural conservatives traditionally execute a methodological sleight of hand to stave off the problem. Can't read all that is out there? Don't need to. All you need to do is convince yourself that it is formulaic and cheap, and 98 % of literature can be tossed out of the window.[3]

The argument is simple—almost aphoristic: once you have read one genre paperback, you have read them all. Naturally, this line of reasoning would be accurate if books were like electrons, every one identical and invariant to the examining eye. It is true, after all, that once you have seen one electron, you have seen them all. Poke it and probe it till Judgment Day and it will still show the same face as today. But books are not like that. What from the Ivory Tower looks like a homogeneous mass, from up close reveals distinctions as profound as those professed on behalf of the literary classics.

Although few intellectuals would state their case so forthrightly, especially nowadays when eclecticism and syncretism rule the day, sooner or later the latent bias comes to the fore. Philosopher and art critic Dennis Dutton typifies this scratch-a-progressivist-and-watch-a-purist-bleed attitude when, laying his aesthetic cards on the table in *The Art Instinct* (2009), he declares that "high art traditions demand individuality".[4] The suppressed premise? The unvariegated masses of pulp fiction do not and can, therefore, be dismissed en masse. Dutton holds these truths to be so self-evident that he does not even argue in their defense, content to advance them as a fiat instead.

Except that popular art prizes individuality no less than high art. No need to look further than arguably the most ossified popular genre of all: crime mystery. It does not take a connoisseur to individuate the urbane quirkiness of Donald Westlake, the gradient-defying villains of Elmore Leonard, the liposuctioned aesthetic of James Ellroy, the post-comradely flavor of Martin Cruz Smith, the jigsaw forensics of Kathy Reichs, the kosher-deli comedy of Kinky Friedman, the Möbius-twisted mind games of Jeffrey Deaver, the public conscience of Ruth Rendell, the Creole gumbo of James Lee Burke, the new Bostonians of Dennis Lehane—and so on, and so forth.

Conceding that crime fiction fosters individuality would make Dutton's argument (tautologically) true at the cost of abandoning his distinction between genre fiction and high art. But his list of literary greats—Homer, Shakespeare, Cervantes, Austen, Dostoyevsky—shows that he is locked up there with Rapunzel in a high tower, lording over a forest of literary entertainment. People make art to please one another, he concedes a little later on. "There is a cool *objectivity*, however, about the greatest works of art: the worlds they create have little direct regard for our insistent wants and needs; still less do they show any intention on the part of their creators to ingratiate themselves with us" (241).

So this is how to differentiate art from schmart. If it disregards human wants and needs, it is a timeless masterpiece. If it ingratiatingly aims to please, it is not. Where does it leave Shakespeare whose Prospero hedges in the Epilogue to *The Tempest* that the players' aim was merely to please, echoing the end of *Twelfth Night* where Feste sings of striving "to please you every day"?[5] In fact, if art funnels something universal in terms of our biological wants and needs—and Dutton's Darwinist theses leave no doubt that such is the case—then great art must do so as well, which in his terms would mean that it is mere entertainment.

OF THE STANDARD OF TASTE

Literary critics can reliably say a number of things about a work of literature, except whether it is good.

The charge that popular fiction is unindividuated and formulaic is true only to the same extent that it is true of highbrow fiction. After all, what is unindividuated and at what level of comparison? All monasteries are alike by dint of being monasteries, yet if you look more closely, no two are identical and most are not even similar. Likewise, no two mysteries are identical, even if all are alike, once you look at them the right way. What is *Macbeth*, after all, if not *Crime and Punishment* meets "The Tell-Tale Heart"? What is *The Great Gatsby* if not *The Godfather* meets *The Count of Monte Christo?* What is *Tough Guys Don't Dance* if not *Kiss Me, Deadly* meets *Naked Lunch?*

Crime writers create within an established aesthetic that attracts readers by advertising the type of game to be played for their pleasure. A clear analogy with sport stems from the fact that, although in football or basketball the rules of the games are also known ahead of time, fans flock to them all the same just because no one can tell in advance how a particular engagement will play out. Unlike sport, of course, writers can tweak the rules of the game in search of the optimal mix of convention and invention. In this, genre fiction is once again no different from high art, which also prizes formula and (self-)imitation, although under the guise of style.[6]

The annual Bad Hemingway and Faux Faulkner contests could never work—and could never be such riots—without readily identifiable formulas to spoof. Taking advantage of the fact that without formula there is no style, the rules are very simple. Entrants submit one-page samples of Papa's or Pappy's style and the most least masterful among them wins the honors. Crime ace Joseph Wambaugh was only one of the countless parodists who, over the years, had run amok with the Nobelists to the appreciative groans from the judges and kibitzers delighted to see styles reverse-engineered and reputations taken down a notch.

When it comes to genre art and to importing highbrow notions of taste where they do not belong, few missteps, however, can rival that of Ruth Bunzel's in her classic ethnographic study of North American pottery of the Hopi nation. Hopi women—only women decorate pottery—are known for their sophisticated aesthetic, the central component of which is their veneration of originality. With ill-masked disdain, Bunzel reported, however, that their painted designs were essentially identical, often differing in elements so minute as to be almost negligible.

Decrying the sterility of the art and of the art-makers' aesthetics, the critic failed to take into account the tradition—that is, the genre—in which the potters worked. Within that genre, the hallmark of originality is the use of variations on inherited elements. It is as if Bunzel decried Wyatt's variations on the Petrarchan sonnet, or Drayton's variations on Wyatt's, or Surrey's variations on Drayton's, or Sidney's variations on Surrey's, or Shakespeare's variations on Sidney's as sterile. Or, for that matter, Leroux's variations in *Le Mystère De La Chambre Jaune* on Poe's "The Mystery of Marie Rogêt", and the rich tradition of variations on the locked-room mystery in the century hence.

Indeed, if you believe Christopher Booker, the infinite variety of literary storylines hides just seven fundamental plots, albeit in a myriad variants, varieties, and variations. As if to highlight the arbitrariness of all such literary structuralism, after advancing the fundamental seven—rags to riches, voyage and return, tragic overreach, rebirth, comic chaos and happy ending, quest narrative, overcoming the monster—Booker added two more "fundamental" categories: mystery/crime and rebellion (never mind that both are quests to overcome the monster).

Another place where this typology bites the dust is the advent of high modernism or postmodernism with its turn toward autotelism and self-deconstruction, manifest in the focus on the act of telling at the expense of the tale. But once you get past the procrustean schematics, the wealth of literary examples, which range over aboriginal yarns, beast fables and fairy tales, epics from the antiquity, operatic librettos, epistolary novels, Wilkie Collins thrillers, Victorian multi-deckers, and Bollywood blockbusters, clearly exhibit similarities that cut across literary kinds, genres, and not least, brows. So much for high art as a paragon of individuality and for genre art as a paragon of sterility.

Story formulas—structures of incidents, as Aristotle called them—hook us afresh because of our interest in the fundamental patterns of human existence. Essentially unchanged since the beginning of history, these insistent wants and needs account for our unflagging pleasure in consuming storylines familiar from time immemorial. This is what the Russian morphologists and formalists intuited already at the beginning of the twentieth century, even though they could not explain it without the tools of modern evolutionary literary studies (evolist).[7]

Today we know that the answer lies is our universal propensity for thinking in stories—so universal, that it forms an inalienable part of our nature and, as such, an inalienable part of both our emotional and intellectual lives. Percipient as ever, back in 1757 David Hume himself appealed to human universals in a bid to tackle the greatest problem in aesthetics and art: the phenomenology of taste. The general principles, he announced in "Of the Standard of Taste", are uniform in all human beings. Recognizing, naturally, that people are actually given to strident disagreements in aesthetic judgments, he concluded that we must be prone to errors.

Although on his account these errors are systematic in nature, they cannot be innate, since that would contradict his major premise of the principles of good taste being distributed uniformly at birth. All misjudgments of taste must, therefore, be attributed to the coarsening of our natural faculties, either due to disuse or ill-use. This neoplatonic position resurfaces in Hume's remark that inadequate knowledge can distort judgment (sample bias can lead to error), even as he conspicuously neglects to specify what counts as adequate knowledge or even as adequate database.

Recognizing that he has painted himself into a corner, Hume executes a stunning U-turn by admitting that different consumers exhibit different humors, and thus contradicting his first premise of uniformity. He then drives another nail into his coffin by admitting the effects of manners and opinions of the age and country on taste, which is another way of admitting that *de gustibus non est disputandum*. In short, for all his analytical efforts, even as great a thinker as Hume is of no help in elucidating how judgments of taste can reliably transfer from one reader to another—the starting point for the "read one, read them all" school of criticism.

Not much has changed during the intervening two centuries and a half. The highbrows' dismissals of the unread mass of popular fiction always come down to the same methodological sleight of hand: how do you know that pulp fiction is formulaic if you have not read it? And how do you know that it is pulpy in the first place? Reliance on other's judgment of taste could be justified only to the extent that there existed phenomenologically transferrable methods of literary comparison and rating. In their absence, one reader's trash will always remain another's treasure, and literary axiology always a matter of personal—which is to say, subjective—taste.

Literary critics can reliably say a number of things about a work of literature, except whether it is good.[8] T.S. Eliot had the presence of mind to laud *The Great Gatsby* even when the book sold just a quarter of the 75,000 copies that Fitzgerald predicted it would. This was the same Eliot who, as the commissioning editor for Faber, dismissed Orwell's soon-to-be-classic *Animal Farm* as jejune and worthless. In fact, the most reliable thing that can be said about our pantheon is that, in some ways, it is a house of cards. Stochastic regularities make it certain that some of the big names in the canon got there mostly by luck and that others who deserved to get there—those known and unknown—did not.

Every field of study shows bias in favor of reporting statistically significant results (and underreporting corrections to the original faulty findings). In the sciences, this bias typically disappears when repeated studies fail because the original spike was a random outlier. In matters of taste we do not have anything like such a self-correcting mechanism. The point is not necessarily that Fitzgerald was for the most part a ho-hum novelist or

Hemingway an intellectual lightweight. But to shrug off the randomness inherent in the infoglut problem is to shrug off that there were—*must* have been—other Fitzgeralds and Hemingways lost in the same random shuffle of literary history that ossified into the canon.

Image 1.1   The Infoglut Problem. "*To shrug off the randomness inherent in the infoglut problem is to shrug off that there were—must have been—other Fitzgeralds and Hemingways lost in the same random shuffle of literary history that ossified into the canon.*"

THE BERMUDA TRIANGLE

All art, whether highbrow or lowbrow, is a product of convention and invention. All artists, from Shakespeare to Scott Turow, dole out types and formulas.

Surrounded by a growing list of appreciative studies of American crime fiction, it might seem as if the Ivory Tower has already fallen down. In reality, while the ramparts may have been breached in a few places, the battle of the brows is far from over. The elite voices may no longer be as fractious and reactionary as in the postwar decades but, as Dutton's example shows, the prejudices are too deeply ingrained to disappear overnight—and too weighty to be skipped over without a word. Given the sympathetic hearing given to crime fiction's aesthetics and politics in the chapters to come, let us then take the quick pulse of the perennial critiques of popular and, by extension, crime fiction.[9]

Pared down to their essentials, they amount to indictments for commercialism, debasement, corruption, and brainwashing. Popular fiction, we are told, is mass-produced by profit-oriented hacks who gratify the base tastes of a paying audience. Popular fiction borrows from serious fiction, leaving debased culture in its wake, and it lures away potential contributors, depleting high culture's talent pool. Popular fiction, runs the next charge, produces spurious gratification at best and emotional and cognitive damage at worst. Finally, pulp fiction is said to lower the cultural level of the reading public and forge passive and apathetic audiences susceptible to demagoguery and propaganda.[10]

All of which is like the Bermuda Triangle: it makes a good story, but the closer you look at the evidence, the less plausible it looks. Take the first charge: genre publishing is nothing but a mass production line hijacked by corporations bent on dumbing down content with the help of profit-driven hacks. None of which is entirely inaccurate, but neither is it the whole truth. Popular fiction naturally operates on the premise of turning a profit. But how much does it differ from the canon where big names function precisely as trademarks to drum up sales?

Who would think of buying a first draft of a self-glorifying safari memoir (*True at First Light*, 1999) if it were not fronted by the name of Hemingway? The fact is that many did for exactly that reason. Bottom-line pressures may be, in fact, more acute for high art, if only because of its low market appeal, especially nowadays when institutional subsidies are more scarce or just more inclined to go pop. In general, the defense of pure art, which fuels the anti-commercial bias of this critique, fails to explain why profit-driven novelists like Faulkner and Fitzgerald would flock to the greenback pastures of Hollywood.

As for uniformity, although highbrows pride themselves on their individuated tastes, as a social group they form such a small and select audience that the fiction they consume is in many ways as—if not more—homogenous. Let's face it: imitation and formula are no less common in highbrow than in genre fiction. An intellectual who sits down with a minimalist story by Marilyn Robinson knows in advance to expect the same kitchen realism as from Anne Beattie: threadbare style, plotless plot, humdrum dailiness.

All art, whether highbrow or lowbrow, is a product of convention and invention. All artists, from Shakespeare to Scott Turow, dole out types and formulas. The only question is which formulas are used—and how. Tellingly, research shows that even such a loose assembly of prestige literature as the Pulitzer winners displays a number of shared thematic, narrative, and agential schemas. On the other hand, studies indicate that there is no sure-fire formula behind a bestseller—or, what amounts to the same thing, it is untraceable over an anisotropic variety of forms, styles, and genres.[11]

As for the alleged uniformity of genre fiction, its sheer volume determines some of its structural and even aesthetic qualities, such as diversity and originality. As part of the infoglut expansion, crime fiction invades every open literary niche in a self-organizing process known as adaptive radiation. Competing to stand out from the competition, while cashing out (and cashing in on) the conventions that appeal to readers, genre fiction refines and realigns formulas and, in doing so, diversifies to a higher degree than highbrow fiction. Adoption *with* adaption is the winning strategy in the race to the readers' hearts and pockets.

Implicitly recognizing that there really is no such thing as genre formula, some critics have tried to deflect attention from the highbrow penchant for imitation.[12] Schemas in popular culture are thus routinely decried as stereotypes whereas the penchant for formula in Elizabethan tragedies or Italian operas are praised as stylizations. When critics like Adorno browbeat genres for being "patterned and pre-digested", they never condemn the Petrarchan sonnet, as patterned a literary form as any. On the other hand, how predigested is Stanislaw Lem's *The Investigation* or his hardboiled "remake", *The Chain of Chance*, which flout the detective story conventions? Or Lynda LaPlante's *Prime Suspect* series which rewrites the book on the police procedural?

This is not to dispute the existence of CAD Harlequin or thriller factories which manufacture thousands of titles every year by filling out story outlines permutated by algos. Nor is the above to be taken as an en masse validation of aesthetic aspirations that often do not come into play for makers of popular fiction. None of this, however, makes genre synonymous with generic. Popular literature constantly mutates, radiates, and diversifies, in the course of the last century alone, creating such novel varieties of that eternal crowd-pleaser—the crime mystery—as hardboiled, lawyer fiction, Harlem detective, police procedural, urban procedural, legal procedural, country noir, tart noir, mob story, narco-lit, or gangsta (not to mention dozens of subgenres and hybrids).

As far as the charge of alienation is concerned, data indicates the opposite of what doomsayers have long insisted is the case. The cliché of highbrows who create purely for themselves and lowbrows who sell their hides to pander to Mencken's booboisie is simply untenable. Ambitious writers like Chandler or Cain *elect* to create in popular genres both for artistic and economic reasons. As the former pointed out in a letter from 1950, to "exceed the limits of a formula without destroying it is the dream of every magazine writer who is not a hopeless hack".[13]

Many genre novelists are highly educated and skilled artists who for complex socioaesthetic reasons prefer to express their individuality within established forms. Before he wrote *The Postman Always Rings Twice* and *Double Indemnity*, James M. Cain had earned a graduate degree in literature and a living as a college professor, editor of *The New Yorker*, and author of *Our Government*, a collection of satirical essays on politics. Chandler was a polyglot, a whiz in mathematics, an expert in Greek and Roman history and culture, and a literary snob. Later in his life, he even reflected on this intellectual background to his publisher, Hamish Hamilton:

> It would seem that a classical education might be rather a poor basis for writing novels in a hard-boiled vernacular. I happen to think otherwise. A classical education saves you from being fooled by pretentiousness, which most current fiction is too full of.[14]

Neither is it true that highbrows do not pander. When on 26 March 1931, the *Memphis Evening Appeal* crucified *Sanctuary* as an "inhuman monstrosity of a book that leaves one with the impression of having been vomited bodily", it reflected the extent to which Faulkner had succeeded in galvanizing the public with crimes and depravity that exceeded even Al Capone's. In general, creators who express their values in the idiom congenial to mass readership often enjoy more creative latitude than their highbrow counterparts. After all, financial success can liberate artists to pursue their cherished projects—which need not at all be highbrow in nature.

Image 1.2   Unemployed men queue outside a depression soup kitchen opened in Chicago by Al Capone, 1931. "*When on March 26, 1931, the Memphis Evening Appeal flailed Sanctuary as an 'inhuman monstrosity of a book that leaves one with the impression of having been vomited bodily,' it simply reflected the extent to which Faulkner had succeeded in galvanizing the reading public with crimes and depravity that exceeded even Al Capone's.*"

Damned If You Do and Damned If You Don't

Borrowing and imitation have always been two-way streets, with intellectuals crossing the tracks for no other reason than to create popular art—and vice versa.

Popular fiction's alleged ill-effects on literary culture are said to be two. First, because genre fiction borrows from highbrow fiction, it debases it. Second, by offering powerful economic incentives, it diverts artists from more esoteric pursuits. One can begin by asking, however, what is wrong with popular creators borrowing from the highbrows? It would seem that such crossovers should be applauded rather than deplored insofar as they introduce aspects of high culture to readers who might otherwise remain outside it. Instead of decrying the glass as half-empty, one should rejoice in it being half-full.

This has often proven too much to swallow for those who would keep the classics a safe distance from the masses. When Emily Brönte's romance *Wuthering Heights* was first printed as a cheap Pocket Book, it sold over 300,000 copies. A few years later, as a comic book, it sold in the millions. Yet, instead of earning kudos for crossover penetration, it was denounced for cheapening a literary classic, proving once again that, as far as pulp fiction goes you're damned if you do and damned if you don't. Recognizing the hypocrisy, during the comic-book wars of the 1950s poet and critic Delmore Schwartz offered this advice in "Masterpieces as Cartoons":

Each adult and literate human being who feels that literature is one of the necessary conditions of civilized existence can set the example of reading *both* the original classics and the cartoon version.[15]

Karl Marx argued that highbrow culture arises from the desire of the elites to distance themselves from the middle classes. As the latter progressively accommodate the highbrow forms, this goads the elites to more esoteric pursuits. Popular forms are, indeed, frequently shunned by the elites until novel forms of entertainment replace them, at which point the entertainment of the past begins to claw its way up into the domain of respectable art. The case could be made for much of today's pantheon, beginning with the theater, opera, and classical music, and ending with poetry, the brash and raucous equivalent of rock music in Plato's day.

If true, this cyclical model suggests that it is natural for high art to alternate between periods of experimentation and accommodation, during which popular culture plays catch-up to the avant-garde. It also suggests that genre fiction does not and could never pose a threat to high culture, despite apocalyptic warnings about its vulnerability to the masses. Indeed, in this picture the lowbrow and middlebrow perform a valuable service as Socratic gadflies that keep high culture on its toes. Accusations of literary debasement are further compromised by their selective bias. Borrowing and imitation have always been two-way streets, with intellectuals crossing the tracks for no other reason than to create popular art—and vice versa.[16]

One of the most popular detective writers in the 1920s USA was S.S. Van Dine, so much so that, while Hammett's stories were coming out in the pulps, Van Dine was selling out hardcover editions. Interestingly, even as he laughed all the way to the bank, he also wrote a literary-aesthetic treatise *The Creative Will* (1916), in which under his real name he flayed popular culture as the province of the vulgar and the ignorant. His detective, Philo Vance, was known for sharing many of the elitist pablums with his creator and in the same Marinist filigree. For all that, in the decade between 1929 and 1939 Hollywood produced no less than eleven Philo Vance movies.

Even if popular literature borrows more from the highbrows—in fact, it is probably the opposite—it may be because its audience is larger and more variegated. At the end of the day, however, the accusation of debasement is undercut by its own logic. Mutual interpenetration and borrowing have been going on for so long that highbrow fiction should by now be utterly debased. In short, either the charge of debasement is wrong, or highbrow fiction penned by highbrow writers and admired by highbrow critics is nothing but debased pulp fiction anyway.

The fact that popular genres attract talent is correct to the extent that we overlook the fact that, attracted by cultural prestige, popular creators also try their hand at more ambitious projects, often in the process of self-discovery as artists. It has never been a secret that the creator of Sherlock Holmes was contemptuous of his famous creation and of adventure stories like *The Lost World* that brought him world renown. In parallel to the exploits of his consulting detective, Arthur Conan Doyle wrote thus reams of historical fiction in the hope that it would bring him the coveted literary credentials.

When that did not work as planned, he devised one of the most drastic measures ever devised to curry prestige, offing Holmes in "The Final

Problem", at the apex of the ace detective's popularity. Professor Moriarty's victory proved, however, to be short-lived. Holmes's demise provoked such an outcry across Britain, with fans sporting mourning bands in public, that he was brought back to life in "The Empty House", with Watson fainting at the sight. In our own time, in the middle of a string of bestselling action thrillers, Nelson DeMille took time out to compose *The Gold Coast* (1990), a contemporary novel of manners and a regionalist humoresque aka *The Great Gatsby* meets *The Godfather*.

This is not to say that all genre practitioners just itch to ditch the mass-market Muse, or that those who actually do invariably pull it off. John McDonald, author of a commercially and critically praised crime series featuring private eye Travis McGee, also tried to write outside the genre that brought him so much success. In "Up From Elitism", even a sympathetic critic like Ray B. Browne was compelled to rate the McGee novels superior to McDonald's "literary" ones. Still, the example shows that popular writers are willing to bet their money on their ambitions, even when such ambitions do not always go hand in hand with their talents.

The same goes for the other side of the equation. Not every artist who tries his hand at slumming it has the wherewithal to pull it off, as Fitzgerald quickly found out during his first two try-outs in Hollywood. The art of writing in popular genres is exactly that, with Philip Roth's *Operation Shylock* (1993) a more recent case in point. While the jacket boosts it as a spy story and a political thriller, it is little more than a literary dog chasing its own tail. A hokey plot of the narrator chasing his double, a never-use-one-adjective-when-three-will-do style, and a parade of diatribes reminiscent of Irving Wallace's *The Word* makes clear that Roth should leave spy-fi to pros like Len Deighton or Larry Bond.

Generally speaking, writers who notch up a bestseller or two do not necessarily turn their noses on ambitious projects afterward. Quite the contrary. The commercial precariousness of the literary métier is a byword, and most authors, including Shakespeare, had other sources of income to buy themselves the creative space they needed. Some of the biggest names in the canon have been deans of cathedrals, customs officers, doctors of medicine, government clerks, insurance executives, journalists, or commercial editors. Some have been successful writers of pulp fiction.

Despite seductive rhetoric that opposes Art and Mammon, most of the time they work together and, more to the point, they work well. The same can be said for book publishers, where prestige and popular fiction have traditionally worked side by side, with little to suggest that one was corrupting the other. André Deutsch kept both V.S. Naipaul and Peter Benchley (of *Jaws* fame) in his stable, while Jonathan Cape printed Kingsley Amis in parallel with Ian ("my name is Bond") Fleming. That same Kingsley Amis, after Fleming's death in 1964, penned a Bond novel called *Colonel Sun* and published it with—who else—Jonathan Cape under the penname of Robert Markham.

HEADS I WIN, TAILS YOU LOSE

> Genre fiction is like a rotten fruit that fools consumers who would otherwise feast on nutritious produce high up on the cultural tree, leaving them with emotional indigestion, intellectual cramps, and cultural diarrhea.

Popular fiction's alleged ill-effects on society at large assume a number of incarnations. First, led by crime fiction, it is said to be emotionally debilitating by providing spurious gratifications and brutalizing with gratuitous sex and violence. Next, it is said to be intellectually debilitating owing to its escapist content, which inhibits the readers' ability to cope with reality. Finally, it is culturally debilitating because it prevents consumers from partaking of high art. In short, genre fiction is like a rotten fruit that fools consumers who would otherwise feast on nutritious produce high up on the cultural tree, leaving them with emotional indigestion, intellectual cramps, and cultural diarrhea.

All this is predicated on the presence of the effects posited by the critics and on popular fiction promoting, or at the very least inducing, these effects. Both of these myths are belied by available data.[17] First of all, there is no generic reader of genre fiction—readership is distributed fairly evenly across the social, educational, and income spectrum. Crime fiction buffs are quite simply avid readers who often also consume vast amounts of belles lettres as well as nonfiction. They make complex and discriminating judgments about the relation of what they read to their personal lives, and are in no way pathological escapists.

Although diversion from daily stresses and sorrows is reported to be an important factor in turning to fiction, highbrow and lowbrow, numerous multilayered and sophisticated motivations come into play in readers' contacts with either. Popular fiction enthusiasts also report a relatively high incidence of re-reading, linking them even more closely to highbrow consumers.[18] Indeed, favorite whodunits are re-read with a passion that vitiates condemnations that they are consumed solely for the purpose of outing the criminal. Evidently, there are parameters of the phenomenology of the mystery genre that take it in the direction of literature *tout court*.

Sociologists, anthropologists, and a growing number of literary scholars document any number of critical and discriminating attitudes among genre fiction readers, something that curators of high art like to arrogate just to themselves. In general, there is no evidence that individuals who regularly consume genre fiction are criminally inclined escapists incapable of getting a grip on reality. Data from community and leisure studies indicate that the lower-middle and middle-middle classes—that is, those most "at risk"—are not isolated brutes living out escapist and violent fantasies but, typically, integrated members of family, peer, and social groups.[19]

This is not to deny that some novels exhibit the antisocial—by and large sex-and-violence-related—characteristics for which they are flogged. My only point here is that content attribution, the standard critical practice of inferring readers' attitudes from textual content, is a singularly unreliable and demonstrably fallible method. Moral decay, of which crime fiction has been accused at every turn, is a moral decoy insofar as the same method, if applied even-handedly, would find plenty amiss with the canon.

Exposing the double standard of highbrow critiques of lowbrow culture in "Against Ethical Criticism", Richard Posner adduces example after example of murder, gratuitous violence, sadism, human sacrifice, animal sacrifice, pillage, slavery, rape, misogyny, sexism, homophobia, racism, and bestiality in classics that range from Homer to Shakespeare to Dickens to Mann. Indeed, the amount of lascivious or violent content compiled for Michael MacRone's *Naughty Shakespeare* (1997) puts the bard on a par with the baddest of the baddest. In all these depraved and debased works, the antisocial behaviors depicted often in loving detail give the lie to content attribution differentiating art from shmart.

In reality, popular fiction, which by and large addresses itself to the dominant social and sexual ethos of the middle class, frequently ends up being more conservative and puritanical than high art.[20] Not to look far, when *Classics Illustrated*, the comic-book giant of the 1940s and 1950s, brought out *Crime and Punishment*, it felt compelled to clean it up for the sake of a mass (often juvenile) reader. The removal of the prostitute Sonia ignited censures of tampering with the classics, giving fresh ammunition to those who see popular culture trashing as a game of heads-I-win-tails-you-lose.

The supply-and-demand forces of the literary marketplace form a feedback loop. There are good reasons to believe that popular fiction, instead of diverting gullible readers away from serious art, responds to the demands of the reading public, or at least to what genre writers and their publishers perceive these demands to be. If preference for genre art is at least in part a matter of choice rather than a Pavlovian response, the charge that Ellery Queen, Chester Himes, or Sue Grafton are the major obstacles between an average reader and *Crime and Punishment* or *The New York Trilogy* is simply untenable.

Genre aficionados select literary content to fit their aesthetic tastes, not least because, just like the highbrows, they need to filter the glut of cultural information beating daily at their doors. They do not generally throw their money away on whatever tops the bestsellers rack but rather select books that satisfy their discernible, if not always explicitly articulated, social needs and aesthetic values. As a rule, they are also less attuned to the verbal and symbolic content of the "pulp" they read, making them, if anything, less susceptible to its effects.

Readers who flock to genre stories, whether for entertainment or enlightenment, hardly pattern their lives after the books they read with so much abandon. There are no Madames Bovarys in real life, despite a few hard-up criminal defendants blaming gangsta rap for real murders with claims that it deadened their sensibilities and incited violence (all with zero success).[21] For people who enjoy popular fiction as a breather from everyday life, a fast-paced dose of action or faraway fantasy serves the purpose much better than navel-gazing avant-garde.

Vice and Its Victim

Even though art history is traditionally written by the highbrows, the latter have always situated themselves and mobilized critical justification in opposition to the prevailing mode of cultural exchange which, in America at least, has always been popular and commercial.

Finally, it is alleged that genre fiction lowers the general cultural level of the reading public, forging a passive and apathetic audience that can easily fall victim to propaganda and dictatorship. Except that, over the course of the twentieth century, the general cultural level in the USA has actually risen from lower-middle to middle-middle class, in stark defiance of the myth that popular culture—which, needless to say, flourished during the period in question—is a one-way ticket to the skid row.[22]

Conservative critics who protest that the reading culture has taken a turn for the worse since the advent of mass culture need only take stock of what English and American mass consumers mass-consumed in the nineteenth century. Running the gamut from the sensationalism to the sentimentalism of penny-dreadful bestsellers like *Vice and its Victim; or, Phoebe, the Peasant's Daughter* (1854), the highlights of the lowlights are atrocious enough to deserve their own campy tributes on the literary equivalent of *RiffTrax*.

Only tendentiousness in contrasting the highest achievements of the past with the mediocre of the present allows critics to allege that popular culture leads to a decline in standards. By now a raft of studies have shown that even the despised Victorian sensation novels have been anything but artless instantiations of genre formula. Champions of the form, such as Charles Reade, Mary Braddon, Wilkie Collins, and Ellen Wood routinely destabilized the very conventions they employed with consummate skill. Frequently drawing on newspaper reports of criminal trials and the proceedings of the Divorce Court, they not only tackled pregnant social issues, but also disputed conventional notions about criminality, morality, and even melodrama itself.[23]

This is not to deny that, like any cultural product, popular fiction is not immune to being infiltrated by latent ideological content that can pacify consumers by obscuring the top-heavy character of power hierarchy in society. In less highbrow terms, we are talking here about preempting political dissent or just social discontent by dealing cultural opium to the masses. Except that when it comes to being susceptible to spin, research shows that the highbrows are prone to the same range of biases and fallacious beliefs in the rationality of their decision making as everyone else. The lowbrows are not that different from the elites, it turns out, especially when the advertising budget is large enough.[24]

This last point exemplifies the nature of modern culture where mutual borrowings, adaptations, and outright appropriations bedevil any facile opposition between cultural highs and lows. Globalization and free trade may be the contemporary buzzwords in geopolitics and macroeconomics but in popular culture they have always been parts of the landscape. Today, more than ever, boundaries between taste levels and artforms are not only increasingly difficult to detect but, as seen from critical efforts to come to terms with the literary middlebrow, even to define.[25]

Interpenetration between popular and highbrow art has always taken place with or without approval from the curators of the particular version of the canon. Little wonder that those interested in preserving the purity of high art often find themselves stymied when tracking its origins. Space-age communication, multichannel mass marketing, and a zettabyte culture of creative imitation make this more difficult by the minute. The experience is like trying to draw the line between sand and water on Arnold's Dover beach. With the tide high, then low, and single waves thrashing playfully about, who is to say where one ends and the other begins?

According to the basic axiom of mass-culture warriors, popular fiction has scant social or aesthetic merit, and therefore scant claim to a place in art history. This is why, where once there were low comedies closing the day for Hellenes tired of high drama, the canon now venerates stage classics from antiquity. Canonized they may be, at times by virtue of no more than having had the luck to survive to the modern era, but ancient Greek comedies were the scandal sheets, gossipy satires, and shameless self-promos of their time. The eliterary culture accepts entertainment from the past but not as literature of entertainment—though the 2015 induction of Vera Caspary, Helen Eustis, Dorothy B. Hughes, Elisabeth Sanxsay Holding, Charlotte Armstrong, Patricia Highsmith, and Dolores Hitchens (crime writers of the 1940s and 1950s all) into the Library of America may be a sign that this is slowly changing.

In the end, institutional dogma apart, crime fiction created for the mass enjoyment of mass readership may be as true a medium of literary artistry and aesthetic continuity as the canon precisely by virtue of circulating and recycling plots and characters that have proven their value over time. Aesthetic innovation, let us remember, emerges in all communities, from the nomad cultures and pre-Columbian Americans down to the rhyming poetry of modern rap and the mosaic of popular genres, which supply writers with preset patterns within which they can develop their individuality and even artistry.[26]

On the other hand, high-art aesthetics is less like a static picture of crystalline purity and more like a moving picture of life itself: a time-specific accretion of impressions, changing winds of fashion, and elitist aspirations. The historical contingency of the value—which is to say the utility—of our classics is a matter of historical record. Belying claims to their transcendence, the boom-and-bust cycle of Shakespeare's literary stock over centuries of shifting aesthetic paradigms is no more a secret than the frailty of the claims to aesthetic immanence made on behalf of *Mona Lisa*.[27]

Buffeted by the vagaries of literary taste and distaste, as well as a raft of extraliterary factors that can range from personal connections or even dumb luck to status-seeking and geopolitical tensions, an artist's stock is always in a flux. In our times it is exemplified by the career of William Faulkner, which owed as much to his talent and tenacity as to the intellectual one-upmanship of Cold War politics.[28] Even though art history is traditionally written by the highbrows, the latter have always situated themselves and mobilized critical justification in opposition to the prevailing mode of cultural exchange which, in America at least, has always been popular and commercial.

BEACHBOOKS FOR INTELLECTUALS

Studies of crime fiction have made big strides in legitimacy since the days of Father Knox and, at the other end, T.S. Eliot—a highbrows' highbrow, an enemy of mass culture, and a closet devotee of Sherlock Holmes.

Rather than constitute a cultural menace, mass-market fiction plays an integral role in society as a popular entertainment and, on occasion, as art. As such, it deserves to be examined in its own right, free of elitist preconceptions on the one hand and of anti-canonical backlash on the other. Most genre fiction is no more than the only thing it ever tries to be: gripping but ephemeral entertainment with no aspirations to bowl over the literati. But to appreciate how much some genre bestsellers have in common with the classics and how much some of our classics owe to genreflecting, we need to better appreciate their nobrow design.

Studies of crime fiction have made big strides in legitimacy since the days of Father Knox and, at the other end, T.S. Eliot—a highbrows' highbrow, an enemy of mass culture, and a closet devotee of Sherlock Holmes. Often working against the critical grain, they have brought the native variety of crime story up from the basement while documenting the raw power of its storytelling and the lingering darkness of its social vision. Building on these critical foundations, *American Crime Fiction* takes a step further by arguing for viewing American crime fiction as a form of art—nobrow art, to be exact.[29]

The masses of readers of murder mysteries do not argue much for their tastes—they know they are not going anywhere. What is there to argue about, anyway? To accept the terms of the culture wars is to accept that literature falls into two categories. One is said to be good for you but is at best an acquired taste, like Brussels sprouts, whereas the other tastes good but can only make you sorry in the end, like New York cheesecake. Put differently, highbrow is snobbish while lowbrow is slobbish, and never the twain shall meet. Tell it to the nobrows who, combining highbrow tropes with mass-market appeal, bring together authors and readers who believe that there is nothing oxymoronic about genre art.

It would be wrong, however, to associate this crossover aesthetic with our century and millennium. As an identifiable cultural formation, nobrow has been around since the early years of the twentieth century, not coincidentally the time when the entire phrenology-based partition gained in notoriety in the wake of Van Wyck Brooks's essay "Highbrow and Lowbrow" (1915).[30] Pointedly, even as he acknowledged the appeal of the thesis and antithesis, Brooks was suspicious of both, arguing for their nobrow synthesis:

> One admits the charm of both extremes, the one so fantastically above, the other so fantastically below the level of right reason—to have any kind of relish for muddled humanity is necessarily to feel the charm in both extremes. But where is all that is real, where is personality and all its works, if it is not essentially somewhere, somehow, in some not very vague way, between?[31]

Still, for much of the twentieth century, attempts to leave behind the aesthetic straitjacket of elites-versus-masses have been fraught with risks. As neither lite diversion nor heavy-duty art, instead of being seen as the best of both worlds nobrow has often ended up being shunned by both, largely vindicating the satirical wisdom that the only thing worse than being talked about is not being talked about. Given that absence of evidence is often cited as a critical evidence of absence, it is an essential part of my project to historicize the aesthetic that openly straddles the high-low binary in search of pulps with gravitas.

Whether they end up being feted or filleted, all the crime writers who star in my book work hard to split the difference between the mass consumer and the discerning connoisseur. Spinning testosterone-dripping action in literate and, on occasion, even literary prose, they contest the stereotype of whodunit blockbusters by engaging not only in political polemics or for that matter economic statistics but, at other times, in self-parody and even deconstructive *jouissance*. Keeping one eye on the commercial and the other on the artistic payoffs, they exemplify the power of vernacular art that resonates with mass audiences.

Entertaining, enterprising, and exuberantly eclectic, the prose poets of America's hoods in the 'hood hang a big question mark on the entire highbrow-lowbrow dialectic, proving that in some cases there is little virtue in separating literature into art and bestsellers (which is not the same as saying that all crime mysteries are art or that all sleepers are not). My interest in them lies, in fact, in direct proportion to their hybrid of high aesthetics and popular appeal—in short, to their nobrow quotient.

Addressing American crime fiction as an artform that expresses and reflects the socioaesthetic values and preoccupations of its authors and readers, I investigate the many ways in which such authorship and readership are a matter of informed literary choice rather than cultural brainwashing or degenerate moral and aesthetic standards. Asking, in effect, a series of questions about American crime fiction as art, I thus employ a selection of notable novels by notable American writers to shed light on the historical hazards and cultural rewards of trafficking between popular forms and high-end aesthetics.

Fixated though they often are on lurid violence, cut-rate sleaze, and homicidal psychopathology, American crime mysteries deserve to be approached as artistically ambitious and ideologically complex on their own terms. Starting from this premise, *American Crime Fiction* weaves together the cultural history of an iconic American genre and, *mutans mutandis*, the cultural history of the country with which it is indissolubly linked. In the process it stakes a claim for distinguishing nobrow as a creative strategy and as a literary formation that puts art back in entertainment and the other way round—which is to say, as a form of artertainment.

Crime fiction dominates the literary market today, making up a quarter of all the books bought in the USA. My bet is, however, that crime fiction—represented in the chapters below by the classic and self-parodic hardboiled, the legal, police, and urban procedural, and the mob story—is not untypical of the creative moves of other American genres, from romances and westerns to sci-fi, spy-fi, horror, fantasy, technothrillers, and what not. In short, I take crime fiction to be a representative species of what their fan, George Orwell, almost apologetically called good bad books, but which I prefer to call beachbooks for intellectuals.

SEX, MONEY, AND REVENGE

Like other types of contemporary fiction, crime novels provide complex articulations of prevailing national concerns, social fears, and fantasies.

Historically, much as American literature has tried to dissociate itself from the untutored productions of the street, the hash house, and the court-house, it has always ended up being defined by them. Be that as it may, despite a growing interest in crime fiction as a social and even ideological force and a liberalization of attitudes toward genre fiction in general, both continue to be viewed askance in some quarters. In 2008 Pulitzer winner and on-and-off crime novelist Michel Chabon could not hide his dismay:

> Entertainment has a bad name. Serious people learn to mistrust or even revile it… Intelligent people must keep a certain distance from its produc-tions. They must handle the things that entertain them with gloves of irony and postmodern tongs.[32]

Of course, an argument could be made—and is made by means of this book—that crime fiction is the realistic and even the naturalistic literature of our times, having invaded and perhaps even conquered some of the territory traditionally occupied by the psychological novel. To be sure, murder mysteries on the whole tend to fixate on behaviors that shade into psychopathology. But among genre paperbacks that model the layers of motive behind the homicidal Big Three (sex, money, and revenge), some conjure up complex life histories that rival the canon in psychological and social nuance.

Approaching crime novels as a variety of realistic fiction helps explain some of the psychological foundation of "immense popularity with all sorts of people of the novel about murder or crime or mystery", as Raymond Chandler put it back in 1948.[33] In an eloquent testimony to this popularity, a recent bibliography of crime novels from the years 1749–1900—way before the advent of the pulps, cylinder presses, and mass-market paperbacks—lists upward of 80,000 titles, not counting short stories in more than 4500 collections. There is also the *Mammoth Encyclopedia of Modern Crime Fiction* which, limited only to the postwar decades, comes in at more than half-a-thousand pages of magnifying-glass print.

At the other end of the spectrum, acclaimed artists who turn their hands to fictional crime are also as common as bread in a prison meatloaf. Even more than Faulkner, Hemingway, and Fitzgerald, one might mention Akira Kurosawa whose ironically titled film *High and Low* (1963) adapted one of Ed McBain's police procedurals, *King's Ransom* (1959), with Tokyo subbing as the suburban tangle of New York City. Indeed, from Eudora Welty to Ludwig Wittgenstein, the roster of big names big on crime fiction makes a virtual *Who's Who* of twentieth-century artists and intellectuals.

Naturally, in the age of infoglut no one can hope to take under the literary microscope more than a small subset of any popular genre at any given time. The problems of selectivity and representativeness loom even larger in the case of crime fiction, hands down the biggest player on the American (and probably global) literary market today. Determined to write a book and not an encyclopedia, just because no one reads *those*, I thus sacrifice the extraneous in order to focus on the central storyline: the nobrow artistry of crime fiction in particular, and genre fiction in general.

The complex interplay between lowbrow and highbrow elements in twentieth-century crime fiction and the concomitant emergence of the nobrow aesthetic is crucial, in my opinion, to the understanding not only of this quintessentially American genre but of American literature at large. My method is thus to work back and forth between text and context, using books to illuminate the social and cultural history of the country, and the other way round. In this sense my project aligns with those of other crime fiction scholars who have brought history, race, and class to the fore in an effort to reconceive the genre along those lines. Trials of being immigrant, nonwhite, or poor in America give us good purchase on the genre through the ways in which it deals, or for that matter fails to deal, with these historically disfranchised groups.[34]

When they make an appearance in the chapters below, however, they do so in the context of complex articulations of popular art striving to leave a mark on its historical present. Tracing the cultural history of the making of twentieth-century genre art, *American Crime Fiction* traces how the plasticity and elasticity of a genre frequently disparaged as a paradigm of banality allowed some of its practitioners to forge a distinct—because nobrow—form of art out of a cross-cultural palette of sources and influences. No less important, it traces how the writers themselves understood what they were doing in precisely these terms, taking equal pride in mastering the formula and in ditching it in the interest of telling an even better story.

These strategic premises dictate the tactical moves made in the book. For one, my interest in the adaptations of the nobrow aesthetic requires that, instead of dwelling on the classic hardboiled novel and the tart noir, as many previous investigators do, I cast my net wider. Beginning with—what else?—Hammett and the ur-hardboiled *Red Harvest*, I subsequently direct the spotlight on the hardboiled metamorphoses in Grisham, the highbrow appropriations by Faulkner and Hemingway, the self-ironic deconstructions by Chandler, and the evolution into the police procedural, the urban procedural, and the mob story.

As importantly, the writers and the books I selected for in-depth analysis dovetail into a panoramic survey of the twentieth century and of what we have of the twenty-first. Hammett's literary career marked a milestone in the early 1920s with the release of the first Continental Op story, followed by the end of the decade with *Red Harvest*. Faulkner's *Sanctuary* straddles the late 1920s and the early 1930s, during which it morphed from a modernist art novel into a nobrow bestseller. *To Have and Have Not*, Hemingway's stab at crossing a proletarian novel with a hardboiled thrills takes us into the late 1930s, by which time Chandler was writing for *Black Mask*.

Chandler's career comes to an end almost exactly three decades later with his experimental and self-parodic *Playback*. By then, McBain has already launched the 87th Precinct series of urban procedurals that would eventually span half a century. In the 1980s he was joined by the wonderboy of legal procedurals, John Grisham, who continues to churn out bestsellers to this day. McBain himself passed away in 2005, three years before Nelson DeMille released his "take two", *The Gate House*, on his original "take two", *The Gold Coast*, which in a cunning playback of Fitzgerald's *The Great Gatsby*, takes us full circle back to the mobsters of the Jazz Age.

Like other types of contemporary fiction, crime novels provide complex articulations of prevailing national concerns, social fears, and fantasies. But, to their credit, they never forget that their job is not to autopsy America's collective psyche or its social ills but to tell a good story to candy-assed urbanites who, as a rule, never come face to face with violent crime outside the pages of the books they consume with so much passion. Out of the timeless menu of lawless racketeers, two-timing femmes, and larger than life truth seekers, they spin fantasies that, like those spun by the bards of yore, grip you by the throat and don't let go—unless it is to get another fix.

NOTES

1. See Swirski, "The Zettabyte Problem" (2015).
2. See Sorensen, et al.
3. Data from Swirski (2005); for background, see Woolf; Rosenberg; Lowenthal; MacDonald.
4. Page 232; below, next quote, 241.
5. Act 5, scene 1: 394–5.
6. On nobrow and the golden mean of convention and invention, see Swirski (2016); below; on creativity and algorithms, Swirski (2013).
7. Also known as literary Darwinism; see Carroll; Swirski (2007), (2010), (2011); Dutton.
8. See Swirski, *Literature, Analytically Speaking* on analytic foundations of literary aesthetics.
9. On apocalyptic and integrated scholarship, see Eco.
10. For a review of these and numerous other critiques, see Gans; Browne (1981); Swirski (2005).
11. Stuckey (1981); Mott.
12. Kaplan; Adorno, 38.
13. Chandler (1972), "Introduction"; see also Bauer.
14. *Later Novels and Other Writings*, 1024.
15. Page 471; see also Davis (1984); below, on accommodation, see Hammill.
16. See Hawkins (1991); Swirski (2005).
17. See Gans, especially Chap. 9; Tötösy de Zepetnek and Kreisel.
18. Barsch.
19. Data are consistent over the decades, from Katz and Lazarsfeld (1955) to Gans (1974) to Zuidervaart and Luttikhuizen (2000); on the literary side, see Swirski (2005); Driscoll.
20. The same argument in the context of American movies—in this case early Westerns—is made by Sklar in Chap. 2, "Nickel Madness".
21. Philips.
22. See classic studies by Dalziel (1957); Gans (1974); this stratification is predicated on the classical social model of five classes—see BBC News (2013) on seven social classes in the UK.
23. Knoepflmacher; Briggs; Hughes; Boyle; Sodeman. For a clear expose of critical tendentiousness, see Shafer; for our-standards-are-in-decline, Jacoby.
24. Mardsen; Fiske; Anderson, "Popular Art"; Swirski (2015); for decision making priming and biases, see Kahnemann and Tversky; Kahnemann.
25. See Driscoll; also Rubin; Mangum; Lassner.
26. See Tatarkiewicz's mammoth *History of Aesthetics*; Anderson (1990); on the aesthetics and economics of rap, see Swirski (2015), Chap. 4.

27. Levine; Boas.
28. Lawrence D. Schwartz; Végső.
29. See Swirski (1999), (2005), (2015); McCann.
30. It actually precedes it by decades; see Troubridge, 169.
31. Van Wyck Brooks.
32. Page 1.
33. In Gardiner and Walker, 53; next sentence, Hubin.
34. McCann; O'Brian; Horsley; Cassuto; Breu.

CHAPTER 2

Briefcases for Hire: Dashiell Hammett and John Grisham

THE PAUPER AND THE PRINCE

Although it may not be obvious at first glance, the chief difference between the gumshoe from the pages of tough-guy fiction and the lawyer-hero of contemporary courtroom procedural may be that one is packing a gun and the other a briefcase.

Take a shopworn, hardboiled dick, softened with bourbon, rumpled at the edges, a piece snug under his arm, a cigarette dangling from the corner of his mouth. Take an Armani-suited attorney at law, all courtroom urbanity and legalese elocution, a smartphone at his ear, a Gucci briefcase dangling from his impeccably manicured hand. What could they possibly have to do with each other? We are talking night and day, the pauper and the prince, the marginal and the mainstream, right?

Not quite. Although it may not be obvious at first glance, the chief difference between the gumshoe from the pages of tough-guy fiction and the lawyer-hero of contemporary courtroom procedural may be that one is packing a gun and the other a briefcase. This goes against the grain of the commonly held assumption that the two genres—hardboiled mystery and legal thriller—have precious little in common, starting with their historical timeframe. After all, hardboiled prose peaked in popularity in the 1930s and 1940s, while legal procedurals did not go nova until the 1980s, enjoying their phenomenal success to this day.

© The Editor(s) (if applicable) and The Author(s) 2016
P. Swirski, *American Crime Fiction*,
DOI 10.1007/978-3-319-30108-2_2

And yet, unexamined assumptions can sometimes lead astray. Take a look at the heroes, for example. Both are fast-talking urban cowboys who daily wade into the shark tanks of city streets and city courtrooms. Both are for hire for a fee plus expenses. Both are slow to get heavy but, when push comes to shove, neither the PI nor the attorney at law will back down from a tangle with the bad guys—or bed-eyed dames, for that matter. As even this thumbnail sketch suggests, the hardboiled hero might be more closely related to the hero of the modern legal procedural than is usually allowed. Could this correspondence be more than a coincidence?

For the answer we can turn to two novels, one undersized, the other bulky, that embody their respective eras, zeitgeists, and schools of writing. Samuel (Dashiell) Hammett's ur-hardboiled *Red Harvest* (1929) and John Grisham's legal blockbuster *The Rainmaker* (1995) exemplify the apparent differences and the underlying similarities between them. A closer look at their cultural roots and narrative strategies reveals the debt that the legal procedural owes to Hammett, Cain, and other hardboiled masters.

Retracing the footsteps of the prime mover of the hardboiled and courtroom mystery—the truth seeker—we can see how the juxtaposition of "hardboiled lawyer" plays out in modern-day legal procedurals represented by Grisham's arguably best and most ambitious novel. For better or worse, legal procedurals today provide a universal forum for the propagation and assimilation of ideas central to American society and culture. Commenting on almost all aspects of contemporary life, they end up informing and on occasion even forming the background of many citizens' values and beliefs.

A good case in point is the sensational 1927 trial of Ruth (Momsie) Snyder and Henry Judd (Lover Boy) Gray, in which both were convicted of murdering Ruth's husband, Albert Snyder. Even though every paper, from the Hearst tabloids to *The New York Times*, hyped up the twists and turns of the hearings, no one today remembers much about Snyder v. Gray. But the millions of readers familiar with James M. Cain's hardboiled classics, *The Postman Always Rings Twice* (1934) and *Double Indemnity* (1936), will have no trouble recalling the details of the case.

Understandably, the names have changed on the way from real life to fiction. Cain, a seasoned journalist who was covering the Snyder trial on assignment, remodeled Ruth, Henry, and Albert to Cora, Frank, and Nick in *The Postman Always Rings Twice*, and to Phyllis, Walter, and Herbert in *Double Indemnity*. But outside this perfunctory disguise, the courtroom and the novels both served the same tabloid cocktail of a bored sex-tigress housewife, her milquetoast lover, and a dullard husband whose sole claim to notoriety was being clandestinely insured by his wife "for $48,000, with a double-indemnity clause in case of accidental death".[1]

Cain was nothing but accurate in grafting the hapless Albert Snyder onto a first-generation Greek restaurant owner, Nick Papadakis. The dead giveaway? In the novel, Nick survives two prior attempts on his life before the lovers—his straying wife Cora and the drifter Frank—finish him off on the third-time-lucky attempt. One of the revelations from the hearings was that Ruth had tried to murder her husband on prior occasions, by poison and asphyxiation.[2] Now, put your finger on the fast-forward button, zoom from Cain to Grisham, and it is clear that during the intervening decades pulp fiction has lost none of its talent for publicizing and even fomenting public attitudes to the law.

A former trial lawyer, Grisham typically builds his plots around real cases, notably in *The Confession* (2010), which fuses elements of a number of death-row appeals that crossed his desk on the Board of Directors of the Innocence Project. Writing about social issues dressed as legal precedents, from child rape and vigilante justice in *A Time to Kill* (1989) to political conspiracy in *The Pelican Brief* (1992), to the war on the homeless in *The Street Lawyer* (1998)—or more recently the crooks and hooks of campaign contributions in *The Appeal* (2008), big class-action suits and Big Pharma in *The Litigators* (2011), and the ravages of the Great Recession in *Gray Mountain* (2014)—he draws rapt audiences in thirty languages worldwide.

Grisham topped all the bestseller lists of the 1990s—the decade that brought out *The Rainmaker*—with cumulative sales of sixty million copies (60,742,288 to be exact). These colossal numbers dwarfed both the king of horror Stephen King and the queen of romance Danielle Steele, who came in second and third with thirty-eight and thirty-seven million respectively. Today he is racing toward cumulative sales of a third of a *billion*, not to mention eight feature adaptations (with plans for at least three more), and a couple of TV series spun in mid-1990s off *The Client* and in 2011–2012 off *The Firm*.[3]

The point of all this is not, of course, that bestsellers are invariably best writers. Most, as a matter of fact, go in one eye and out the other and are designed to do so. But, like a knockout blonde with a smoking gun, the legal procedural warrants close attention. From the exponential rise of the "I'll sue you" mentality to the right to be Mirandized and have an attorney present, legal fiction lurks at the back of many Americans' attitudes to law, legal justice, and even society at large. This includes academics and other intellectuals, many of whom are consumers and even producers of popular culture. For, as one of us pleads guilty, "while we seem to be taking only innocent pleasure in our popular readings, we are always at the same time inserted into a cultural value system".[4]

THE TOAST OF HOLLYWOOD

> Suddenly, Tinseltown PIs were all Bogey's Spade: dashing, debonair, and as such nothing like their shabby, low-key offscreen prototypes.

Just as all roads used to lead to Rome, all roads from the legal procedural lead back to Hammett's *Red Harvest*. After all, if not Hammett, then who? Although many crime writers such as Carroll John Daly, Raoul Whitfield, George Harmon Cox, Frederick Nebel, Brett Halliday, and Michael Collins plied their craft alongside him, he was the only one to leave a lasting mark on American literature and culture. While Sam Spade and the Continental Op keep popping up in books, movies, animés, and graphic novels, to say nothing of critical monographs, most of his competitors from the pulps era have by now dissolved into the mists of obscurity.[5]

Even crime fiction buffs would be hard pressed today to remember Daly's less-than-unforgettable detective Race Williams or Whitfield's not-so-memorable gumshoe Jo Gar. Some hired guns, it seems, were destined to disappear from the cultural supermarket as swiftly as their creators, and not even subsequent imitators like Mickey Spillane and his lantern-jawed Mike Hammer were able to dent Hammett's staying power. The Thin Man, on the other hand, remains as popular and as readable today as when he was the toast of Hollywood.

All of his novels—*Red Harvest* (1929), *The Dain Curse* (1929), *The Maltese Falcon* (1930), *The Glass Key* (1931), and *The Thin Man* (1934)—are in print, reissued by Vintage Crime/Black Lizard. His critical standing is even more assured today than a generation ago, when he was celebrated as "the foremost exponent of the American 'hardboiled' detective story".[6] The best evidence of his stock going through the roof is the addition to the prestigious canon of Library of America in two volumes: *Complete Novels* (1999) and *Crime Stories and Other Writings* (2001). Not bad for a writer of private eye mysteries in which the only thing faster than a bullet is one-line wit.

Hammett also left his imprint on American cinema through John Huston's 1941 adaptation of *The Maltese Falcon*, selected by the American Film Institute as one of twenty-five Greatest American Films. Everyone knows the picture's all-star cast—Humphrey Bogart, Mary Astor, Sidney Greenstreet, and Peter Lorre as chypre-scented (gay) Joel Cairo—although theirs was only version number three. Barely a year after publication, *The Maltese Falcon* became a proto-sexploitation flick *Dangerous Females*, and five years later a Bette Davis comedy *Satan Met a Lady*. But it was the 1941 version that imprinted itself on Hollywood and on the public mind. Suddenly, Tinseltown PIs were all Bogey's Spade: dashing, debonair, and as such nothing like their shabby, low-key offscreen prototypes.

Huston's noir came on the heels of an entire string of translations of Hammett's action-packed adventures onto the big screen. In fact, all five of his novels were swiftly made into pictures: from *Roadhouse Nights* (1931), based on *Red Harvest*, to *The Glass Key* (1935, and again in 1942), to *The Dain Curse*, which was even made into a TV series in 1978. The biggest hit of all, however, turned out to be *The Thin Man*, with William Powell and Myrna Loy on the marquee, which spawned no less than five sequels: *After the Thin Man* (1936), *Another Thin Man* (1939), *Shadow of the Thin Man* (1941), *The Thin Man Goes Home* (1944), and *The Song of the Thin Man* (1947).

It seems logical, then, to begin with the writer who detached private investigators from the yellowy pages on which they strutted their stuff and reshaped them into figures larger than life—in one word, into archetypes. This is not to say that there was little detective fiction before Hammett. By the end of the nineteenth century, with ballooning cities hungry for city-centric prose, crime stories enjoyed a wide following in dime novels, pulp magazines, and in the new type of quality periodicals—the slicks. *Collier's*, *McCall's*, *McClure's*, *Munsey's*, *Saturday Evening Post*, and *Cosmopolitan* all in a textbook nobrow fashion printed mass-appeal fiction side by side with journalism.

Closely paralleling the meteoric rise of penny papers like the *New York Sun* and its arch-rival the *New York Herald* in the 1830s, the slicks sold for a dime, which was less than the cost of printing, making a profit from advertising instead. In one success story, *McClure's* began in 1892 with a circulation of 8000. Two years later it had more than a quarter of a million subscribers. Its reporting was routinely the product of investigative journalism: muckraking, hard-hitting, poking the sleazy underside of society. But there was also a fair amount of original fiction, frequently written by staff members, who continued to stigmatize vice and corruption in stories about organized crime, venal politicians, crooked police, and hard-nosed detectives.

Muckraking was the buzzword of the day: hot, catchy, and pushing sales through the roof. The hard edge and topical realism reflected the fact that crime in America was no longer seen in terms of isolated pockets of brutality perpetrated by society's dregs, but rather as an open-ended series of violation of a corrupt system requiring urgent and active response. With the approval of their owners and editors, muckraking journalists carried the reformist banner by attacking social injustice, documenting business abuses, and drawing the general public's attention to political complicity.

For a while even Teddy Roosevelt embraced the muckrakers' progressivist agenda, at least until *Cosmopolitan* ran a series of articles called *Treason in the Senate*, which censured some of his political allies. Incensed, in a speech (later printed in the *New York Tribune*) the president tarred the crusading journalists by putting them at the level of the muckraker in Paul Bunyan's allegory *Pilgrim's Progress*, eventually turning the tide of public support against the pen-wielding crusaders. Be that as it may, during the first fifteen years of the twentieth century the muckrakers could claim an extraordinary degree of success in exposing and, ultimately, reforming an endless roster of corrupt social, political, and business practices.[7]

Among others, their reporting brought about the dismantling of the convict and peonage systems in some states; substantial prison reforms; the passing of a federal pure food act and a federal employers' liability act; setting aside of forest reserves and the passing of the Newlands Act which reclaimed millions of acres of land; and saving the Niagara Falls and most of Alaska from uncontrolled exploitation. As importantly, the muckrakers were behind the adoption of partial child labor laws, eight-hour workday laws for women, and mothers' pension acts in select states; the passing of workmen's compensation laws by almost half of the states; dissolution of monopolies such as the Standard Oil and the Big Tobacco companies; and legislating better insurance laws and packing-house laws.

What set Hammett apart from these contemporaries was that, as an ex-Pinkerton operative, he had years of experience in the business to draw upon. The young Dashiell joined the Baltimore branch of the Pinkerton Detective Agency (then located in the Continental building) back in 1915.[8] He enjoyed going undercover and working gang disputes, until one day he was obliged to use a gun. Guarding a powder magazine, he spotted a thief scaling the fence and, after a few shouted warnings, there was little left to do but to follow instructions and fire. Struck, the man fell off the fence and fled, clutching his arm. Hammett reported terror at the sight of blood and at the fragility of life. He would never carry or use a gun again.

Publicity stunts cultivated (in every sense of "cult") by writers such as Hemingway invite readers to project his first-person narrators—especially those portrayed realistically in a biographically accurate milieu—onto the flesh-and-blood author. Although projecting hardboiled attitudes to guns and violence could hardly work in Hammett's case, there is no doubt that the years as a Pinkerton operative shaped much of his prose, starting with the figure of Continental Op. Neither would this first-hand intimacy with the nuts and bolts of enforcing the law and with the workaday moves and countermoves of a trained professional be lost on Grisham.

Image 2.1 Dashiell Hammett/John Grisham. *"Although projecting hardboiled attitudes to guns and violence could hardly work in Hammett's case, there is no doubt that the years as a Pinkerton operative shaped much of his prose, starting with the figure of Continental Op. Neither would this first-hand intimacy with the nuts and bolts of enforcing the law and with the workaday moves and countermoves of a trained professional be lost on Grisham."*

WALDRON HONEYWELL

Hammett's first detective, Waldron Honeywell, would make a point of proving that the Sherlock Holmes mysteries would have been cracked by routine methods of ordinary policemen. Soon, however, even he would step aside for a more realistic and influential creation: the Continental Op.

After a few years with Pinkerton, during which he witnessed ghastly acts of brutality perpetrated on and by union labor, Hammett quit and became a successful writer of advertising copy and a reviewer of detective fiction for local magazines and papers. The experience as a commercial ad man may have contributed to his development as a writer: knowing the value of each word, knowing how to play to the audience, and knowing the concerns of the average man.

His readings from the time were that of a nobrow autodidact, from the pulps to Aristotle, Flaubert, and Henry James, all the while convinced that he could identify quality irrespective of whether it was dressed up as a crime story or psychological drama. Perhaps more importantly, he reveled in thirteenth-century Icelandic sagas. What he found in them was akin to his own literary inclinations: laconic and grim realism, highly structured but action-driven narration, sophisticated appreciation of social hierarchy, preoccupation with loyalty and honor, and not least heroes: granite hard, taciturn, not given to emotional excess.

In 1920 H.L. Mencken and his partner, George Nathan, founded the lowbrow magazine *Black Mask* in order to subsidize their highbrow *Smart Set*. Hammett became an avid reader and, soon after, regular contributor to the magazine that already featured one hardboiled detective created by Carroll John Daly. Even so, Daly's Race Williams stories were more in the Bond vein: action melodramas full of international intrigue and espionage. It would be up to Hammett to take the hardboiled hero and drop him right smack into the gangland streets of Prohibition America.

Both in his fiction and nonfiction, Hammett came down hard on the old-fashioned detective story. The brainy sleuth who rarely leaves his room, yet unerringly identifies the murderer from esoteric clues, struck him as utterly ridiculous. Hammett had skulked in too many cold doorways and had been taken too many times by surprise to put much stock in armchair detectives. He knew how often real-life investigators are stumped trying to piece together what happened, and he knew that they were not gentlemen of leisure with eccentric hobbies but low-priced drudges on twenty-four-hour call.

Hammett's first detective, Waldron Honeywell, would make a point of proving that the Sherlock Holmes mysteries would have been cracked by routine methods of ordinary policemen. Soon, however, even he would step aside for a more realistic and influential creation: the Continental Op. Years later Hammett explained that the Op was never given a name so as to stand for every operative. "I've worked with several of him", he said.[9] Physically the Op was modeled after James Wright, assistant manager of Pinkerton's Baltimore office and Hammett's former boss. The short, thick-bodied, rough-spoken Wright used to drill into his underlings that morality was a strictly personal affair. When on the case, a detective may lie, cheat, remove evidence, and emotionally manipulate suspects so as not to disadvantage himself vis-à-vis men who abide by no code of honor.

The Continental Op made his first appearance on 1 October 1923, in a story called "Arson Plus". By the end of the decade, the squat, gruff, middle-aged detective had become a regular, featuring in no less than thirty-six stories, all but two in *Black Mask*. The readers' reaction was enthusiastic: in a 1930 poll they voted Hammett one of the magazine's best liked writers. Even more than the stories, however, it was Hammett's first novel that made his hero a detective icon. The backstory of its famous title is recorded in a letter from Hammett to his publisher Blanche Knopf:

> Somehow I had got the idea that "Poisonville" was a pretty good title, and I was surprised at your considering it hopeless—sufficiently surprised to ask a couple of retail book sellers what they thought of it. They agreed with you, so I'm beginning to suspect which one of us is wrong. Here are the only new titles I've been able to think up so far: THE POISONVILLE MURDERS, THE SEVENTEENTH MURDER, MURDER PLUS, THE WILLSSON MATTER, THE CITY OF DEATH, THE CLEANSING OF POISONVILLE, THE BLACK CITY, RED HARVEST [Y].[10]

Notwithstanding praise from Joseph "Cap" Shaw, the editor of *Black Mask*, which by 1927 had reached crescendo proportions, Hammett might have never written *Red Harvest*, had it not been for Shaw's insistence that his writers publish book-length fiction, indirectly boosting the prestige of the magazine. The rest, as they say, is history. Hammett's crime-riddled, slang-riddled, hyperbolical gangster story caught on, attracting audiences to this day, not least in the Coen brothers' stylish adaptation as *Miller's Crossing* (1990).[11]

Whence this stunning success—reprised a year later by *The Maltese Falcon*, which sold out seven reprints in 1930 alone? Some critics suggest that Hammett masterfully translates motifs from romantic fiction into the setting of the modern city. According to this recipe, *Red Harvest* is a tale of a knight errant who slays the dragon (or, alternatively, cleans the Augean stables), whereas *The Maltese Falcon* is a modern-day treasure hunt. Although true, even more truth is to be found in the blunt realism that beckons from every page of *Red Harvest*. It is not quite a procedural yet, but then Ed McBain would have the great benefit of coming a quarter century after the Thin Man.

WHO FRAMED ROGER RABBIT?

Anything but a conventional idea of a heartthrob, much like Bob Hoskins in *Who Framed Roger Rabbit?*, he is nevertheless attractive to women, especially when he shows vulnerability, as when he fears he might be going blood simple.

At the beginning of *Red Harvest* the Op gets hired by Donald Willsson, son of a local tycoon, but before he can suss out what this case is about, his employer is shot dead. Never one to waste an opportunity, the Op cons Donald's father, Elihu—the Tammany Hall-type mayor of Personville, aka Poisonville—to hire his bureau, the Continental Detective Agency, to clean up the corrupt burg for ten grand. While playing hard to get with the local femme fatale, Dinah Brand, the detective plays the bad guys off each other, even as bodies pile up (by any count, close to thirty). Having done his job, in the last scene the Op hands the cauterized city back to old Willsson, the rotten king of the rotten city.

Red Harvest provides a perfect snapshot of Hammett's anti-heroic hero. Although he holds his own in the face of superhuman odds, the Op cuts an unflattering figure. A short, stubby man of forty, he tips the scales at 190 pounds and owns to a "chubby middle" (106). Predating Kurt Vonnegut's *Slaughterhouse 5*, Hammett makes certain that no one could confuse his protagonist with a Hollywood leading man. After all, in Dinah Brand's words, how many bankable actors (beside, perhaps,

Edward G. Robinson) would fit the role of a "fat, middle-aged, hard-boiled, pigheaded guy" (85)?

Efficient and durable in scuffle after scuffle, the Op may call on the bureau for assistance but remains essentially a solitary bull of a PI. Where Race Williams and Jo Gar were youthful, classy acts not given to pinching pennies, Hammett's stubby, middle-aged cheapskate stands a world apart from them and from the later brood of detectives of the silver screen. Film PIs, like in Arthur Penn's 1975 *Night Moves*, are frequently romanticized into knights pursuing truth for its own sake, with the telltale wordplay on "night". In contrast, the Op is a workhorse for hire, not particularly mindful of the law. Half-modern urban lawman and half-classic western outlaw, he will ride again many decades later as Rudy Baylor, the legal beagle from Grisham's *The Rainmaker*.

And yet, partly justifying the claims that Hammett was transposing romantic motifs to modern urban reality, there is something Byronic about his hero. The Op has no past, no attachment to the place he arrives to, and no attachment to the place he comes from except for loyalty—you could almost say fealty—to his Boss. A lone wolf, he is incorruptible in his quest. Anything but a conventional idea of a heartthrob, much like Bob Hoskins in *Who Framed Roger Rabbit?*, he is nevertheless attractive to women, especially when he shows vulnerability, as when he fears he might be going blood simple.

The analogies to the romantic tradition carry only so far, of course, since the differences far outnumber the similarities. There is, for example, not a hint of romantic love, no tragic hero or tragic ending, not to mention that the Op is nobody's idea of a romantic lead: drinking hard, lying like his life hung on it (which it does), and riding Dinah Brand like no hero in the Provençal troubadour tradition ever would. Hemingway and other hardboiled writers often romanticized their protagonists into heroic bulwarks in an amoral world. For Hammett heroics are irrelevant in a world deprived of moral codes. The Op never looks less a hero than when, after all the bloodletting, it turns out that he had no intention of reforming Poisonville.

Unattached, self-reliant, plainspoken, unschooled but quick-witted by nature—the hardboiled detective owes in many ways to the national character as it has come to be mythologized in American history, including literary history. Much of his character can be traced as far back as Daniel Boone and the Leatherstocking tales of the clash between the frontier and the civilization. In this sense the Op is, indeed, an urban recreation of an

Indian fighter and a Tombstone lawman. In the same vein, his hostility to the avatars of America's capitalist society—the robber barons, politicians, cops, and gang and union bosses—owes much to frontier populism, a para-political (nowadays also paramilitary) attitude that, hand in hand with the repudiation of the federal government, sanctions vigilante justice.

The detective story is essentially a morality play, with the detective and the criminal often personified as two halves of the same psyche. The crime allegorizes an archetypal human impulse, whether revenge, lust, or greed, whereas the solution reintegrates the rent social fabric. In contrast, even as the Op returns the town to its former state, that state is shown to be corrupt and evil. In the classic detective story murder is an aberration from the social norm (remote locales reinforce the notion that crime can be solved without affecting society). *Red Harvest* is set in the heartland of America, but it is a heart so degenerate that organized crime and a harvest of death are no news to anyone.

In line with Hammett's loosely Marxist leanings, some elements of *Red Harvest* could be construed as an indictment of capitalist society. On the other hand, the novel advances no real platform for social reform or for raising political consciousness. Naturally, there is nothing amiss with that because writers of fiction have a different job description from politicians or social philosophers. In fact, even though much ink has been spilled over Hammett's Marxism and the price he paid in the wake of the House Un-American Activities Committee (HUAC), the *Red Channels*, and eventual blacklisting and imprisonment, in reality his later politics could be described as disillusioned populism (or even Op-ulism).

POW, YOU ARE THERE

> The hardboiled speech is such a potent yet adaptable invention that all characters employ it: gangsters, tycoons, detectives, bootleggers, labour organizers, politicians, bank clerks, boxers, hustlers, dames, and not least Continental operatives.

Hammett not only reclaimed what was even then threatening to become a stereotype of a detective hero but also perfected a style that would come to be synonymous with the American crime story, if not American literature *tout court*. The brisk, brusque narration, crammed with side-of-the-mouth slang, is a worldwide trademark of the genre. One critic put his finger on the heart of the matter: "Take the violence and take the hardboiled hero away and you can still have a hard-boiled story if you have the style... Pow, you are there with the staccato sentences, fragments of sentences and fresh verbs made out of nouns."[12]

Although detractors might see in *Red Harvest* a relic of its times, in truth few contemporary action thrillers can match the nervous energy of Hammett's prose. Take, for example, this fusillade of jump cuts: "I kicked the pooch out of the way, made the opposite fence, untangled myself from a clothesline, crossed two more yards, got yelled at from a window, had a bottle thrown at me, and dropped into a cobble-stoned back street."[13] Or how about this Op ed: "He looked around the room, smiled nervously, crossed to the open bathroom door, peeped in, came back to me, rubbed his lips with a tongue, and made his proposition."

Like in the beheading song from *The Mikado*, Hammett's whiplash-short phrasing is designed to deliver a succession of short sharp shocks. With exposition pared down to the minimum, pages upon pages of rapid-fire dialogue are punctuated only by scenes of rapid-fire action. How much *Red Harvest* is action-driven can be calibrated from the preponderance of verbs, a mind-boggling 20 % of the total word count. With some sentences packing only three or four words, the dash of events and the verbal rat-a-tat are diced into chapters sometimes only three or four pages long.

Much like Hammett's stories, where three-quarters of his lexicon is monosyllabic, *Red Harvest* is dominated by short vernacular Anglo-Saxon diction. It is also littered with slang, an essential part of today's aesthetic, but a risqué move in the 1920s. When Sinclair Lewis, the first American to receive the Nobel Prize for Literature, published *Babbitt* just seven years earlier, many critics crucified it for its liberal use of slang, even though it was nowhere near as roughshod as *Red Harvest*. Hitching the hardboiled novel to the same star that guided Whitman, Harte, Twain, and the fin-de-siècle naturalists, Hammett's decorum entailed correlating speech with the social milieu.

A man alone in a hostile burg, the Op gets chummy with crooks and hoodlums in order to turn them against each other. As part of this divide-and-conquer tactics, he has to pry information out of tight-lipped mouths while guarding what he knows, which fosters a self-conscious attitude toward language. Indeed, in contrast to most real-life detectives, Hammett's hero is surprisingly articulate for a hired gun. The wiseguys, too, are as prone to shoot back with a wisecrack as shoot you in the gut, often indulging in a round verbal sparring when their fists or gats should be doing the talking.

The hardboiled speech is such a potent yet adaptable invention that all characters employ it: gangsters, tycoons, detectives, bootleggers, labor organizers, politicians, bank clerks, boxers, hustlers, dames, and not least Continental operatives. This homogeneity is justifiable to the extent that all of them are steeped in the same criminal environment, interacting and communicating daily with one another. A tool of survival of the fittest and the wittiest, the streetwise idiolect adds to the cinematic feel to the plot, with people constantly on the move and action taking place in the streets, in contrast to the closet dramas of armchair-detective fiction.

The hardboiled style is such a distinct creation, in fact, that one can frequently recognize it just by looking at the page—whiter than most, since pared down to tit-for-tat dialogue interspersed with bursts of action. It is a style recognizable by the speed with which it is (meant to be) read, fuelled by predominantly monosyllabic vernacular replete with action verbs. It is a style that displays less than it means: tough, spare, understated, brimming with litotes. And, not least, it is a style that aims to please: colloquial, fast-moving, chock-full of action and urban wit.

At the end of the day it is also a style bespeaking the transformation of the USA from an agrarian to a hyper-industrial nation, boxed in unruly, unsafe, and ungovernable conurbations. Consonant with it is the fact that *Red Harvest* is hardly a murder mystery at all. As a whodunit, it should have ended with the solution of the murder of Donald Willsson, which comes a quarter of the way through. Instead, it grafts this opening murder onto a plot that, just like in *Sanctuary*, caroms through the entire history of modern crime in America: mafia racketeering, police corruption, assassinations, political sellouts, labor strike-breaking, bootlegging, fight fixing, gambling, bank robberies, and gun fights, to name just a few.

When at the beginning of the twentieth century, Lord Acton took on the editorship of the magisterial *Cambridge Modern History*, he vowed to chronicle our excesses and errors in the name of his own aphorism that, if power corrupts, absolute power corrupts absolutely. Not surprisingly, *Red Harvest* is also preoccupied with absolute power and absolute corruption. Old Elihu Willsson, an oligarch who owns the legislature, the courts, the police, and the state senators, is a metonym of American capitalism. Halfway through the book, the Op jeers: "don't kid yourself that there's any law in Poisonville except what you make for yourself" (119). By now, most Americans have internalized this point of view, regarding public officials and the institutional structures which they serve as irredeemably fraudulent and corrupt.[14]

SEVEN THOUSAND LIQUOR CASES

The gritty, crime-spattered picture from the pages of hardboiled fiction evolved in response to its times and social conditions, just as the legal procedural did in lockstep with our white-collar corporate decades.

Before we look at how Grisham adapted the hardboiled conventions for his legal procedurals, let us set the scene by taking a short detour through the streets of the USA between the two World Wars. Even a perfunctory sketch makes apparent that the gritty, crime-spattered picture from the pages of hardboiled fiction evolved in response to its times and social conditions, just as the legal procedural did in lockstep with our white-collar corporate decades.

In the years between *The Great Gatsby* and *The Grapes of Wrath*, America faced a tidal wave of criminal violence tied to Mafia syndication, institutional corruption, political graft, and economic malaise of the Great Depression—all of them attendant on the chaos of immense urban growth. Where in 1810 there were just nineteen cities with over 100,000 residents, in 1880 there were fifty. Between 1880 and 1900 alone New York City grew from under two million people to three and a half million. Within the same period Atlanta, Buffalo, Detroit, Omaha, Toledo, Indianapolis, Columbus, Cleveland, and Milwaukee more than doubled their populations.[15]

Immigration reached an all time high: almost fifteen million people staggered onto the shores of Ellis Island between 1890 and 1920. Where in 1900 one-third of Americans lived in cities, by 1920 country dwellers were a minority. The bigger the shark, the bigger the pilot fish, and crime levels swelled along with the cities. In 1926 alone there were 12,000 homicides for 117 million Americans—more than 10 homicides per 100,000. Today, with a population of 317 million, that rate is less than half of what it was then (which still amounts to a murder every half an hour).

During the Prohibition crime and especially violent crime "matured" in nature. No longer restricted to unrelated felonies committed by violent but unorganized perpetrators, lawlessness assumed the dimensions of out-and-out racketeering, especially after the constitutionally mandated thirty-six states ratified the Eighteenth Amendment in January 1919, making the sale and distribution of intoxicating beverages a federal offense (eventually all states except Rhode Island and Connecticut signed on that one-of-a-kind social experiment).

Almost overnight the relationship between politicians and gangster bosses assumed a new dynamic. Previously politicians protected gangsters who, using muscle and organization, helped them ensure electoral success in turn for protection and lucrative contracts. During the 1920s and 1930s, Prohibition and criminal syndication (following the territorial settlement among the so-called Group of Seven—Lucky Luciano and Tom Pendergast among them) changed all that.[16] Why bother greasing politicians to make a few dishonest bucks by overcharging the city for construction contracts or trash disposal when bootlegging will make you rich overnight? Big money sent big gangsters on a nationwide shopping spree, buying Democrats and Republicans left and right.

In 1929, the year of *Red Harvest*, in many cities real power lay in the hands of crime bosses, so much so that Frank Loesch, President of the Chicago Crime Commission, actually asked Al Capone to help Chicago hold an *honest* election.[17] Holding entire cities in their pockets, kingpins like Hammett's Elihu Willsson were copied wholehog from the front pages of scandal-larded tabloids. How did Willsson differ from Tom Pendergast, perhaps the most feared power broker in the country who, as Kansas City's Democratic party boss, routinely "elected candidates by stuffing ballot boxes, bribing businesses, and beating and intimidating voters"?

If the politicians and political kingmakers were crooked, they could have been learning their trade from the police. It is estimated that, during the Prohibition, nearly two-thirds of the Chicago police were on the take, and in some precincts 100 %. It was futile to make arrests. Witnesses testified at their own risk, many of them intimidated, others bought, more than one silenced with a bullet. Many judges were owned by gangsters, so that of almost 7000 liquor cases that went before the New York courts, 400 never went to trial and more than 6000 were dismissed, giving a risible conviction rate of 7 %.

Also in 1929, the National Commission on Law Observance and Enforcement publicly stated: "The general failure of the police to deter and arrest criminals guilty of many murders, spectacular bank, payroll, and other hold-ups and sensational robberies with guns, frequently resulting in the death of the robbed victim, has caused a loss of public confidence in the police in our country."[18] The police were not merely corrupt but brutal toward the poor and helpless. Officers broke in new recruits with: "Boys, there's more justice in the end of this nightstick than there is in all of the courts of the land."

Image 2.2   Orange County Sheriff's deputies dumping illegal booze, Santa Ana, 1932. "*Many judges were owned by gangsters, so that of almost seven thousand liquor cases that went before the New York courts, four hundred never went to trial and more than six thousand were dismissed, giving a risible conviction rate of seven percent.*"

Seen in this light, the *Red Harvest* that on the first reading seems so contrived in its over-the-top violence and hyperbolic corruption begins to look like a photographic, if distilled and condensed, likeness of its times. Indeed, all the building blocks of its plot—indiscriminate murders, pitched gun battles in the streets, degenerate police force, power sharing between politicians and gangster bosses—are altogether factual. To be sure, thirty stiffs (roughly one every seven pages) seems extreme until you remember that every year every metropolis would chalk up scores of homicides, most of them unsolved. Poisonville's double-dealing mayor having a sit-down with assorted crime bosses and Police Chief Noonan are as all-American as a Norman Rockwell painting.

As audiences would rediscover on the pages of the legal procedural, the hardboiled decades with their crisp prose, romantically anti-romantic heroes, and muckraking appetite for social dysfunction were neither gone nor forgotten. Their bestselling formulas certainly ring familiar: authentic

street lingo, credible rendition of the criminal underworld, gritty out-
look on life, shades-of-gray morality, jaded picture of law and justice,
quick wit and verbal skirmish, and not least self-effacing understatement.
Reinventing popular fiction for contemporary readers, the legal procedural would also reinvent the concept of American justice while integrating legalese into the American vernacular.

VACANT NICHE IN THE MARKET

> If Watergate is a historical watershed when the nation en masse lost faith in
> its lawmakers, it is also a symbol of a new breed of law breakers who now
> called the shots.

The metamorphosis of the rough-and-tumble private eye into a Harvard-
groomed attorney occurred neither overnight, nor in a linear fashion.
After all, many postwar purveyors of courtroom drama—Jack Ehrlich,
George V. Higgins, William Harrington, Harper Lee, and the perennially
bestselling Erle Stanley Gardner—elected not to follow in the Thin Man's
footsteps. It was not until the 1970s, and even more so the 1980s, in fact,
that lawyer heroes began to forfeit some of their postwar polish and evince
more than a casual resemblance to the old guns for hire.

Whence the change? Why would legal eagles begin to resemble Sam
Spade and even the Continental Op, instead of remaining as honorable
and gallant—not to mention celibate and substance-free—as Atticus Finch
in *To Kill a Mockingbird*? One account of the genesis of modern legal fiction goes like this:

> The startling success of the lawyer procedural since the late 1980s (and
> the relative lack of such outstanding forerunners of Turow and Grisham as
> George V. Higgins) can be related to massive changes in the historical condi-
> tions which underpin the production and consumption of suspense fiction.
> The collapse of the Soviet Union, the disintegration of the Eastern bloc and
> the end of the Cold War made the old-style NATO spy thriller obsolete. The
> lawyer-procedural stepped into this vacant niche in the market.[19]

This putative etiology, whereby the legal procedural came into being to
replace the hole created by the spy thriller, is questionable for a number
of reasons. First of all, chronological correlation does not entail causality.

Every time I brush teeth after supper it gets dusky outside, yet I would be a fool to attribute nightfall to my dental hygiene. Next, the theory ignores a welter of counterevidence. As the careers of Len Deighton and John le Carré in England, and Robert Ludlum and Tom Clancy in the USA (not to mention their numerous rivals, clones, and in the case of the latter two thriving franchises) bear out, espionage fiction has enjoyed colossal popularity during the 1970s and 1980s, and ever since.

Moreover, if any genre were to fill the allegedly vacant spy-fi niche, it would not be legal fiction, whose protracted courtroom proceedings have no analogues in Bond-style escapades, but the police procedural, premised as it is on murderous riddles wrapped inside investigative enigmas and on plotlines more akin to the intrigues and mind games of espionage novels (to say nothing of the action quotient of fistfights, gunfights, and shadowy encounters in the dead of night). Finally, the theory is falsified by the fact that by the 1980s courtroom procedurals, epitomized by Gardner's Perry Mason, have been celebrating more than half a century of solid sales and readers' loyalty.

On balance, the contention that the merger of hardboiled sensibility and procedurals about the ins and outs of the American legal system owed to massive historical changes in post-Cold War Europe does not stand up to scrutiny. One need not even look as far as Sidney Lumet's *Twelve Angry Men* (1957) to realize that, far from being a post-Berlin Wall phenomenon, America's fascination with the hooks and crooks of the law is rooted in the same muckraking impulse that gave birth to the hardboiled noir. Its love affair with legal shows old and new is splashed all over TV channels and their quotidian fill of *Perry Mason, Law and Order, Street Legal, Boston Legal, Night Court, Ally McBeal, Matlock, Judge Judy, The Practice, The Associates, 100 Centre Street, Against the Law, Common Law, The D.A., Court Martial, Suits, L.A. Law, The Jury, Partners,* and dozens of others.

Guns have always been the way of life (and death) in America, and especially as violent crime surged during the Prohibition and Depression era. But after World War II, gun-toting mafiosi gave way to another breed of criminal, bigger and better protected than anything America has seen before. Corporate villainy, which gave us robber barons like Rockefeller, Vanderbilt, Carnegie, Gould, Fiske, and Stanford in the days before Enron, Halliburton, Fanny Mae, Freddy Mac, and Bank of America, has been around from the birth of the nation. But in parallel with the postwar boom, corruption and white-collar crime took off on a scale undreamed of even by the mob.

If Watergate is a historical watershed when the nation en masse lost faith in its lawmakers, it is also a symbol of a new breed of lawbreakers who now called the shots. Suave, dressed to the nines, with a spin doctor and speech-writer on either side, their turf was no longer the mean street but a manicured boardroom where they hatched corporate rackets and political cover-ups.[20] The times were indeed a-changin' and, despite public affection for affable members of the bar *à la* Andy Griffith, in a world run by hinky politicians and their corporate cohorts only no-holds-barred legal grit could stand up for victims of "victimless" crimes perpetrated by banks, corporations, and law firms (not coincidentally, Grisham's first smash hit was called *The Firm*).

Luckily, the hardboiled hero was still for hire, even though by now he had to swap his trademark fedora for a brand-name tie, the trench coat for the latest in Armani blazers, and the Tommy gun for a Tommy Hilfiger briefcase. Just as predators evolve in sync with their prey, exacting justice from the "suits" called now for an attorney-at-law capable of going after the bad guys on their own legal and illegal terms. The only thing that changed, it seemed, was that they were now billing by the hour instead of by the day (plus expenses).

THE BANZHAF BANDITS

> A fresh-faced and inexperienced law student goes all by himself after a mammoth corporation, at the end of the day exacting legal justice and a multi-multimillion-dollar verdict in his client's favor. Could anything be more trumped up?

As a new class of courtroom procedural began to outsell crime fiction, and as lawyers began to steal the limelight from private and police detectives, the same critical voices that faulted hardboiled mysteries for purveying escapist fantasies began to snipe at legal fiction. Claims from the *integrati* that legal procedurals dealt in urban realism and social justice, narrating events that in the best documentary tradition mirrored precedent-making cases from real life, met with critical remonstrations against contrived and unrealistic plots.[21]

Not to look far, *The Rainmaker* seems to be a textbook case of trite melodrama dressed as legal storytelling. A fresh-faced and inexperienced law student goes all by himself after a mammoth corporation, at the end of the day exacting legal justice and a multi-multimillion-dollar verdict in his client's favor. Could anything be more trumped up? The Spiro Agnew case from 1968, filed against the then Vice-President of the USA, is a useful benchmark of how much (or, in reality, how little) credence to accord such criticisms.

As Governor of Maryland in 1967, Agnew handed out construction and engineering contracts to numerous friends, who repaid his largesse with generous gifts. What riveted the country about his high-profile trial was not even the offender himself—he was, after all, a politician—but the legal team that brought him to court: three young law students from George Washington Law School. Dubbed the Banzhaf Bandits (after their professor, John Banzhaf III), they successfully lobbied Maryland residents to press charges against Agnew on behalf of the state.[22]

Taking on the entire political machinery rolled out by the second-highest office in the land, against impossible odds the Bandits succeeded in stripping the offender of the protective cloak of elected political office. Even though the jury proved reluctant to convict, Agnew beat jail only by pleading *nolo contendere* (no contest) to a $10,000 fine and three years of unsupervised probation. Eventually forced to repay more than $268,000 to the state of Maryland, he chose voluntarily under duress to resign from the White House on 10 October 1973.

Another landmark case that highlights the documentary veracity of Grisham-type legal melodrama is the historic 1977 Ford Pinto trial. The Ford Motor Company had for years been aware that the Pinto's gas tank could easily rupture in rear-end collisions. Loath to cut into profits, they refused to address the problem, even though "making improvements on existing tanks cost from $5.08–$11 per car".[23] By the end of the day, the corporation's laxity in safety standards led to more than half a thousand lawsuits. Most were conveniently settled out of court, but there was one particularly ghastly incident that even Ford could not keep under wraps as it made headlines around the world.

Mrs. Lily Gray and her thirteen-year-old passenger, Rick Grimshaw, were driving in her Ford Pinto when it was rear-ended. The explosion was practically instantaneous and, by the time rescue crews converged on the smoldering wreck, Mrs. Gray was already dead. The boy was barely alive, covered by third-degree burns. The Gray family and the maimed teenager hired prosecutor Mike Consentino and filed a suit against Ford for what was commonly perceived as disregard for human life. In February 1978 the legal and automotive worlds were stunned "by the milestone decision of a California jury to award more than $128 million in damages in connection with a fatal fire in a 1972 Pinto".[24]

Despite the triumph for the plaintiffs, there was not to be a happy ending, in a denouement echoed by Grisham in *The Rainmaker*. Although the jury ruled that the Ford company must pay $600,000 to the survivors of Mrs. Gray, on top of $2.8 million in actual and $125 million in punitive damages, all this was later slashed to $3.5 million. Three and a half million dollars sounds like a lot when planning a Club Med vacation, but does not even approach compensating for a life lost and another disfigured beyond repair. All was not in vain, however. In what the media typecast as a David v. Goliath face-off, the prosecution succeeded in permanently changing the rules of conduct for corporate malpractice. The Ford trial established both a precedent and a legal ruling that corporations can be held accountable for failing to warn customers of potential hazards and, even more to the point, that they "can be prosecuted for any crime, including homicide".[25]

A landmark victory for an attorney who showed the average citizen how to wring justice from white-collar killers. But justice could be exacted even without being a member of the bar. In a 1993 lawsuit that may have inspired the plotline of *The Rainmaker*, a legal clerk with little more than dogged persistence built a winning case against the Pacific Gas and Electric Company of California. Her name has since become the title of a blockbuster Oscar winner and a synonym for real-life Davids stomping on corporate Goliaths: Erin Brockovich.

From Union Carbide's manslaughter of 4000 employees in an explosion at their Bhopal plant (linked to criminally shoddy production practices), to the Iran-Contra scandal when seemingly the entire American government lied to Congress in full view of the nation, to the reification of Gordon Gekko-type rapacity on Wall Street and Main Street—during the decade that breathed new life into the legal procedural, justice was once again up for grabs. The only difference between this lawless renaissance and the Prohibition was that, this time around, there were enough good lawyers to go after the bad guys.

America has always offered a fertile ground for violence and social lawlessness, but the last two generations, raised on media-fanned scandals and prosecutions, highlight a society tangled up in a paradox. With violent crime ebbing, the tide of white-collar crime reached tsunami proportions, and as felonies and corporations behind them got bigger and harder to fight, an attorney-in-shining-armor found himself called in to the rescue. In parallel, as the more and more litigious country turned to professionals versed in the art of war and the letter of the law, lawyer fiction came into its own, turning away from the docility of *Matlock* and toward a picture of the law more worthy of Faulkner's *Sanctuary*.

WORST OF PAGES

> There is no denying that despite so many critics complaining that Grisham's prose is awful, much of the time it is awful.

In spite of his penchant for bourbon and taking the law in his own hands, there was only one man fit for the job and, fortified with a law degree and a ritzy wardrobe, the hardboiled hero found himself employed once more. Few, however, employed him with greater panache and success than the legal procedural's wunderkind, John Grisham. Although the genre boasts a long array of brand-name authors such as Scott Turow, William Deverell, Richard North Patterson, David Baldacci, John T. Lescroart, Andrew M. Greely, and Lisa Scottoline, Grisham wins every popularity contest hands down, with all of his sixteen (and counting) legal procedurals making—and often topping—*The New York Times* bestseller lists.

Many of his early bestsellers, including *A Time to Kill*, *The Firm*, *The Pelican Brief*, *The Client*, and *The Chamber*, also became Hollywood blockbusters, right down to Francis Ford Coppola's tear-jerker adaptation of *The Rainmaker* (1997). With Hollywood heavyweights like John Voigt, Matt Damon, Mickey O'Rourke, Danny DeVito, Roy Scheider, and Danny Glover on the marquee of just that one film, and more adaptations in the pipeline, Grisham easily contests, if not exceeds, Hammett's celebrity at the peak of his fame.

Naturally, with the status of the star author in the genre comes his share of criticism. On the cusp of the millennium, *Newsweek* poured scorn on *The Testament*: "The big criticism that dogs the appearance of every new Grisham novel is that he's writing the same book over and over (David and Goliath go to court)."[26] A year later *People* magazine pulled even fewer punches in the review of *The Brethren* eloquently titled "Worst of Pages": "Grisham is guilty of creating unlikable characters, implausible plot twists and dull writing. A thriller minus the thrills." Ouch—even for a publishing goliath who outsells the competition many times over.

There is no denying that despite so many critics complaining that Grisham's prose is awful, much of the time it *is* awful. Justifying a 2009 quasi-compliment about "a skilled craftsman cranking it out on auto-pilot", he dishes out reams of wooden prose, replete with verbal splinters.[27] Nor is he ever going to win awards for characterization. As far as plotting goes, however, critics forget that at a deeper level all fictions look alike. If at a certain degree of thematic and structural abstraction all legal procedurals are indistinguishable from one another, so are Shakespeare's sonnets, the Brontës's *romans fleuves*, or Dickens's comedramas.

It is thus entirely correct of Mary Beth Pringle to observe that most of Grisham's thrillers feature a legal hero who "embodies the good that can come from law in a democracy, whereas the other lawyers in the novels often embody the larger obstructive legal environment against which the good lawyer struggles".[28] But the critics who would do their homework will note that each of his bestsellers introduces new elements into the familiar genre framework. In fact, it is these seemingly inexhaustible variations on the theme that bring readers back year in year out in anticipation of novel twists to the true-and-tried formula.

Grisham's first foray into fiction, *A Time to Kill*—according to him, influenced by *To Kill a Mockingbird*—tells the story of two lawyers, Jake Brigance and his assistant Ellen Roark, who represent a black man in the heart of the racist South. African-American Carl Lee Hailey, the avenging father of a brutally raped ten-year-old daughter, murders in cold blood the two white perpetrators. Harassed in the manner of *Mississippi Burning* by the predominantly white townsfolk and the local chapter of the KKK, the legal duo put their lives at risk to do right by the accused.

Grisham's second novel and first bestseller, *The Firm*, stars a young hotshot, Mitch McDeere, who discovers that the legal firm that employs him is owned by the mob, with the corollary that partners who try to quit have a nasty habit of turning up dead. Stuck between the rock and a hard place—sell his soul to the devil and risk jail, or assist the FBI and risk death—McDeere contends with his conscience as much as with the wiseguys. In *The Client* the protagonist is not even an attorney, but an eleven-year-old boy Mark Sway. When Mark accidentally learns the location of a missing US Senator's body, word leaks out, and soon he is on the run accompanied by his lawyer, Reggie Love, a fifty-something recovering alcoholic. After narrowly eluding their pursuers, the fugitives tip off the DA while the Sway family go into witness protection.

The Chamber represents an even more dramatic departure from the allegedly read-one-read-them-all template. As novice attorney Adam Hill vainly tries to save his estranged grandfather Sam Cayhall from death row, the book ruminates on the legal and moral morass of capital punishment. With each page, Adam has to come to terms with his grandfather's debt to society, the dimensions of guilt and redemption, and the role that lawyers play in the process. Even *The Testament* belies *Newsweek*'s plot recipe, focusing on internecine fighting that often accompanies probation of wills. Because billionaire Troy Phelan left most of his pile of gold to just one of seven heirs, illegitimate daughter and missionary Rachel Lane, a burnt-out lawyer Nate O'Reilly nearly dies trekking across the Brazilian rainforest to reach her before the will is eviscerated in court—only to find she is dead.

A growing number of Grisham's recent books, including *A Painted House* (2001), *Skipping Christmas* (2001), *Bleachers* (2003), *The Broker* (2005), *Playing for Pizza* (2007), and *Calico Joe* (2012), are not even legal fictions. *A Painted House*, which broadens Grisham's novelistic canvas to the rural South, deserves a special mention, alongside *A Time to Kill*, *The Chamber*, *The Last Juror*, *The Summons*, and—in another creative stretch— a short story collection, *Ford County* (2009). In the manner of Faulkner, all of them assemble a picture of a fictional northwest Mississippi town of Clanton in the no less fictional Ford County. *Sycamore Row*, a 2013 sequel to Grisham's first novel, continues to flesh out his Yoknapatawpha and its "hill people": poverty stricken sharecroppers, hardscrabble cotton pickers, immigrant toughs, good ole boys, white trash, uneducated blacks, physical and mental cripples, all immersed in a simmering culture of violence.

Exhibit A

Time and again the plot cools its heels while the narrator detours the reader through the ins and outs of *Law For Dummies*.

As even this quick survey reveals, Grisham's palette of plots, intrigues, and denouements is not as monochromatic as his detractors claim. But there are other aspects of his procedurals to suggest that this former lawyer, who practiced criminal law for a decade (for six and a half years in parallel with serving in the House of Representatives in Mississippi), may be pursuing artistic goals in conjunction with monetary. Were Grisham no more than a former litigator dabbling at literature, there would be little to explain why he takes stylistic chances in *The Rainmaker*, writing it almost completely in simple present, or why so many of his men and women dedicated to the law renounce it before his novels' end.

To better grasp the oddity of such denouements, picture Auguste Dupin, Sherlock Holmes, or Hercule Poirot forsaking their *métier* after wrestling with a particularly troubling case. Yet, in what must count as a self-reflexive statement on the profession, Grisham has Mitch McDeere of *The Firm* desert the bar after his ordeal, opting for a peaceful life instead of trying to recapture the opulent one he lost. In *The Pelican Brief* Darby Shaw outruns and outsmarts her enemies, only to abandon her law career as she goes into hiding. By the end of *The Testament*, Nate O'Reilly turns to spirituality instead of litigation. And it is no different in the denouement of arguably the most ambitious of Grisham's thrillers, *The Rainmaker*.[29]

The novel opens with the fresh-faced, fresh-out-of-law-school Rudy Baylor getting evicted from his apartment. Without a job and penniless, he finds lodgings with an aging lady, Miss Birdie. He also finds his first client—the Black family. Donny Ray Black is at death's door: his family cannot afford a complex but potentially life-saving treatment for leukemia. His mother purchased health insurance from Great Benefit, but the company insists that their policy does not cover leukemia. Maneuvering the Blacks through a bad-faith lawsuit, Rudy does his David bit against the defense team's Goliath while falling for a young abused wife, Kelly Riker.

When Kelly finally musters the courage to file for divorce from her maniacal husband, a savage fight ensues and Rudy kills him. He lets Kelly takes the blame, gambling correctly that she will be acquitted on grounds of self-defense. Rudy eventually wins the suit against the insurers, but the ending comes out of Sophocles rather than Aristophanes. Donny Ray is dead and the company files for bankruptcy, walking away without paying a penny. Bruised by the trial and his personal tribulations, the unconvicted killer drives off with Kelly into the sunset, planning a career change from lawyer to high school teacher.

Even considered in isolation from other Grisham procedurals, *The Rainmaker* shows amply that his aesthetic entails more than a courtroom tug of war between the good, the bad, and the ugly. Low on testosterone and adrenaline, the story delves into the personal challenges and ethical dilemmas of the legal *métier*. With the litigation anchoring the narrative structure, the bulk of the novel is devoted to relationships among people, the emotional paralyses they suffer, and the ways in which they struggle to glue back together their shattered lives. And, of course, there is the script-flipping hero who gets away with murder after manipulating the crime scene and the justice system for his own ends.

In the year he wrote *The Rainmaker*, Grisham found himself on the receiving end of a lawsuit from another lawyer-turned-writer who alleged that *The Chamber* plagiarized her book about representing serial killer Ted Bundy (she lost both in a lower court and on appeal).[30] It may be that the experience hardened even further Grisham's view of American legal profession—assuming it was possible in the first place. After all, as he scoffed in October 2014, the American judiciary has gone crazy during the last thirty years, incarcerating more and more people for less and less defensible reasons. What is certain is that, looking for a new aesthetic with which to depict the tortuous nature of contemporary justice, he went back to the hardboiled school.

At first glance, of course, youngblood Rudy looks poles apart from Hammett's middle-aged detective. But if you care enough for pulp fiction to spare it a second glance, you will notice the extent to which not only the heroes, but also the attitude, speech, and styles of both novels are cut from the same cloth. It is not just that Rudy and the Op are, by nature of things, truth seekers. Both narrate their stories in the same first-person, laconic, understated voice-over. Both own up to being work-driven, parsimonious, and cynical. Both team up with associates, even as they remain essentially loners. Both kill in the name of higher justice and, when needed, play dirty without looking back. Both leave town once their job is done.

Reading *The Rainmaker* after *Red Harvest* is, in fact, an experience familiar to connoisseurs of rap: the latter novel appears to liberally sample from its antecedent. Where the Op haggles with Dinah Brand over a dime, penny-pincher Rudy does yardwork for his landlady to cut the rent. Where the Op is a workaholic who forfeits sleep—a cold shower and cold bourbon take up less time—Rudy is equally averse to recess, "living at the office over the weekend, napping only a few hours, then returning like a lost sheep to the office" (463).

Both share a soft spot for dames with a heart of gold, and where the Op is gruff and super durable, underneath the kinder and gentler exterior Rudy is every bit the same ten-minute egg. Neither is loath to hit where it hurts, so much so that in the heat of the combat it gets hard to tell them—or their authors' prose—apart. "Before he can cock the bat, I lunge at his face with a right hook. It lands on his jaw and stuns him just long enough for me to kick him in the crotch." And: "I socked Jerry twice, kicked him, butted him at least once, and was hunting for a place to bite when he went limp under me."[31] Trading punch for punch and word for word, both show a strong sense of street and poetic justice, not to be confused with the law.

Like Hammett, who salts his pages with street talk and street walk, Grisham seasons his with legal jargon and procedure. Time and again the plot cools its heels while the narrator detours the reader through the ins and outs of *Law For Dummies*, to the point of elucidating the meaning of terms like deposition, trial unit, sanction, acquittal, and so on. For tens of millions of his fans, this is a priceless opportunity to get the inside view of courtroom tactics, the trade jargon, and the kitchen perspective on the profession that increasingly dominates public discourse.

Why pay a small fortune for *Barron's Dictionary of Legal Terms* when, for only a few bucks a pop, any Sunday reader can learn as much as any Sunday reader can from the reigning king of legal procedurals? To wit, a deposition is a standard method of pretrial discovery which consists of a stenographically transcribed statement by a witness under oath, followed if needed by a cross-examination, with attorneys present. A trial unit is an autonomous task force of lawyers, secretaries, and paralegals assembled by the firm to handle a case. A sanction is a reward or punishment for both civil and penal actions. An acquittal is a legal finding that a defendant is not guilty and thus to be set free.

It is through novels like *The Rainmaker* that the public learns about ambulance chasers, those much derided injury lawyers who circle hospital wards like sharks do a sinking raft, looking to sign up plaintiffs. But most of all, the reading public absorbs attitudes toward law from its star witness— a former trial attorney whose picture of American justice is frequently as hardboiled as Hammett's. As for the latter, *Red Harvest* encapsulates his view of the legal system in the figure of Dawn, a seedy shyster who speaks in filigree like S.S. Van Dine's sleuth Philo Vance (whom Hammett gutted in a review for *Saturday Review of Literature*).

ONE PART HAMMETT, TWO PARTS GRISHAM

The parallels to Hammett—the tidal wave of crime and the failure to sweep it from the streets included—are equally apparent when it comes to narration.

Even as he entertains his readers, Grisham educates them on the nuances —loopholes, in the parlance—of the American legal labyrinth, sometimes at the price of condensing information into mini-lectures embedded in the narrative, such as on the process of fast tracking:

> In response to years of criticism by laymen and lawyers alike, the rules of procedure were changed not long ago in an effort to speed up justice. Sanctions for frivolous law-suits were increased. Mandatory deadlines for pretrial maneuvring were imposed... Created in this mass of new regulations was a procedure commonly known as "fast-tracking," designed to bring certain cases to trial faster than others... The parties involved can request that their case be fast-tracked... usually done when the issues are clear, the facts are sharply defined but hotly in dispute, and all that's needed is a jury's verdict. (204)

Far more than for verisimilitude and local color, Grisham employs the procedural to comment on the American legal and judiciary systems. This didactic dimension seems to be of equal importance to him and to his readers, adults and children. To better reach the latter, in 2010 Grisham launched a series of legal fictions for teens, starring Theodore Boone, a thirteen-year-old with precocious legal savoir faire. "I'm quietly hoping", affirmed the writer what a generation of readers has come to expect of him, "that the books will inform them, in a subtle way, about law". No wonder that, when he speaks out on American law, he is listened to, as witnessed by the 2014 brouhaha over his remarks on child pornography.[32]

Instructing his readers about the fine points of the legal matrix, his books also instruct them about the United States of America, a country which boasts per capita the highest number of lawyers in the world. For an art historian, this is popular art in the service of mimetic representation. For an urban sociologist, this is popular culture bringing the visible world to Conradian justice. For a literary critic, this is popular fiction dishing out contemporary realism in the guise of high-octane crime drama, whether in its hardboiled or legal-procedural incarnation.

The parallels to Hammett—the tidal wave of crime and the failure to sweep it from the streets included—are equally apparent when it comes to narration. Innovatively for him, in *The Rainmaker* Grisham even attempts to write in the hardboiled style. Admittedly, his prose is for the most part a dim shadow of the fervid pace of *Red Harvest*, the analytical leanness of *The Maltese Falcon*, or the bon vivant gaiety of *The Thin Man*. But within its limited stylistic means, *The Rainmaker* gets better-than-average mileage out of crisp, staccato phrasing distinctly reminiscent of Hammett:

> I step outside. I close the door quietly behind me, and look around for nosy neighbors. I see no one. I hesitate for a moment and hear nothing from inside the apartment. I feel nauseated. I sneak away in the darkness. (571)

Not only are Grisham's sentences as bold and rhythmic as in *Red Harvest*, but about as caustic (not to say hardboiled) in their attitude:

> I'm about to strike gold, to destroy Great Benefit in open court, and I struggle every hour to control these thoughts. Damn, it's hard. The facts, the jury, the judge, the frightened lawyers on the other side. It's adding up to a lot of money. Something has got to go wrong. (462)

Even thematically Grisham positions himself closer to vintage Hammett and the hardboiled school than his detractors allow. Even as all of his procedurals are concerned with the miscarriage of justice, they are even more concerned with loyalties, like in Chandler, almost always divided and almost always betrayed when put to the test.

It is true that *The Rainmaker* might initially appear as over the top as *Red Harvest*, what with its byzantine intrigue, hyperbolic villainy, tear-jerker plot, and a climactic David v. Goliath showdown. In an endgame for the soaps—which corroborates many reviewers' opinion that not only the Boone series, but every one of Grisham's legal fictions is geared to the 8–13 age bracket—the Black family win a landmark courtroom victory, only to end up without a cent in their pockets. But if you think this is phony, recall how the Grey family had their compensation slashed by $121.5 million at a stroke of a gavel.

If you allow for the poetic license in the narrative condensation and tele-scoping of events, Grisham's drama is as realistic and as deeply rooted in today's litigation practice as Hammett's *Red Harvest* was in the lawless 1920s. Consonant with this mimetic impulse, *The Rainmaker* drives home a number of civic lessons, beginning with the dispossession of the lower-middle class to the fact that, under American law, once a company files for bankruptcy, it will typically receive enough protection to escape creditors and quickly begin cheating elsewhere. After all, Enron and all the "too big to fail" mortgage and financial scam artists are Great Benefit in everything but name.[33]

Like Great Benefit, all were innovatively defrauding their clients in a manner that put a sardonic spin on Enron's six-time title of America's

Most Innovative Company. As a business venture, Enron did not, after all, produce anything. Instead it acted as a go-between for energy transactions (in lumber, steel, oil, etc.), amassing a fortune while selling nothing except deception—for a while anyway. Hammett and Grisham would have been proud: judging by the returns from stock markets, Enron's stories were bestsellers too. It was not until its unorthodox business "solutions" blew up in the faces of the legion of faithful that Enron admitted to overinflating profits, exotic accounting, and all-out lying about its various ventures.

No fiction was too outrageous, no story too wild. In one example, Enron claimed that their plant in Teesside, UK, was earning millions while still under construction. In another instance, Enron executives in Valhalla, New Jersey, filed paperwork documenting oil trading worth $1.7 billion (which led to a colossal increase in stock price), although no trade had taken place at all. Naturally, once the investors smelled a rat, the lengthy process of filing lawsuits commenced. On cue, in a crude but effective move that defanged potential reparations, Enron, who must have stolen a page from Grisham's Great Benefit, filed for Chapter 11 protection. No longer liable for its grand larceny, it was soon reinventing itself as a "newer, stronger, albeit smaller" company (and no doubt kinder and gentler too).[34]

As Grisham's legion of fans testify with their wallets, his seemingly contrived plots vindicate him, like the hardboiled muckrakers of yore, as a chronicler of American corporate corruption and white-collar felony. After all, as the Prohibition and the Great Depression gave way to the postwar manufacturing boom and advertising blitz, readers and writers began to move away from the corner of Mean Street where the hardboiled hero used to rent an office. With the better-trained and better-equipped police better poised to enforce the law and keep neighborhoods safe, old-style PIs had to retire from the scene until business picked up again. And so it did when lawmen went aggressively after crime syndicates in the 1950s and 1960s.

Suddenly, another species of criminals started to get caught in the dragnet. Camouflaged in dapper suits and boardroom chatter, they were every bit as pernicious as the syndicated gangsters of yore. Even the public caught up with the fact that, in a fight against a multinational corporation or a government bureaucracy, you needed an apparent oxymoron: a good lawyer. In was time for a new type of American hero: a one-man or one-woman posse who could talk the legal talk and walk the courtroom walk. Throw the muckraking and the hardboiled tradition into the equation, and you have the formula for *The Rainmaker*: one part Hammett, two parts Grisham, a twist of lemon, and a whole lot of excitement.

NOTES

1. Engel, 102; thoroughly revised, parts of this research are based on Swirski and Wong (2005).
2. See Engel, 104.
3. Figures from CNN; Grisham official website; BBC News "Grisham".
4. Porter, 121.
5. See Geherin, 26.
6. Blaha, 801.
7. For background, see Regier; for the pulps, as opposed to the slicks, see Paula Rabinowitz.
8. For background, see Johnson.
9. In Geherin, 18.
10. 20 March 1928; in Hammett (2001), 45.
11. See Restaino; Mooney.
12. Panek, *Probable Cause*, 114.
13. Page 199; next quote, 174.
14. See Swirski, *Ars Americana*, (2011), and (2015).
15. For background, see Swirski (2007).
16. For Chandler's fascinating piece on Luciano, see Hiney, 250–255.
17. Panek, 96; below, Abadinsky, 83.
18. Panek, 100; below, Abadinsky, 109.
19. Hefferman, 190.
20. See Swirski, *Ars Americana*, (2011), and (2015).
21. On integrated versus apocalyptic scholarship, see Eco; on lowbrow versus highbrow, see Swirski (2005); Swirski (2016); Swirski and Vanhanen (2016).
22. See Banzhaf.
23. McCaghy, 295.
24. Strobel, 21–22.
25. Strobel, 272.
26. Jones (1999), 65; *People*, 46.
27. In Rayner.
28. Pringle, 23.
29. For Grisham's rare comment on the book, see Margaret.
30. Nelson; below, BBC News (2014).
31. Grisham (567); Hammett (184).
32. BBC News (2014); quote below, in Middleton.
33. Enron's illegal activities are extensively chronicled in Wuensche.
34. Quoted from Enron's official website: http://www.enron.com (2003). Shortly thereafter, Enron has deleted this phrase, then the entire website.

CHAPTER 3

Boilerplate Potboilers: William Faulkner and Ernest Hemingway

GOOD GOD, I CAN'T PUBLISH THIS

> Not to beat around the bush, *Sanctuary* boasts enough scandalizing or just plain pornographic material to rival Hearst's tabloids of the time.

In the notorious introduction to the 1932 Modern Library edition—axed on his behest from later Random House reprints—Faulkner took an unusual step for a serious writer, declaring that *Sanctuary* had been conceived as a potboiler. Having penned several books that got published but not bought, he confided, "I began to think of them in terms of possible money. I took a little time out, and speculated what a person in Mississippi would believe to be current trends, chose what I thought would be the right answer and invented the most horrific tale I could imagine and wrote it in about three weeks."[1]

Caveat emptor when buying into authorial confessions, especially into Faulkner's. To begin, *Sanctuary* (1931) took him not three weeks but four months to complete (the manuscript is dated January–May 1929; the typescript 25 May 1929). Neither did he invent it from scratch. The pivotal event, for example, was lifted from a Memphis newspaper report of a local mobster, "Popeye" Pumphrey, who had allegedly raped a girl with a pistol. There is no doubt, on the other hand, about the horrific nature of the tale. On finishing it, the publisher is said to have protested: "Good God, I can't publish this. We'd both be in jail."[2]

© The Editor(s) (if applicable) and The Author(s) 2016
P. Swirski, *American Crime Fiction*,
DOI 10.1007/978-3-319-30108-2_3

Apocryphal or not, this last part of Faulkner's account jibes with the resurgence of moral policing in America during the Great Depression. Its epitome was the new set of restrictions in motion pictures, quickly dubbed the Hays Code, after Hollywood's censorship czar. None of this, in the end, deterred his publisher, Hal Smith, from taking a chance on a manuscript so clearly packed with commercial dynamite. Neither did it deter MGM from reeling in the up-and-coming litterateur on a contract, capitalizing on his new-found notoriety *and* on his highbrow credentials.

In the summer of 2005 Oprah created a literary ado of her own by selecting *As I Lay Dying*, *The Sound and the Fury*, and *Light in August* for her distinctly lowbrow book club. While the nod from the High Priestess of Self-Help to the recondite *The Sound and the Fury* raised questions about high art and mass consumerism, it raised even more questions about why the infinitely more readable *Sanctuary*—from the same "golden period" in Faulkner's career—was left out. It certainly had nothing to do with violence, which is far more graphic in *Light in August*, beginning with the castration scene. On the other hand, none of the threesome that received Oprah's imprimatur was anywhere near as salacious.

Not to beat around the bush, *Sanctuary* boasts enough scandalizing or just plain pornographic material to rival Hearst's tabloids of the time. It goes beyond impotent Popeye's rape of a teenager with a vegetable to cross into the realm of sacrosanct psychosocial and sociobiological taboos. Insinuating that the protagonist, lawyer Horace Benbow, hides incestuous longings for his sister *and* his daughter-in-law, Faulkner portrays the rape victim as a nymphomaniac who calls her violator "Daddy" and revels in sex with a stud he finds for her, while Popeye himself whimpers and slobbers at the foot of the brothel bed.

Perhaps as disturbingly, flanked by four heavies and a mob shyster, she perjures herself when summonsed to court. Her testimony fingers an innocent man for her rape and for the murder of Tommy, a good-natured if slow-minded bootlegger, who had protected her right until Popeye blew his face off and deflowered her with a corncob. Ironically, the serial killer himself is eventually caught and hanged for a homicide he did not commit, in a denouement reprised hence in the Maigret *policiers* and in the Martin Beck procedurals.

Organized crime, racketeering, police corruption, political venality, labor breaking, bootlegging, gambling, prostitution, witness intimidation, guns spitting lead at a drop of a hat—there is enough crime and hardboiled justice in *Sanctuary* to fill *Red Harvest*, an obvious model for a bestseller-seeking writer in the days when Hammett was the rage. This is what may have also drawn them to each other in Hollywood, where during the 1930s they became fast drinking buddies, with Hammett going crazy that Faulkner, as big a lush, could knock off novel after novel while his own creative powers were drying up.

For all that, Faulkner's own harvest of violence and death, much as the quixotic investigation carried out by his attorney, is played out in the melancholy key of vintage Chandler. Moreover, even though like Grisham Faulkner follows the erratic course of retributive justice, instead of dicing up procedural niceties he wields the law like a microscope with which he examines the compulsions and cruelties inherent in basic human instincts. Indeed, whereas Hammett and Hemingway are direct and almost pure in their depictions of violence, Faulkner gravitates to its more brooding and twisted manifestations, much like Poe and Baudelaire before him.

This eclectic—not to say nobrow—array of literary registers fits with Leslie Fiedler's argument that one of Faulkner's greatest accomplishments in *Sanctuary* is engaging "two audiences, each unaware of the fact, much less the grounds, of the other's appreciation".[3] Selling well is emphatically not the same as selling out and, if Faulkner's hunt for a bestseller between literary highs and lows sounds like the latter, it is just another Ivory Tower canard. Not everyone can write in popular forms for popular audiences, as borne out by Fitzgerald's spectacular flameout in Hollywood.

A reader of Henry James, Faulkner would have known the latter's story "The Next Time" in which, having published a series of distinguished works, a litterateur sits down to write a potboiler, only to produce another unpopular art novel. Even as James meant to reify the myth of Pure Art, incorruptible by such base motives as making money, for Faulkner it would have meant just the opposite. As critical of James as he was of Hemingway for sticking to their formulas and failing to take creative chances, he would become his own Pygmalion and his own Galatea and recreate himself as a nobrow bestseller.

It is worth remembering that his apprenticeship as a popular artist took him years during which, try as he might, he could not make a living writing for the slicks. Rejection after rejection made abundantly clear that editors did not think much of his commercial fiction (the silver lining was that it left him with plenty to cannibalize from in the later years).[4] Even the perennially anthologized "A Rose for Emily", written around the same time as *Sanctuary*, was originally turned down by *Scribner*'s and had to appear in the highbrow *Forum*.

This is why Faulkner's eventual success in placing his stories even in the über-slick *Saturday Evening Post*, where they would sell copy side by side with Fannie Hurst, Edna Farber, and Fitzgerald, marks not his failure but his measure as an artist. This is also why, far from being a manqué member of the Faulkner canon, *Sanctuary* marks its high point, developing an aesthetic that would take popular audiences where they would never have ventured on their own. Albert Camus, Nobelist himself, concurred. Calling Faulkner the greatest American novelist, he called *Sanctuary* his greatest novelistic achievement.[5]

GUTS AND GENITALS

Insofar as Faulkner's creative intentions can be read off his revisions, all three major lines of them are consistent with refurbishing an art novel into a courtroom noir.

Faulkner's determination to hit the commercial bull's eye may have gained in urgency in the wake of marrying up in 1929. It may have been further intensified by his missing mortgage payments, having to heat the house with firewood he had to chop himself (it had no running water or electricity either when he bought it in 1930), or putting in twelve-hour night shifts in the university power plant, wheeling coal from the bunker to the boiler. Ironically, the job afforded a lull of about five hours, during which he would improvise a table from the wheelbarrow and crank out a chapter of *As I Lay Dying* and then *Sanctuary* a night, giving a novel twist to the meaning of "potboiler".

Yet, to be even in a position to appraise what Faulkner achieved by means of *Sanctuary* presupposes approaching it as a result of art-creative decisions and not of merely financial pressures. Economic determinism, whether Marxist or market-capitalist in origin, denies the very possibility of artistic critique. In spite of occasional claims to the contrary, pragmatic and pecuniary considerations do not automatically invalidate aesthetic ones—with *Sanctuary* the best case in point. After all, even as it attests to Faulkner's determination to make a buck, it equally attests to his determination to work in the popular idiom without compromising his artistic standards.

The proof lies in the proofs. After Faulkner received the galleys in mid-November 1930, he reported being appalled at the very impulse that caused him to write the book. But what was that impulse? Given how unreliable Faulkner is in other parts of his account, his post-hoc claims of starting out with the idea of a potboiler must be taken with a grain of salt. Indeed, what scant evidence there is points to the contrary. With Faulkner reading from the manuscript to his then friend and mentor Phil Stone, the latter was convinced that *Sanctuary* was another art novel.[6]

Was the original impulse that caused Faulkner to write *Sanctuary* to add another high-modernist chapter to the Yoknapatawpha saga? If so, as likely as not he rewrote the proofs out of artistic considerations, seeing as his impecunious circumstances had not changed in the meantime. If, on the other hand, he had been gunning after a potboiler from the get-go, his shock at the proofs could only have come from the shock at his ineptness in browing down despite the effort he poured into it, about which he made no bones:

> I made a thorough and methodical study of everything on the list of best-sellers. When I thought I knew what the public wanted, I decided to give them a little more than they had been getting; stronger and rawer—more brutal. Guts and genitals.[7]

Indeed, insofar as Faulkner's creative intentions can be read off his revisions, all three major lines of them are consistent with refurbishing an art novel into a courtroom noir. For one, the galleys version suffers from a distinct dichotomy of purpose, grafting the rape-and-homicide trial onto a Sartoris family saga—or the other way around. The revisions streamline the plot by shearing off reams of historical interpolations that threatened to turn *Sanctuary* into a digressive performance like its sequel, *A Requiem for a Nun* (1951).

Equally, where the galleys try to graft a Freudian study of Benbow's sexuality onto the camera-ready story of Temple and Popeye, the canonical version thins the Freudian subtext to a few residual hints, so much so that readers unacquainted with *Sartoris* (1929), where these matters get more play, may dismiss or even miss them altogether. Finally, better economy of purpose is achieved by deleting the frequent and often spurious jumps in chronology, together with poorly integrated shifts in setting and point of view.

None of the changes, on the other hand, make the book any less of a literate potboiler. The canonical version is, if anything, even more violent, adding a mob lynching to more than half a dozen murders that take place on and off screen. There is still porn, sadomasochistic and hardcore, and a Southern Gothic gallery of feebs, freaks, and crips, beginning with Popeye, whose chinless face is deformed like the rest of his body. Then there is broad comedy and deadpan one-liners that would be right at home in Hammett or DeMille ("whut you want to kill him fer? You caint eat him, kin you?").[8]

There is even gallows humor, when Popeye asks the sheriff to fix his hair, only to hear "Sure" as the latter springs the trapdoor. *Sanctuary* even sports that ultimate stamp of commercial fiction, the O'Henry hook, which ironically reverses Popeye's fortunes on the final pages. Indeed, given this coherence of vision in the revisions, Faulkner's success as an artist must be measured by his success as a genre artist, who assembled a literate crowd-pleaser from—as the editor of the eventually restored original tallied up—"Eliot, Freud, Frazer, mythology, local color, and even 'current trends' in hard-boiled detective fiction".[9]

Reviewers and fellow novelists, such as the future French Minister of Cultural Affairs André Malraux, all acknowledged this nobrow melange, even throwing classical tragedy into the mix. Whether Faulkner's final cut lives up to his aesthetic bravado is, of course, another story. To be sure, for the most part his prose rolls along as smoothly as a tear on a penitent's cheek. From time to time, however, it lapses into the type of grand guignol, murkiness, and adjectival logorrhea that makes the annual Faux Faulkner competition for the best (worst?) parody of the master's style such a hoot. Viscid, surfeitive, or fulgent, anyone?

Faulkner's strong suit is his dialogue, whether it is Benbow's hollow non sequiturs or Tommy's untutored drawl. Even so, he falls short of legal proceduralists or hardboiled writers when it comes to rendering the milieu in authentic street jive or lawyerese. Tellingly, there is almost no slang in *Sanctuary* on either side of the law, although the presence of tough mugs, whether under glass or in the zotzing streets of Memphis, would beg for a few twists, wikiups, and roscoes. In this respect, Hammett's and Grisham's verbal resources trump Faulkner's just because, having walked the walk, they can talk the detective and courtroom talk.

SOUTHERN GOTHIC

It is for no other reason that the Gothic is sometimes classified as a proto-detective novel, wherein Fate and not the law is called upon to right the past wrongs, much as in *Sanctuary*.

Elevation to the canon has frequently less to do with literariness than with historical contingencies and institutional or individual self-interests (*1984* is a *very* bad great novel). Adding to the muddle that is literary axiology is the fact that prejudgment about a book's bloodline—highbrow or low-brow—can significantly affect perceptions of aesthetic quality. In terms of the high-low divide, at least, readers typically find what they have been primed to find: artistic invention in one, generic convention in the other. Reverse the background assumptions and you will be surprised how the new frame alters the picture.[10]

Few institutional curators are keen to publicize such embarrassing facts as that, not long before Faulkner was awarded the 1949 Nobel Prize in Literature, the faculty at the Ole Miss dallied with the idea of awarding him an honorary degree, only to scuttle it in light of a conspicuous lack of support. Primed by the Swedish Academy, however, generations of readers have been primed to genuflect to what Hemingway disdained as his rival's verbosity, opacity, and scarcity of control—only to be dissed back for self-imitation and timidity in experimenting with linearity and point of view: in short, with what Faulkner considered style.

Even as critics concede Faulkner's indebtedness to popular genres, the opinion that *Sanctuary* is a good novel despite, rather than because, of its lowbrow pedigree remains a rule rather than an exception.[11] It is a rule, however, that might be more honored in the breach than the observance. After decades of critical labors dominated by psychoanalytic gibberish or, conversely, dismissals as a potboiler and thus second-grade literature, it is time to celebrate *Sanctuary* as a genre novel, not least because it allows us to appreciate its author's creative intentions and, as such, his artistry in every sense of the word: highbrow, lowbrow, and nobrow.

Sanctuary brought Faulkner the sought-for commercial *and* critical success, cemented that same year by his first Hollywood contract ($3000 over six weeks). It outsold everything he had published before and, likely, would have made him rich had not the publisher gone bankrupt during the Depression. It proved a perennial draw even during Faulkner's pro-longed decline in popularity, when nearly all of his books went out of print before the nod from the Nobel Committee gave them a new lease on life. Indeed, its imagery became so iconic that, in his letters and eventually in *Across the River and into the Trees* (1950), Hemingway would malign his rival as "Corncob".[12]

Of course, *Sanctuary* is more than the sum total of the moves and countermoves of the plot. Like Hemingway, Faulkner models responses to trauma, but where the former has his eye on the instinctual and physical, Faulkner homes in on the moral. This is why much of *Sanctuary* is filtered through the sensibilities of a protagonist who is as much of an antihero as the Op, if for dramatically different reasons. Well-meaning but defeated all around, Benbow founders as an agent of justice because he is incapable of waging war on men—and women—morally lesser than he is. Lacking the hardboiled gutsiness of a James Wright or the crass vitality of a Snopes, he admits as much: "The machinery is all here, but it wont run" (17).[13]

The opening chapters unfold in the moonshiner's hideout known as the Old Frenchman Place, decrepit and ominous in the manner of Horace Walpole's *The Castle of Otranto* (1764). Even as the popular imagination associates the classic Gothic with the specter of assault on maidenly virtue, Walpole's plot equally conjures up the specter of unavenged crime. It is for no other reason that the Gothic is sometimes classified as a proto-detective novel, wherein Fate and not the law is called upon to right the past wrongs, much as in *Sanctuary*.

Faulkner fills the Old Frenchman homestead with a supporting cast of outlaws and misfits who send Benbow, Temple, and Popeye on the way to their respective destinies. The biggest outlaw and misfit in their midst is, of course, the diminutive serial killer. Encased in black suits that set his deformed bloodless face in relief, stunted from birth from a syphilitic mother so that he needs to wear his pants rolled up, his grotesqueness is mirrored in his doll-like hands from which a cigarette or a pistol are rarely absent.[14]

Popeye is both a likeness and a caricature of Dutch Schultz, another mob-connected bootlegger whose readiness to settle all accounts with a gat made him into a gangster icon of the Prohibition. Faulkner's psychological brilliance is evinced by the fact that, four decades before the birth of FBI's Behavioral Science Unit, he sketches the life history of a serial killer with the exactitude of a modern-day criminal profiler: familial and social abuse, pyromania, maiming animals, stints in foster homes and juvie institutions, violence-warped sexuality, and that almost relieved passivity once in the hands of the law.[15]

Into this Southern Gothic blunder a couple of intruders from high society, a young lawyer Gowan Stevens and his college flirt Temple Drake. A pretty, vacuous flapper, she is as much a victim of her own nature as of Popeye who, in a scene more elliptical than the orbit of Mercury, rapes her with a corncob. Debriefing her in a Memphis brothel, where the gangster eventually installs her as his moll, Benbow is staggered to hear her recount the assault "with actual pride, a sort of naive and impersonal vanity" (216). But, while Gowan and Temple epitomize the new South, so does Benbow's widowed sister Narcissa, one of the chief engineers of her brother's defeat in and out of court.

Although a Sartoris, with all that entails in terms of Faulkner's binomial allegory, her expedient morality is akin to that of Senator Clarence Snopes, a corrupt and venal representative of his voters in more ways than one. Living in the brothel, Temple comes under the wing of its madam, the fleshy Reba Rivers who, in her hardnosed likeability, shares something with Miss Jenny, an aged great aunt in the Benbow household. A shrewd observer of human follies, Miss Jenny's occasional council to Benbow is the closest thing to authorial intrusion in a novel that changes angles and styles of narration as often as a guilty man changes his testimony.

The storyline, spread over a few summer weeks of 1930, splits into three parts, with the Old Frenchman ruin as the backdrop to the first, and Jefferson and Memphis to the latter two. Alternating between the city and the big city, it juxtaposes Benbow and Popeye, two central players in the courtroom drama in which one is conspicuously present as counsel for the defense and the other conspicuously absent. One impotent existentially, the other sexually, both the truth seeker and the evildoer underscore the complexity of good and evil. It is possible for a good man to be a bungling lawyer and an incestuous voyeur, and it is possible to feel a touch of pity and understanding for a very bad one.

The mood and structure of the first part, which ends with Tommy's death and the rape of Temple, is patterned on classical tragedy, as grim and ineluctable as any of Sophocles. Carrying their fates with them, Gowan and Temple exemplify Oscar Wilde's aphorism about being able to resist anything except temptation. The self-professed Virginia gentleman cannot stop drowning himself in alcohol, while the girl courts disaster by ignoring repeated warnings to lay low. As simple-minded Tommy wonders why the men around the house cannot leave her be, his repeated curse "Durn them fellers" sounds, like the banjo riff in *Deliverance*, a thin note of impending catastrophe.

MURDER CAPITAL OF THE USA

Like *Red Harvest*—or for that matter any good novel—even as it condenses and hyperbolizes, *Sanctuary* holds a mirror up to reality, cataloguing the collateral damage of the worst social experiment in American history, one that made the Jazz Age a bootlegger's and gangster's paradise.

The law in Faulkner is what it is in Grisham: a normative social system, a machinery of behavioral control and social engineering, a self-interested and almost self-governing institution, and a species of vice lodged deep in the heart of American culture. Historically, the USA has been the brain-child of lawyers, with nearly half of the signatories of the Declaration of Independence and thirteen of the first sixteen presidents trained in the law. Their stranglehold on the life in the country continues in the present, with the number of attorneys and the volume of litigation between one and two orders of magnitude greater than in other capitalist countries, notably in Japan. "The problem as I see it", quips the hero of Nelson DeMille's *The Gate House*, "is fast-food chains and lawyers. Too many of both" (136).

Although, in contrast to Grisham, Faulkner had no legal training, he was surrounded by generations of family members, friends, acquaintances, and even hunting buddies who practiced law. It is not for nothing that his hometown of Oxford, Lafayette (a stand-in for Jefferson, Yoknapatawpha) has been described as "almost overrun with lawyers".[16] Indeed, the way his works crawl with attorneys and men dedicated to the law as a way of life—their enumeration would take half a page—Faulkner could be mistaken for a legal proceduralist. Whether he is a better exponent than Grisham of the values of American society as viewed through the prism of the law is, of course, another question.

If the presence of lawyers and the law is felt throughout Faulkner's canon, it is especially so in the Yoknapatawpha novels (with the exception of *As I Lay Dying*). It is not a coincidence that, during the days when he was writing and rewriting *Sanctuary*, Memphis reigned as the undisputed murder capital of the USA, overshadowing even New York and Chicago in the volume and depravity of violent crime. Be that as it may, even more than a gangster thriller, stripped to its core *Sanctuary* is a courtroom drama, not least because, stripped to *its* core, any courtroom showdown is a life-scripted morality play.

Like Grisham, Faulkner indicts the social rituals of exacting justice which, more often than not, are more intent on going through the motions than on fulfilling their legal and moral obligations. Justice in *Sanctuary* is blind alright—to the truth, that is. Even the idealistic Benbow warns his client: "you're not being tried by common sense… You're being tried by a jury" (132). At the end of the proceedings, which deliver the usual farrago of high rhetoric and low blows, the jury finds a blameless man guilty on the word of a messed up teenager. When, during the night, the mob takes the law into its own hands and torches him and the jail, Faulkner rounds out a picture of American justice as sordid as anything in his canon, including *Wild Palms* (1939).[17]

The same travesty is in evidence during the hearings that condemn Popeye to death for another man's murder. Both mistrials, in which both of the accused place no faith in the discharge of justice, are mirror images of each other. To ensure that the parallels are not missed, Faulkner goes for symbolic overkill: both juries take exactly eight minutes to arrive at the same wrong verdict. Elsewhere, he is again as subtle as a Jehovah's Witness, juxtaposing a black rat and black-clad Popeye before the rape, and red and white coloration in its aftermath. Bleeding in Popeye's motorcar, Temple is framed by white tree blossoms, both echoed in the powder and rouge she lays on thick onto her pale face set in relief by red curls.

Just as outright lawlessness, miscarriage of justice is symptomatic of the corrosion of social machinery. Like *Red Harvest*—or for that matter any good novel—even as it condenses and hyperbolizes, *Sanctuary* holds a mirror up to reality, cataloguing the collateral damage of the worst social experiment in American history, one that made the Jazz Age a bootlegger's and gangster's paradise. Not that the Prohibition was supposed to achieve *that*, or indeed anything less than a moral renaissance across the country. Its roots went back, after all, to the Anti-Saloon League founded in 1895 to lead the crusade against the corner saloon, blamed for degrading workers into lives of vice and crime, not to mention impairing their productivity.

Even before the Prohibition there were local and even state options, so that by 1918 two-thirds of the country were already legally dry. Under pressure from the war economy, which was gobbling up all stores of grain and sugar, in January 1919 the requisite thirty-six states ratified the Eighteenth Amendment. During the Jazz Age (also known as the Lawless Decade) the ban became, of course, such a howling failure that in 1928 the high-profile Wickersham Commission was convened by president Hoover to suggest a way out of this mess. Its *Report on the Causes of Crime* came out in 1931 and it was a doozy: the Prohibition, it concluded, was unenforceable but should be enforced. Only with the election of FDR, with a tidal wave of reforms about to engulf the country, the Eighteenth Amendment was killed and buried in nine months.

In the context it is funny that, even as everyone around him drinks and carouses ("jazzing" was slang for whoring), bootlegging Popeye gripes that there should be a law against alcohol. His counterpart, Benbow, on the other hand, starts out full of faith that the law will perform rationally and humanely even as individuals serving it may be less than honorable. By the end of his trials he is reduced to a shell of a man, crushed by the collapse of the illusion that justice is what the law is about. His pipedream of society made cooperative and cohesive by virtue of the state, the church, and the law withers in the wasteland typified by the utilitarian mores of Senator Snopes: if they don't see you, it did not happen.

A big part of Benbow's defeat comes from his head-on collision with organized religion. Trying not guilt but conformism to Baptist orthodoxy, like in *A Scarlet Letter* holier-than-thou Savonarolas pervert the Christian spirit by turning persecutors and eventually even murderers. In vain does Benbow console his client's common-law wife: "God is foolish at times, but at least He's a gentleman" (280). Hounded by the zealots of Jefferson, she counters with a simple: "I always thought of Him as a man." Her vision of God prone to indelibly human failings is the kindest interpretation of the religiosity in the novel.

Sniping as it does at hypocrisy and injustice, *Sanctuary* spares nary a word, on the other hand, to the trials of the Southern blacks. If anything, throwaway references to Negro servants, Jim Crow train cars, or homicide committed by a gorilla-black husband seem to perpetuate the stereotypes of the era. Even though Faulkner had to contend with accusations of racial condescension, if not worse, they are half-truths at best. Especially later in his life, notably in the wake of the 1955 murder of Emmett Till, he spoke out against white supremacist groups and their campaigns of terror. A year earlier he also publically endorsed *Oliver Brown v. Board of Education of Topeka* and its ruling against school desegregation.

At the end of the day, however, Faulkner is essentially an apolitical writer who, content to leave moralizing to Aesop, deems it his artistic duty to depict prevalent attitudes. Benbow's sister personifies those when she admits that the miscarriage of justice concerns her less than her standing in Jefferson. Her double standard is mirrored by Senator Snopes and DA Graham, two officers of the state and the law by virtue of their institutional appointments. If they have scruples, they hide them well while ingratiating themselves with anyone who smells like money or potential advancement.

Sanctuary Much

Eager to cash in on the sensation created by the novel, Paramount rushed to
buy the rights, only to release a heavily censored ragbag of a gangster story
and romantic melodrama.

Faulkner's narratives revolve not only around the law as a controlling force
in depraved, if not downright lawless, society. Equally they revolve around
history as the controlling force of individual existence. Nothing expresses
it better than his famous—and lately hotly contested in a court of law—
line from *A Requiem for a Nun*: "The past is never dead. It's not even
past."[18] Lingering over individuals whose traumas play murder with their
present, Faulkner plots their stories onto his *idée fixe*: the disintegration
of the old South and the conditions for its spiritual and political renewal.

Like other installments of the Yoknapatawpha chronicle, *Sanctuary*, a
book in which no one triumphs and everyone fails, sounds a requiem
for the genteel South. As becomes a family soap, the struggle for its legacy and future is enacted by two mythical clans: the aristocratic house
of Sartoris—which includes the families of Benbow and Drake—and the
assorted rabble of the Snopeses, including the DA and Popeye. It does
not matter that the two are not even clan members, or that they make a
name for themselves on the opposite sides of the law. Faulkner's allegory
transcends traditional hierarchies and bonds.

More than status or even wealth, it has to do with comportment and
an ingrained sense of moral decorum. Insofar as the Sartorises exemplify
the romanticized code of honor of the Southern gentry, their patrician, if
not unadulterated, nobility sets them apart from scuzzy carpetbaggers like
the Snopeses. As the Senator whores and connives, his opposite number
in this war of the clans not only seeks truth and justice but, with a *noblesse
oblige* commensurate with his station, looks after a dispossessed mother
and infant like a latter-day Joseph.

Even as *Sanctuary* drives a stake through the myth of the Southern
belle, Popeye's violation of the girl reenacts, in the opinion of some literary critics, the violation of the old South at the hands of a foreign intruder.
Its historical synecdoche is the Old Frenchman Place. Once a grand mansion girded by cotton fields, gardens, and lawns, now it is but a gutted
memory, linked to the present by a thin scar of a road. Personal history
twines with Southern history right up to the title for, just as Temple finds

no sanctuary in the present, there is none to be found in the plantation-era past, save for scarred memories of old-time glory.[19]

Personifying this sense of history is Miss Reba, the bordello keeper, who cameos through Faulkner's canon right up to his farewell *The Reivers* (1962). Together with other regulars, from Benbow to the lawyer-historian Gowan Stevens, she links Yoknapatawpha into one of the great American literary series or, in the parlance, soaps. Predating McBain, Faulkner locks his leading and supporting cast into a stable grid of relationships onto which he projects a kaleidoscope of life stories and social histories. This is why already in 1931 he admitted to the need for cross-checking for internal consistency and for accuracy of events and characters borrowed from real life, eventually even admitting to writing "the same story over and over".[20]

Sanctuary forms a link in a chain of novels and stories, notably "A Rose for Emily", that study morality in a controlled setting of a small-town social circle where private lives can be very public, indeed. Research shows that, whether in cities, towns, or hamlets, people average the same number of friends and acquaintances in the same number of loosely overlapping social networks, neither of which has changed much since the beginning of tribal socialization. Humans evolved to live in small communities of about 100–150 people, and today the social brain that evolved with them remains fundamentally unchanged. The result? The average size of an individual's social circle is remarkably stable at about 100–150.

Beyond this number the rest of humanity are regarded or, more to the point, disregarded as strangers to rub shoulders with in the street but without seeing. Indeed, for many individuals city life is defined by feelings of isolation and alienation which are, not surprisingly, common themes in art and literature. Look at any metropolis through a social microscope and watch it dissolve into an ever-changing mosaic of 150-size subdivisions in which scuttlebutt and intolerance of outsiders and nonconformists are as commonplace as in Faulkner's fiction. Blowing the lid off a darling town like Jefferson, *Sanctuary* shows it to be Memphis writ small.

Temple's schoolgirl taunts about the Snake being there even before Adam presage a chain of events that leave no doubt about Faulkner's belief that evil is endemic to human psyche. But even as he conjures up an orgy of degeneracy and malice aforethought, he has no truck with nihilism. It is one thing to agree with the existentialists, theodiceans, and sociobiologists that, as one literary critic put it, evil "is a necessary condition of existence which cannot be destroyed without destroying life itself".[21] It is another to accept that no sanctuary from injustice or crime can be found in society. "I refuse to accept this. I believe that man will not merely endure: he will prevail", affirmed Faulkner in his Nobel address.

The year 1951 saw the publication of *Sanctuary* reloaded, aka *A Requiem for a Nun*. The story picks up eight years after the rape and the murder trial, with Temple married to Gowan Stevens, with whom she has two children. In a tragic turn of events, the younger one is murdered by Temple's black servant (the titular "nun") in a last-ditch attempt to stop her mistress from embarking on a path of dissolution *à la Sanctuary*.[22] Prolonged flashbacks reveal compromising letters with which Pete, younger brother of Alabama Red (Temple's stud in Miss Reba's cathouse), reawakens her demons. Just as she is ready to steal away with Pete, the nanny kills the baby, forcing the mother to reexamine her life.

The experimental narration alternates between prose segments that flesh out the history of Yoknapatawpha and dramatic scenes that form, in effect, a mini-play. Thematically, the central part of *Requiem* is the middle of its three Acts, called "The Golden Dome", in which Temple undertakes a lengthy confession in front of the Governor and her husband's uncle, the ubiquitous Gavin Stevens. Revisiting the grand guignol of *Sanctuary* from Temple's point of view gives Faulkner a chance to play it back in a more abstract and impressionistic voice characteristic of his later period.

Besides his own, there were two other attempts to wring more juice from the same orange: a 1933 Paramount film called *The Story of Temple Drake* and a 1961 adaptation of Faulkner's *Sanctuary* and *A Requiem for a Nun* marketed by Fox as *Sanctuary*.[23] Eager to cash in on the sensation created by the novel, Paramount rushed to buy the rights, only to release a heavily censored ragbag of a gangster story and romantic melodrama, with Benbow, Temple, and Popeye (whose name is changed to Trigger) played by William Gargan, Miriam Hopkins, and stony-eyed Jack La Rue.

The second film, directed by Tony Richardson (who later disavowed it), transfers to the screen the staid drama of *A Requiem for a Nun*, juiced up by the jazzier sections of *Sanctuary* to boost its box-office potential. Unfortunately, not even the presence of Lee Remick as Temple and Yves Montand as Cajun gangster Candy (Popeye) can hide that the end result is

Image 3.1 Carl Van Vechten's iconic 1954 photo of post-Nobel William Faulkner/Faulkner's Underwood Universal Portable typewriter in his office at Rowan Oak, now a museum. *"Revisiting the grand guignol of* Sanctuary *from Temple's point of view gives Faulkner a chance to play it back in a more abstract and impressionistic voice characteristic of his later period."*

another over-the-counter sleeping pill. Structured as a series of flashbacks that flesh out Temple's dual character, the picture is so unmoving that two generations of film critics proposed to change its tagline to *"Sanctuary* much, but no thank you".

WORSE THAN DRESDEN

During the 1930s Hemingway was casting about for artistic direction, all the while savagely resenting the success of writers like John Dos Passos, who in 1936 became the first of his generation to make the cover of *Time*.

Even as their literary lives were infused by similar passions and ambitions, their personal lives also ran on parallel tracks to a remarkable degree, not least when it came to playing fast and loose with the truth about their alleged wartime valor. Hemingway fabricated elaborate fictions about soldiering with the Italian Arditi, a far better story than being hit by mortar shrapnel while driving a behind-the-lines supplies truck full of chocolate and cigars. Faulkner went a step further, lying not only about his wartime service (he never left Canada), but also about his alleged injuries.

As literary start-ups, both apprenticed under Sherwood Anderson, who midwifed their first publications. Both turned on him once they began to find their stride, though Faulkner carried out his literary patricide with a restraint and even a token of gratitude manifestly absent in Hemingway. Both sojourned in postwar Paris, one quietly soaking in the ambiance, the other hobnobbing and networking the expat circles. Both eventually made their way back to the USA to shake up the American letters and, ultimately, the literary world at large.

Both made the cover of *Time* within two years of each other, going on to win the Nobel Prize in Literature within five (Faulkner collected his 1949 award in 1950; Hemingway skipped the 1954 ceremony citing health issues). Both were chronic drinkers and notorious drunks, even as one was as private about it as the other was not. Both were avid fishermen, hunters, and outdoorsmen for much of their lives. Although there was no love lost between them, mid-career they even edited and adapted each other's work, with Faulkner's "Turnabout" appearing in Hemingway's collection *Men at War* (1942) and *To Have and Have Not* adapted by Faulkner for Howard Hawks's eponymous film noir (1944).[24]

If there was ever any doubt about their awareness of each other's writings, not to say a grudging appreciation of each other's talents, their personal libraries dispel them once and for all. In his Key West and Cuba houses, Hemingway accumulated more than a dozen of his rival's major works, beginning with *Sanctuary* (which, he wrote later, he could never bring himself to re-read). Faulkner returned the favor by keeping *To Have and Have Not* as well as several other of his rival's fictions and nonfictions—notably the uncorrected proofs of *The Old Man and the Sea*—on his bookshelves at Rowan Oak.[25]

Both perpetrated myths that, as in the case of *Sanctuary*, would on occasion take on a life of their own. Hemingway, of course, ended up forging a myth so much larger than his life that it would come to cast a deep shadow over his writing and even his death.[26] One of its persistent strands is that he, rather than Hammett—let alone the earlier contributors to *Black Mask* or the fiction-plying muckrakers—pioneered the hardboiled style. Exhibit A in this literary paternity suit is *In Our Time* (1925) with its tautly restrained prosody, concrete imagery, and a slice of life served gritty side up.

The facts of the matter tell, however, their own history. Hammett's first Continental Op story appeared in October 1923. "Indian Camp" from *In Our Time*, frequently cited as an avatar of Hemingway's hardboiled style, was not completed until February 1924.[27] Furthermore, it had been soundly rejected for publication in the USA, after which Hemingway decided to print it himself in Paris-based *the transatlantic review*, where he was a subeditor (until the appearance of *The Sun Also Rises*, he could not sell a short story back home).

Another abiding part of the myth is that his writing style has spawned generations of imitators, but no equals. The editors who perpetuate this contention on the front leaf to the Arrow Classic edition of *To Have and Have Not* have apparently never heard of James Ellroy's *L.A. Confidential*, the second-last novel of his celebrated L.A. Quartet. Racing forward with a grace and a growl of a Detroit muscle car, it easily out-Hemingways Hemingway with a telegrammatic style, predicate-less sentence equivalents, and a dog-eat-dog conscience—all of which earned Ellroy the nickname of Demon Dog.

Over the course of their parallel careers, Hemingway and Faulkner have come to define not only the quintessence of American modernism but also its polarity, "Papa" with his mimetic minimalism and "Pappy" with his expressionistic experimentation. In this context, it is only fitting that one of their favored tropes was parallelism. Employed by Faulkner structurally, mostly on the level of a chapter or scene, it was often used by Hemingway stylistically on the level of a sentence, identifiable by his rolling cadences, multiple conjunctions, and an almost classicist equipoise.

Yet, for all these affinities, when it came to reinventing themselves as artists in the 1930s, they approached it with very different mindsets and from very different directions. Where the critically lauded Faulkner looked to go commercial and engage the mass reader, the commercially successful

Hemingway looked to go engagé and prove something both to the literary pundits who accused him of anti-intellectualism, and to the Marxists who derided him for the cult of the individual in the age of the masses.

The results could hardly have been more different. Where Faulkner walked away with a nobrow tour de force, Hemingway bombed worse than Dresden. Summing up the long and short of it, Delmore Schwartz trashed *To Have and Have Not* as "a stupid and foolish book, a disgrace to a good writer, a book which should never have been printed".[28] With reviewer after reviewer crucifying it as naïve, a piece of propaganda, and a flat-out failure, Malcolm Cowley's concession that it was "the weakest of Hemingway's books—except perhaps 'Green Hills of Africa'" was notable only for its restraint. What was it about the hardboiled story of Harry Morgan, gun-runner, rum-runner, man-runner, that turned literary criticism into contact sport?

The 1930s were politically synonymous with the Great Depression, which did not lift for good only after the USA's entry into World War II. In art it was the decade of social commitment, and in literature the decade of the proletarian novel. How did Hemingway fit into this picture? Having remarried into a well-to-do Pfeifer family, he luxuriated in African safaris, fished off his 40-foot ocean-going yacht, and thumbed his nose at the Left which alternately wooed him and booed him for his disregard for the Cause. Worse for a writer, he had not written a novel since *A Farewell to Arms* (1929) and, if his magazine fiction told a story, his nova was settling into a dull glow.

Literary tributes, such as Archibald MacLeish's "Famous at twenty-five: thirty a master", did little to hide that during the 1930s Hemingway was casting about for artistic direction, all the while savagely resenting the success of writers like John Dos Passos, who in 1936 became the first of his generation to make the cover of *Time*.[29] In many ways, *To Have and Have Not* was thus to be a literary statement as much as a work of literature. Not incidentally, it would also be only his second book set in America, if only in its rugged southern tip—the Florida Keys.

BROTHER, CAN YOU SPARE A DIME?

Throw in three-sheets-to-the-wind vets who brutalize one another as casually as if it were a Hanna-Barbera cartoon, Cuban desperados who spit out slogans about tyranny and revolution, snide government officials, and ham-handed swipes at effete litterateurs and degenerate "haves", and you have Hemingway's novel of the decade.

As Key West became Hemingway's winter domicile in the early 1930s, this domestic backdrop may have kindled his domestic concerns, including the plight of World War I veterans working on the construction of a highway linking the islets with the mainland. On Labour Day, 1935, a hurricane tore up the Keys, flattening a Civilian Conservation Corps labor camp and drowning several hundred men. After rushing in supplies on his own boat, incensed Hemingway penned an article for the Marxist *New Masses*, calling it "Who Murdered the Vets". In it he demanded to know why the men had been left at the camp despite early hurricane warning, in effect accusing the Florida bureaucrats and the Roosevelt administration of manslaughter.

Projected on a broader canvas of Depression-era despair and decay, Hemingway's concern for the underdog may have justified in his mind the ideological crudities and solemn editorializing that turn the final chapters of the book into so much boilerplate propaganda. But it is actually in the short Part II that Harry's negro deckhand nails the ghost of the economic implosion. "Prohibition's over. Why they keep up a traffic like that? Why don't people be honest and decent and make a decent honest living?" (51), whines Wesley, as the two men bleed from gunshot wounds sustained in a botched rum-smuggling crossing from Cuba.

The shortest answer is that honest work, if you were fortunate to get it, brought starvation wages. The 1930s were synonymous with breadlines, soup kitchens, packing-box shantytowns (dubbed Hoovervilles), insolvent banks, boarded up storefronts, businesses buying civil-order insurance at Lloyd's in London, middle-class garbage picking, and panhandling so rife that newspapers mockingly campaigned to adopt "Brother, Can You Spare a Dime" as a new national anthem. National suicide rates shot up 20 % and insanity rates almost doubled among reports of magnates who made millions and filed no income reports.

Before it all happened, the figures had been impressive, just like the figures that testified to the unsinkability of *Titanic*. Industrial production grew by leaps and bounds, from well under thirty billion dollars in 1909 to well over eighty billion in 1929. In the first thirty years of the century the GNP increased fourfold and, although in the same period the population in the country exploded from 75 to a whopping 125 million, per capita wealth more than doubled. So did the number of millionaires during the decade or so between the Great War and the Great Depression.

Then, seemingly overnight, the American Dream got laid off, lost a place to dwell to foreclosure, and left town on a freight train with an army of hoboes. By 1932, as the wheel swung to the bottom of the cycle, a semi-permanent class of drifters and beggars, more than two million strong, was criss-crossing the country looking for jobs or handouts. National income nosedived to half of what it had been before Black Tuesday. Fixed salaries dropped 40 % and wages 60 %. More than a hundred cities threw in the towel, declaring they had no relief funds left. Unemployment swelled to twelve million, a number Hoover refused to believe.

When his successor spoke in his inaugural address about one-third of a nation ill-housed, ill-clad, ill-nourished, he could have been speaking of Hemingway's Conchs hiring out for starvation wages or former cops like Harry turning outlaw when the tanking economy put charter fishing on the bum. Throw in three-sheets-to-the-wind vets who brutalize one another as casually as if it were a Hanna-Barbera cartoon, Cuban desperados who spit out slogans about tyranny and revolution, snide government officials, and ham-handed swipes at effete litterateurs and degenerate "haves", and you have Hemingway's novel of the decade.

To Have and Have Not labors to overcome the handicap of being stitched up from two magazine stories—"One Trip Across" (*Cosmopolitan*, 1934) and "The Tradesman's Return" (*Esquire*, 1936)—plus Part III, added on and off during the Spanish Civil War summer of 1936. This piecemeal origin and the consequent lack of coherence, which led some reviewers to murmur that the book's only unity was in the binding, was no secret to the author who lobbied to print it as an omnibus with his previous hits "The Snows of Kilimanjaro", "The Short Happy Life of Francis Macomber", and "The Capital of the World". Unpersuaded, Scribner's printed the book as we know it, although not before deleting lengthy sections that libeled his erstwhile friends, notably Dos Passos.[30]

But saying farewell to his political indifference, Hemingway has not transcended his political ignorance. His critique of America's upper crust, which lapses by and large into charges of impotence or, conversely, sterile promiscuity, has all the insightfulness of a bright adolescent. Reinforcing this impression are the comic-book contrasts between the haves and have-nots like Harry, who happens to own a house, good furniture, a piano, a car, and a big-ass twin-engine boat. Even *The Nation*, the self-described flagship of the Left, did not pull its punches: "Nothing could be more inept here, more lacking in true insight."[31]

Given how the book fails as a socioeconomic allegory, a study of the poor, a satire on the rich, and even as a novel, it is hard to understand how anyone, let alone anyone on the Left, could take it at face value. That they did, despite Hemingway's patent unease about Stalin-type terrorism or his hero's curt "F—his revolution" (118), shows that some Marxists were even greater political dopes than he was.[32] The same must be said of Hoover's COINTELPRO, who targeted Hemingway for his agitprop for the Loyalists during the Spanish War, in particular on the one-reeler *The Spanish Earth* (1937).

As artist engagé, Hemingway flops with every crude volley he fires at the rich. At the bottom of the barrel that is *To Have and Have Not* flicker, however, a few flecks of gold. One of them is the visceral unease about the Cuban revolution, which is spinning its last wheels today as Brother Castro and Uncle Sam aim to restore full diplomatic relations. From time to time, there is even a glimpse of the old iceberg. When the US Navy docks in New York, gloats one boozy masochistic war veteran, "there's old guys with long beards come down and you can piss in their beards for a dollar" (146). This throwaway remark about men hiring out as pissoirs says more about being poor than pages of righteous indignation. Everyone knows that Depression stinks. Well, here is what it stinks of.

.38 POLICE SPECIAL

> The plot builds up to a Reservoir Dogs-type climax in which everyone goes down in a hail of bullets from every conceivable type of firearm, including two icons of the gangster era, a Tommy gun and a sawed-off.

Following the success of *Black Mask*, the 1920s and 1930s saw a tidal wave of hardboiled fiction printed in a seemingly endless line of pulp magazines. Fans could slake their thirst for tough-guy homicide for a dime (later two bits) in *Action Detective, All-Detective, Black Aces, Black Book Detective, Clues, Crime Busters, Detective-Dragnet, Detective Tales, Dime Detective, Detective Story Magazine, Double Detective, Greater Gangster Stories, Nickel Detective, Phantom Detective, Pocket Detective, Popular Detective, Racketeer Stories, Scotland Yard, Spicy Detective, Strange Detective, Thrilling Detective, Top Notch, Triple Detective, 10 Detective Aces, Secret Agent X, The Complete Detective, The Shadow*, and scores more.

Although Hemingway did not hide his respect for Chandler's brand of hardboiled prose, he always chafed at being lumped with the school. In almost every way, however, the first two-thirds of *To Have and Have Not* are a testosterone and adrenaline-pumped action adventure, from the first shootout to the last smuggling run. Peppered with shady deals hammered out in flinty dialogue, not to mention one ice-veined murder after another, the action shuttles between boat decks and the back of Freddy's bar, itself modeled on Sloppy Joe's bar in Key West (from 1981 an annual site of the Hemingway lookalike contest).

It was there that Hemingway repeatedly boasted that his first and, in the end, only novel of the decade would be a winner. True to his word, it sold out four printings in a couple of months, made the *New York Times* bestseller list, and earned him his first appearance on the cover of *Time*. How could he be so sure of success? Piece of cake. As he joked a few years later, *To Have and Have Not* was,

> a frail volume devoted to adultery, sodomy, masturbation, rape, mayhem, mass murder, frigidity, alcoholism, prostitution, impotency, anarchy, rum-running, chink-smuggling, nymphomania and abortion.[33]

In short, a made-to-order chart burner. More to the point, as in the case of *Sanctuary*, its commercial prospects coincided with the popularity of the hardboiled genre that Hemingway, author of "The Killers" and "Fifty Grand", could count on to sell with the public. Sure enough, *To Have and Have Not* stars a ten-minute-egg equivalent of a hero knee-deep in a pool of blood and violence. The plot builds up to a *Reservoir Dogs*-type climax in which everyone goes down in a hail of bullets from every conceivable type of firearm, including two icons of the gangster era, a Tommy gun and a sawed-off.

A better part—and, at the same time, the better part—of the book is a textbook illustration of the hardboiled style: dialogue that stops only for action, clipped colloquial narration, authorial presence effaced to next to nothing, and everything held together by almost ritualistic violence. Even when things get more descriptive, figures of speech are frequently of urban or military origin, as when a gargantuan marlin is described in terms of a depth bomb or a submarine. Add to this short—some as short as two pages—chapters, minimum exposition, and an edgy waterfront attitude, and you have a hardboiled thriller that leaves little to be ashamed of.

All the same, with Faulkner looking over his shoulder, Hemingway tries out different angles of narration, sometimes more and sometimes less nimbly. Part I is—as it was in *Cosmopolitan*—all first-person Harry. Part II switches to third person, with Harry at the crosshairs. Part III anticipates the more variegated storytelling in *For Whom the Bell Tolls* (1940) with its blend of first-person, internal monologue, and omniscience going into and out of sundry minds. Among pseudo-modernistic extracts set in italics, it even experiments with stream of thought, a more coherent type of stream of consciousness.

Ironically, much as Hemingway may have wanted his hero to stand as an individual, Harry emerges as little more than a type of rogue outlaw, with the Gulf as the frontier, or a type of tough egg that would feel at home in any detective pulp magazine. There is nothing subtle about it, either. He hires out for a fixed price a day plus expenses, talks laconic, and takes the lives of career criminals, from a human traffic kingpin to a gang of Cuban bank robbers. This checks with his being an ex-Miami cop who still packs a Smith & Wesson .38 police special and thinks like a detective, if only to crook the law for his own ends.

This is not to overlook several exceptions to the private eye formula. For one, Harry is happily married to Marie, a big-boned, bleached-blonde ex-hooker, with whom he has three daughters. He may be as pitiless and as much a loner as the Continental Op but, in sharp contrast to Hammett's crimebuster, he acts and kills not in the name of what is right but in the name of what is right for Harry. Be that as it may, when he pleasantly tells a young Cuban bandit, "Don't be so tough so early in the morning. I'm sure you've cut plenty people's throats. I haven't even had my coffee yet" (4), his lines come from the same playbook as the Op's and Sam Spade's.

Outwardly, of course, he is more Spade than the Op: tall, hulking, blond, with an arresting face. Needless to say, women find him irresistible because there is something piratical about him. Not for nothing Harry's namesake, Henry Morgan, was a legendary buccaneer who, before being knighted, pillaged and terrorized the Caribbean, even capturing the city of Panama. As related by John Steinbeck in his little known first novel *Cup of Gold* (1929), although betrayed and sold as an indentured servant, in time Morgan organized a seaworthy band of cutthroats and set about robbing the rich.

In the end, however, deserting his brothers in arms, he sold out to the very haves he used to rail against. Accepting a pardon and knighthood from the British monarch, he settled in Jamaica with a well-bred wife and served out his days as a Lieutenant Governor. Another of Harry's real-life prototypes may have been Joe Russell, a Key West skipper, who earned his name smuggling rum during the Prohibition. There is also Hemingway's anonymous hero of a 1932 story, "After the Storm", another tough-minded and hard-fisted Key West boat captain.

Image 3.2   Ernest Hemingway posing in the 1930s with a marlin, Havana Harbor, Cuba/Rum runner schooner *Kirk and Sweeney* with contraband stacked on deck. *"Another of Harry's real-life prototypes may have been Joe Russell, a Key West skipper who earned his name smuggling rum during the Prohibition. There is also Hemingway's anonymous hero of a 1932 story, "After the Storm", another tough-minded and hard-fisted Key West boat captain."*

Reflecting the book's shifting center of gravity, other characters of note are introduced in the longest Part III, in which Harry gradually yields the stage to two groups that typecast the contrast between America's rich and not. The first are the tourist layabouts and the owners of luxury yachts moored alongside the piers of Key West. Among them: a rich playboy and his boy toy, a grain broker on the lam from the Internal Revenue, an aging sex-starved starlet and, to round up the picture, a dull family of a Horatio Alger-type tycoon who earned his millions with honest industry. The have-nots are the rowdy barflies, be they war vets or labor organizers, and the mostly faceless army of poverty-line locals.

In a 1958 interview Hemingway grandstanded: "The most essential gift for a good writer is a built-in, shock-proof shit-detector."[34] Assuming that he was a good writer, his own shit detector was patently out of order when he penned *To Have and Have Not*, especially the parts that viciously slam Dos Passos, ill-concealed as the author of proletarian novels, Richard Gordon. Ironically, Hemingway's accusation of trading in stock characters and clichés while being despised by real laborites, not to mention being a drunk and a cad, applies to the author of *To Have and Have Not* rather than the author of the masterly epic *USA*.

The Great American Paradox

The same antitheses beat at the heart of the Great American Paradox: the cult of the individual in a country built on mass production, mass culture, and mass-culturally produced beliefs, starting with the belief in self-reliance and individualism.

For a writer who liked to sneer that writing is architecture and not interior decoration, the wonky structure of the book reflects the mid-course change from a hardboiled story of an individual to agitprop about social polarities. It calls to mind an old joke about equal amounts of meat in a horse-rabbit hamburger: one horse, one rabbit. Indeed, enough remains of the protean design for Harry to dominate the whole. Like *Oedipus Rex*, the hero starts out at the top of the wheel of fortune, and his efforts to dig himself out of a hole are similarly tinged with a premonition of doom, cued by the subtitles of the three parts. In Spring Harry suffers a bite wound. In Fall he loses an arm. In Winter, his life.

If in Spring he appears in control of his destiny, refusing to smuggle revolutionaries into Cuba, by Winter he is sufficiently down on his luck to do exactly that. Symbolically, his decline is also paced out by his escalating losses: fishing tackle, money, contraband liquor, arm, boat, and finally life. But if Hemingway's allegory is as overdone as a half-hour steak, so is his irony. Stiffed by a client, Harry is reduced, in his own words, to peddling his *cojones* to make a living. Chapter 24, the crux of the engagé part of the book, opens with an inner view of a gigolo, who peddles his *cojones* to a well-heeled patron, albeit without metaphorizing.

As for politics, Harry's turn to crime presumably illustrates the All-American spirit of self-reliance and civil disobedience, in this case against the government welshing on laissez faire by overtaxing alcohol. Ironically, as an exponent of free-market capitalism, Harry occupies the same boat as big-time operators like Joseph P. Kennedy, who made a fortune smuggling Prohibition whisky from Montreal distilleries, in the process becoming the very image of a self-made man and the head of America's top political clan. The sole difference between them is that Kennedy greased too many hands to fear the long arm of the law, while small fry like Harry washed out and up on the shores of the Great Depression.

Sunk by the same economic storm that threatened to sink the whole country, Harry personifies the limits of self-reliance and individualism in twentieth-century plutocratic and bureaucratic America. The only problem with this interpretation is that Harry could not care less for the Iron Heel. As indifferent to fostering solidarity among the dispossessed as he is to the simmering revolt against the American-sponsored regime in Cuba, he robs Chinese have-nots of the passage they paid for and commits mass murder to steal the cache set aside for the people's revolution. Like Walter Huff in *Double Indemnity*, he tries to buck the system simply because he believes he has the *cojones* for it.

In a 1943 letter to Howard Hawks, who was then readying to shoot *To Have and Have Not*, Hemingway tried to spin his hero as "a man who tried to buck this world single handed and found that it couldn't be done and that men had to stick together to win".[35] His claim might have carried a little more weight had Harry actually done anything prosocial or, for that matter, had not plotted to kill his first and then last deckmates to remove witnesses to his murders. The argument that he kills only the men who rob and kill others leaves out too much to convince. Suffice it to imagine what would happen if men like Harry united to fight for what they thought was theirs to wonder who exactly Hemingway was trying to make us root for.

This fundamental confusion of purpose highlights the paradox that transcends *To Have and Have Not* and even American literature to reach into every corner of the country's cultural and social history. The would-be novel illustrates it well, insofar as the two short stories that make up Part I and II sing the virtues of hardboiled individualism, whereas Part III tries to change tack in favor of class solidarity. The hardboiled horse and the proletarian rabbit pull in opposite directions, and needless to say the horse wins. The same antitheses beat at the heart of the Great American Paradox: the cult of the individual in a country built on mass production, mass culture, and mass-culturally produced beliefs, starting with the belief in self-reliance and individualism.

Rarely absent from Hemingway's writings is the need for a response to violence. The docks are, of course, a microcosm of the urban jungle with their tough guys, tough attitudes, course talk, and dishonest deals colored with the premonition of gunplay. It is a hard environment in a hardboiled story in which thirteen men die sometimes a naturalistically graphic death. But even death feels sometimes only half as hard as the life into which people are seemingly brought in only to take a beating. In a country at war with itself, the only saving grace for those fated to fail may be the style in which they go down.

In this context, Harry's famous last words, "No matter how a man alone ain't got no bloody fucking chance" (158), ring like a banner headline inserted for the sake of giving a proletarian spin to the story. Interestingly, however, the last words in the novel belong not to the hero but to his wife. For readers of *Ulysses*, it is difficult to shake the feeling that her rambling soliloquy is meant to point to Molly Bloom's from the end of Joyce's novel. The link is far less far-fetched when you consider that in 1922 Hemingway went around Paris soliciting subscriptions for *Ulysses*, and even devised a plan to smuggle copies of the banned book into the USA (a real-life Gatsby, his own copy of *Ulysses* had pages cut only in the first half and in the final soliloquy).

In her muted outpour of grief, Marie seems not that different from Frederic Henry in *A Farewell to Arms,* who sees people's lives mirrored in the frantic scramble of ants on a burning log, searching for sanctuary from destruction. Yet, in the spirit of Molly Bloom's life-affirming "yeses", from Marie's despair emerges a kind of resigned acceptance that the sun also rises with or without the people we care for, and no less symbolically, that church bells always toll for thee. None of which, of course, survives in the multiple treatments of the book at the hands of Hollywood, beginning with the 1945 adaptation by Faulkner et al.

The eponymous film is a more or less inaccurate version of Chap. 1 of *To Have and Have Not* (producer-director Hawks did not think much of the rest). With Bogart and Bacall trading double entendres in between a few musical numbers, the picture is little more than a noir vehicle for the star and his satellite rather than an attempt to transfer Hemingway's story, let alone his philosophy, onto the big screen.[36] Next came *The Breaking Point* (1950), with Key West replaced by Newport, California. No political or social subtext here: Harry smuggles illegal Chinese immigrants for Mr. Sing, whom he ends up killing in self-defense—roughly the first part of the book. Still, Hemingway sent notes to the producers to the effect that their hatchet job suited him just fine.

The last Hollywood version, released in 1958 as *The Gun Runners*, had several working titles, including *Rub My Back*, *One Trip Across*, and *Ernest Hemingway's Gun Runners*. Despite the fact that the last two were shamelessly designed to cash in on Hemingway's post-Nobel Prize fame, the movie is some ways more faithful to the original. Sam Martin (played by pouty-lipped Audie Murphy) runs a charter boat, losing valuable fishing tackle to a deadbeat client. Martin then takes up smuggling machine guns to Cuba with a shady operator who, during the last fateful run, tries to double-cross him, only to be killed in the onboard shootout.

In the end, the more things do not change, the more they stay the same. Even though the Roaring Twenties and the Groaning Thirties are no longer with us, the hardboiled fiction that so entertainingly reported their excesses has never gone away—or if it has, it made a comeback with every new generation. Unfortunately, neither have the chronic divisions between America's haves and have-nots. With more and more Americans effectively disfranchised by the political system, with 1 % of the nation owning almost all of its wealth, Hemingway's poor excuse for a protest novel strikes a surprisingly topical chord in the new millennium.[37]

NOTES

1. Both on page vi; see also *Sanctuary*, Vintage edition, 322–323.
2. Ibid, page vi.; see also Cantwell; Collins. On the contract, see Minter, 139.
3. Fiedler (1988), 76; cf., telling remarks on James in "Faulkner at Virginia" (audio file).

4. See Creighton; Moreland; "A Rose for Emily" owes some of its popularity to The Zombies's eponymous 1968 track.
5. Camus, 319; see also Warren, 295. In 1956 Camus adapted *A Requiem for a Nun* for the stage.
6. Whitehurst Stone, 144; Faulkner's report on the galleys in Meriwether and Millgate, 123. Proofs dates as per Blotner (1993); in (1964), Blotner places the receipt of proofs in November; Rampton dates it to January 1931, well nigh impossible given the publication date of 9 February 1931.
7. In Blotner, 234.
8. Page 72; below. The comic episodes are the country rubes in the city (Chap. 21), Red's wake (Chap. 25), and the gossip session starring Miss Reba, Miss Myrtle, and Miss Lorraine (Chap. 25).
9. Polk, 293; below, Malraux, 744.
10. See Kahneman.
11. Nelson, 42; on intentions and intentionality, see Swirski, *Literature, Analytically* (2010).
12. Fruscione, Chap. 4.
13. All page references to the Vintage edition.
14. Popeye's character first appeared in "The Big Shot" (ca. 1929, published posthumously); on American Gothic, see Soltysik Monnet.
15. Established in 1972; nowadays renamed Behavioral Research and Instruction Unit (BRIU).
16. Snell, 171; see also Watson, 3–4.
17. Title chosen by the publisher, Random House; later published under Faulkner's preferred title *If I Forget Thee, Jerusalem*.
18. Act 1, scene 3; for the Faulkner estate lawsuit against Woody Allen (dismissed in 2013), see Leopold.
19. On the map of Yoknapatawpha County Faulkner drew for the flyleaf of *Absalom, Absalom!*, the Old Frenchman Place is in the southeast quadrant.
20. Blotner (1977), 185.
21. Vickery, 114; on the sociobiology of evil, see Swirski (2011), Chap. 4. Faulkner's Nobel speech: http://www.nobelprize.org/nobel_prizes/literature/laureates/1949/faulkner-speech.html.
22. The title could also refer to Temple in a veiled reference to Shakespeare in whose times a "nun" also denoted a prostitute.
23. Seventy and ninety minutes respectively, both black and white.
24. With Jules Furthman and (uncredited) Cleve F. Adams and Whitman Chambers; Faulkner also adapted Chandler's *The Big Sleep*, starring again Bogart and Bacall.
25. Reynolds, 123; Blotner (1964).
26. See Donaldson.

27. Hemingway's first book of fiction, *Three Stories and Ten Poems*, was printed privately in mid-August 1923.
28. In Meyers, 251; see also De Voto, 224; Connolly, 228; Rahv, 241; Kronenberger, 236.
29. MacLeish, 71.
30. Mostly on the advice of Arnold Gingrich; *The Sun Also Rises* benefitted as much, if not more, from excisions and revisions by Fitzgerald.
31. Kronenberger, 440.
32. See Edmund Wilson, in Lynn, 465.
33. In Bercovitch, 219; see also Hotchner, 172.
34. In Plimpton.
35. Baker, 332.
36. In *Key Largo* (1948), also starring Bogey and Bacall, director John Huston used another splinter of the book–the gun fight on the boat–for the climax.
37. Swirski, *Ars Americana*, Chap. 3.

CHAPTER 4

The Not So Simple Art of Murder: Raymond Chandler

No Chinaman Must Figure in the Story

A detective takes no notice of his feelings. He does not ask questions about his own salvation. He is the most perfect realist in the world. As soon as he falls in love, he loses his intellectual integrity.

Emerging in parallel with the modern urban jungle, modern crime fiction became an instant hit with the public, by 1905 boasting its own heading in *The Reader's Guide to Periodical Literature*.[1] Almost from the beginning it also began to draw the attention of literary critics, some of whom, sensing the potential of the genre, tried to correct its formulaic tendencies. One of them was Ronald Arbuthnott Knox, British clergyman, editor, and part-time detective storywriter who, in the Preface to the *Best Detective Stories of 1928–29*, spelled out the ten commandments for crime mystery's Golden Age.

In the days when C.S. Lewis and J.R.R. Tolkien were laying down the foundations of modern fantasy shielded by the highbrow respectability of Oxford greens, Father Knox dispensed structural gospel such as "Not more than one secret room or passage is allowable" and "No Chinaman must figure in the story." Notwithstanding Knox's predilection for humor and even full-blown hoaxes, his decalogue reflected the state of the art in crime fiction—and crime fiction criticism—even as across the Atlantic Hammett, Hemingway, Cain, McCoy, Chandler, and other alums of the

© The Editor(s) (if applicable) and The Author(s) 2016
P. Swirski, *American Crime Fiction*,
DOI 10.1007/978-3-319-30108-2_4

hardboiled school were experimenting with form and style in ways that would transform American fiction for decades to come.[2]

Father Knox's proclamations proved more inspiring than he could have foreseen when in 1973 a Canadian-Czech writer Josef Skvorecky published a collection of ten detective stories called *Sins for Father Knox*. Self-consciously recherché, although popular enough to eventually become a TV series, each story in the series was devised in contravenience of one of the Monsignor's injunctions. Still, not all of the early stabs at the poetics of the detective genre were so silly. One of the more consequential came, in fact, from another Czech litterateur of impeccable highbrow and nobrow credentials.[3]

Karel Čapek's 1924 essay "Holmesiana, or about Detective Stories" took stock of the genre he occasionally practiced with his customary flair. The Czech writer understood that at its narrative center lay not the crime, but the detective. Nor, following Father Knox, did he hesitate to prescribe what kind of sleuth stood at the center of a good crime story. A detective has nothing to do with himself, pronounced Čapek. A detective takes no notice of his feelings. He does not ask questions about his own salvation. He is the most perfect realist in the world. As soon as he falls in love, he loses his intellectual integrity.

If art denies expectations, invalidates rules, and, generally speaking, transmutes water into wine, then Raymond Chandler is a *bone fide* artist, not least because his Philip Marlowe, arguably the most successful literary creation of the twentieth century, is the living antithesis of Čapek's recipe for a successful detective. True, Marlowe may not ask too many questions about his own salvation, but he takes notice of his feelings, not to mention those of others. He is as much a soft-hearted romantic as a hardnosed (not to say hardboiled) realist. And, on the final page of Chandler's final novel *Playback* (1958), he is not only in love but fixing to marry.

On the umpteen pages of Chandler's unfinished sequel, *The Poodle Springs Story* (1959)—completed by Robert Parker and published in 1989 as *Poodle Springs*—he even plays husband to a multimillionaire's daughter without losing any of his intellectual or, for that matter, moral integrity. In fact, Marlowe's resolve to remain true to himself is so steadfast that, as his creator underlined in more than one letter, it might even test the integrity of the marital vows. Playing havoc with Čapek's commandments, just like Skvorecky did with Father Knox's, Chandler shows time and again that the genre is simply too creative, its poetics too flexible, and its characters too complex to conform to any critic's prescriptions or proscriptions.[4]

In his lifetime Chandler's unflagging attention to such *prima facie* highbrow elements of storytelling as style, mood, and diction earned him acclaim from Hemingway, Eliot, Burgess, Perelman, Steinbeck, Maugham, Waugh, Priestley, and Auden, among a legion of other literary luminaries. The *Atlantic Monthly* published his essays alongside Jean Paul Sartre's, Albert Einstein's, and Walter Lippman's. A writer of power and vision and a self-pronounced aesthetic snob, he was, in Auden's words, nothing less than a contemporary novelist whose "powerful and extremely depressing books should be read and judged, not as escape literature, but as works of art".[5]

No less august an opinion-maker than the London *Times* agreed. In what was literally the last word on the matter, its 1959 obituary honored Chandler as a virtuoso who, "working the vein of crime fiction, mined the gold of literature".[6] In 1995 even the Library of America threw its weight behind the hardboiled master, editing all of his novels, most of his stories, many of his essays, and some of his letters in two volumes—sandwiched in between Thomas Paine and Robert Frost—and thereby inducting him into the national Literary Hall of Fame.

Quite an honor for a writer trained in classical literature who self-deprecatingly professed not to care a button for hardboiled fiction, owning only to trying his hand at experimenting with dramatic dialogue. Around the time he was putting the finishing touches on *Playback*, however, in the best understated tradition of the genre he had come to define, he defiantly underscored his contribution to American letters: "To accept a mediocre form and make something like literature out of it is in itself rather an accomplishment."[7]

MAYHEM SPICED WITH NYMPHOMANIA

Chandler may have been unaware of Cary Grant's homosexuality.

When, on the closing pages of his classic *Love and Death in the American Novel*, Leslie Fiedler went gunning after crime fiction, he blasted Chandler in a broadside that reverberates to this day:

Murder laced with lust, mayhem spiced with nymphomania: this is the formula for the chief surviving form of the murder mystery in America, though, indeed, that form has not surrendered its native birthright of anti-feminism. It insists, however, on undressing its bitches, surveying them with a surly and concupiscent eye before punching, shooting, or consigning them to the gas

> chamber. Not only in the cruder and more successful books of Mickey Spillane, but in the more pretentious ones by Raymond Chandler, the detective story has reverted to the kind of populist semi-pornography that once made George Lippard's *The Monks of Monk Hall* a black-market bestseller. (499)

The only problem is that these insults could be cooked up only by someone unfamiliar with Philip Marlowe, a detective principled enough to make Job look like a sellout. From *The Big Sleep* to *The Poodle Springs Story*, the PI is hard as they come when the occasion demands it, he bedevils his share of platinum blondes, but nowhere does he go surveying them with a surly and concupiscent eye before punching, shooting, or consigning them to the gas chamber.

In his well-known 1944 essay "The Simple Art of Murder", Chandler echoed Čapek in arguing that in crime fiction the hero is everything. In his private notebook jottings, released posthumously as "Twelve Notes on the Mystery Story", he was equally resolute: the lynchpin of a mystery story is the detective. Everything hangs on his personality—if he doesn't have one, you have very little, indeed. And in Philip Marlowe, a private eye who from his inception broke free of the hardboiled type, he created one of the most personable characters of the twentieth century.

The creation proved so vibrant that not only Marlowe's personality but even his offstage life become the subject of interest, eventually leading the author to flesh it out for the public. From a 1951 letter to D.J. Ibberson, catalogued by the Library of America as "The Facts of Philip Marlowe's Life", we thus learn that the detective is a northern Californian by birth, is thirty-eight years old, and strikingly good looking in the Cary Grant mold (Chandler may have been unaware of Cary Grant's homosexuality). He has brown hair, brown eyes, a couple of years of college from Oregon, no living relatives, stands over six feet tall, tips the scales at 210 pounds, smokes and drinks practically anything that isn't effeminate, and used to work as an investigator for an insurance company and then for the Los Angeles county DA.

More to the point, he is a sensitive, nuanced, and romanticized hero who has precious little in common with real gumshoes for hire. A real-life PI, scoffed Chandler, is a drudge with no more personality than a blackjack and no more moral stature than a stop sign. In contrast, Marlowe has been cast as an urban knight from the first page of the first novel, *The Big Sleep* (1939). Ogling the Sternwood mansion, he pauses in front of a panel depicting a knight rescuing a lady tied to a tree. "I stood there and thought that if I lived in the house, I would sooner or later have to climb up there and help him", he sighs, hinting at a tradition harking back to the *chanson de geste* and the grail quest.[8] On cue, in the next novel *Farewell, My Lovely*, the detective will search for Mrs. Grayle.

Case after case shows Marlowe to be an errant crusader of romance. By the time of *The Long Goodbye* (1953), he is even a sentimental introvert with a complex inner life, who freely admits: "I'm a romantic. I hear voices crying in the night and I go see what's the matter. You don't make a dime that way."[9] Cruising the big bad City of Angels for a fee plus expenses, he rebuffs all golden handshakes that probe his integrity in one of Chandler's perennial motifs. By everyday standards, he is, of course, an anachronism. As Parker's Marlowe tells his wife in *Poodle Springs*: "I'm a failure. I don't have any money. In this great Republic that's how the judgement is made, darling." Be that as it may, his moral compass never wavers.

As to Fiedler's allegations of nymphomania and semi-pornography, Marlowe's infrequent episodes of lovemaking are invariably understated in lyrical and chaste terms befitting a knight of romance. No need to look further than the opening pages of *The Poodle Springs Story* to find a hint of sexual intimacy elliptical enough to satisfy an astronomical observatory. No more than "a long sigh, and two people as close as two people can get", Chandler's restraint and tenderness are no different from *Playback* where the bedroom darkness yields only "that muted cry, and then again the slow quiet peace".[10]

Image 4.1 The private eye as an anachronism: Robert Elliot Gould in *The Long Goodbye*, directed by Robert Altman (1973). *"By everyday standards, he is, of course, an anachronism. As Parker's Marlowe tells his wife in* Poodle Springs: *'I'm a failure. I don't have any money. In this great Republic that's how the judgement is made, darling.'"*

Projecting his disdain for the genre's formulas onto one of its most celebrated practitioners, Fiedler misses his target by a country mile. Even though Chandler unquestionably belongs to the hardboiled school, he has never belonged to the *Black Mask* ghetto. Back in 1933, for example, when the majority of pulp-fiction hacks hacked a million words a year to scratch out a living, his first story "Blackmailers Don't Shoot" was a harvest of five months of conscientious revisions. Finessed to flush right, as if typeset for publication, it typified his almost obsessive-compulsive attention to detail, his poetic control of expression, and almost boundless command of linguistic resources.

A quarter century later, Chandler's last novel *Playback* was another odd duck. Instead of dishing out familiar formulae, it bid an ironic, if fond, farewell to the entire hardboiled tradition. Depicting a modern America of billboard culture and criminals too well protected to bring within hearing distance of a courtroom gavel, it self-reflexively deconstructed itself and its genre. Its tongue-in-cheek, not to say parodic, playfulness defied readers in search of a hardboiled caper where the wiseguys are all ten-minute eggs and the detectives run at the mouth with bullet-quick wit. Few, if any, were ready to give Chandler credit for experimenting with the rules of the game, or even playing an entirely different literary game altogether.

A BOMBSHELL REDHEAD ON THE RUN

If all these goings-on are too contrived and over the top for a plot of a hardboiled mystery, it is on the word of two generations of literary critics for whom *Playback* is the one Chandler novel they love to hate.

Eleanor King, alias Betty Mayfield, is a bombshell redhead on the run. No sooner does the criminal court rule her husband's death of a broken neck an accident than—exonerated but fearful of her well-heeled and well-connected father-in-law Henry Cumberland—she skips town.[11] Determined to buy herself peace of mind with wads of Cumberland's cash, she gets off the train in a southern Californian town of Esmeralda followed by Larry Mitchell, blackmailer and lounge lizard, and by Chandler's by now middle-aged private eye.

Marlowe tails Betty on behest of Umney, a big shot lawyer with a big checkbook and an even bigger attitude. Once on the case, in no time the detective finds himself on the wrong side of a gun from Mitchell, a whisky bottle from Betty, and another gun from a roughneck shamus from Kansas by the name of Goble. A series of episodic encounters takes him to Betty's plush hotel where Larry the lizard is said to lie dead on her balcony. The circumstances could scarcely favor her less. Blackmailed by Mitchell, she had the motive and the opportunity, and the broken neck makes it look like a nasty case of déjà vu.

Running himself from solitude, Marlowe goes to bed with Umney's expensive secretary in a tender one-night stand. The morning after he goes back to safeguarding Betty, who tries to buy him first with cash, then flesh. Between Brandon, a major-league gangster from Kansas, and Harvest, a tough guy on Brandon's payroll, Marlowe finds his hands full even before another body turns up: Chang, a junked-out watchman found hanging in his slum bedsit. Meantime the detective runs into one of Chandler's most curious characters: an elderly gentleman with a cane in his gloved hands. Mordant and observant, the old hotel habitué holds Marlowe captive with discourse on God, existentialism, and art.

Along the way there is also Fred Pope, an old resident of Esmeralda, who in a chapter-length monologue mulls over the antisocial drift of this erstwhile suburban paradise, while the plot cools its heels. A few chapters later, in an intertextual nod, Marlowe turns down a $5000 bribe from the gangster, just like he turned down $5000 from Betty and another such gift from a would-be friend in *The Long Goodbye*. Then the curtain drops on this murder mystery in which murder does not out, in which no murderer is brought to justice, and in which it is not even certain that there has been a murder in the first place.

Even though Brandon is the prime suspect in the deaths of Mitchell and Chang, lacking evidence or even conviction that their demise had not been respectively an accident and suicide, Marlowe lets him go. Tired from running and from throwing herself at Marlowe, Betty gambles on a future with Brandon. Goble and Harvest, beaten into pulp, fade away. Snubbed and apoplectic, Cumberland the tycoon repairs home. His big shot lawyer Umney is told to go kiss a duck. And Marlowe? Closing the book on this outlandish case with all the verve of a timeworn Sisyphus, staving off the solitaire without and within, he takes a long-distance call from Paris and pledges himself to love and marriage.

If all these goings-on are too contrived and over the top for a plot of a hardboiled mystery, it is on the word of two generations of literary critics for whom *Playback* is the one Chandler novel they love to hate. William Marling is wholly representative of this critical school of hard knocks when he knocks it—and hard—as a "disheartening performance" and "the least of Chandler's novels".[12] As if that were not enough, he approvingly quotes Harold Orel whose own body slam—"dreary trash"—is said to speak for most readers. But if blanket dismissals make for dubious scholarship in general, it is especially so when things are demonstrably not as elementary as any one of these literary-critical Sherlocks would have you believe.

Consider just one of Marling's allegations: "Beyond the semi-satiric portrait of the wealthy retirees of Esmeralda, there is little social criticism or insight."[13] This is plain wrong. Fred Pope's mini-treatise on Esmeralda, which takes up the entire Chap. 20, is only one of several passages where Chandler's social criticism of the erosion of the town's social cohesion hits home with the aplomb of Jackie Robinson. Indeed, Marling shoots himself in the foot when he extols the insights of Bernard Schopen, who himself extols Chandler's social critique and insight. In fact, concludes Schopen, so effective was Chandler's social commentary on life in America, "that social criticism has become a major function of the form".[14]

As for Marling's slam of *Playback* as the least of Chandler's novels, the hardboiled master himself had no qualms acknowledging his shortcomings as a crime writer: "The story has weaknesses. It is episodic and the emphasis shifts around from character to character and it is, as a mystery, over-complicated, but as a story of people very simple. It has no violence in it at all; all the violence is off stage."[15] Tellingly, however, he felt this way not about *Playback* but about his anatomy of Hollywood, *Little Sister* (1949), uniformly praised by Marling and other critics.

Even Jerry Speir, widely regarded as a witness for the defense in the ongoing dispute about *Playback*'s place in the Chandler canon, is difficult to tell from those who trash it as forgettable and hokey. While Chandler's artistic stock has risen over the decades, *Playback* continues to be seen as a write-off, as evidenced by Speir's remark that it offers "certain insights into the author and his attitude towards his work in his later years", which damns it with the proverbial faint praise.[16] Worse, his otherwise discerning semi-chapter on *Playback* falls prey to the same critical myopia that made Marling dismiss the book as virtually without virtue and made Fiedler slander Chandler as a semi-pornographer.

Without providing a shred of supporting evidence, Speir contends, for instance, that Betty becomes involved in a "struggle for power within the mob" (78). Again, this is plain wrong. The better the writer, proposed Chandler in his twelve notes on the mystery novel, "the more subtly he will disguise that which cannot be told".[17] Although some reviewers drubbed the plot of *Playback* as a dog looking for a lamppost, it may take readers some time to figure out, for example, that the real target of black-mail is not Betty but Brandon, making Chandler a more devious plotter than even he allowed.

The point is that he is too devious—or, what amounts to the same thing, too subtle—for Speir, who mistakes the bloody punishment of petty hustlers like Goble for a struggle within the mob. Textual evidence makes it clear, however, that there is no struggle in the West Egg of Esmeralda, only Clark Brandon and his brand of American justice. Brandon will not be pushed around by a greasy gumshoe from Kansas who threatens to mouth about his racketeering past, and Goble has to be taught a lesson he will not easily forget. As for Betty, she may be a deluxe gold-digger in the manner of Dinah Brand from *Red Harvest*, but becoming the big boss's squeeze does not make her a player in a power struggle that just isn't there at all.

When even seasoned critics flounder, it is time to take a fresh look at the source of their interpretive confusion.[18] Revisiting *Playback* means, of course, revisiting the multiple narrative signposts that show Chandler going after a dramatically different effect than a vintage Marlowe mystery. From the title down, *Playback* spells out an invitation to a novel kind of detective game—intertextual, ironic, self-reflexive—and readers who miss the clues run the risk of misinterpreting and, consequently, misjudging the book altogether. Regrettably, all of its harshest critics do just that, taking a straightforward view of Chandler's last mystery that ignores its Olympian playfulness and its complex valedictory to the entire hardboiled school.

THE IS TO WAS MAN

With the title as the symbolic gatekeeper to the garden of forking interpre-tations, *Playback* cautions: look not for an old-fashioned hardboiled mys-tery lest you mistake a self-reflexive deconstruction of genre for a manqué Marlowe caper.

As much as he admired Hemingway's titles, Chandler habitually dithered over his own. Even a partial list of those he contemplated but never used is long and, in its own way, revealing: *The Corpse Came in Person, The Man with the Shredded Ear, A Few May Remember, Zone of Twilight, Parting Before Danger, The Is to Was Man, All Guns Are Loaded, Return From Ruin, Lament But No Tears, Too Late to Sleep, The Cool-Off.* Conspicuous as the novel's central symbol, on the first pass the title of *Playback* seems to pose little interpretive difficulty.

Robert Parker, who himself effected a Chandler playback in a 1991 novel of his own—a sequel to *The Big Sleep*, entitled *Perchance to Dream*—exemplifies the critical consensus by seeing the title as little more than a replay of the tragedy from which Betty flees for dear life. No sooner is she cleared of her husband's death than the chain of events in Esmeralda restages the entire nightmare, with circumstantial evidence pointing the accusing finger right at her.

If that were all, of course, the wordplay would be worth little more than the paper it is printed on. But it isn't, partly because the 1958 novel is itself an intertextual playback of a screenplay Chandler wrote when still in Hollywood. After the triumph of his scripts for *Double Indemnity* (1944; co-credited with director Billy Wilder) and *Blue Dahlia* (1946), Universal-International coughed up an unheard of contract—$4000 a week, points on profits, and minimum supervision—for rights to an original screenplay. Chandler completed the job in 1948, calling it *Playback*.

Knee-deep in postwar recession, the cash-strapped studio never got around to shooting the picture. Yet, even as it stands, more than one critic judges it to be Chandler's finest work for film—no mean accolade, with his two previous screenplays Academy Award nominees.[19] More to the point, the normally reticent writer agreed (even as he disparaged the script while working on it), in 1953 making the first stab at adapting it into a Marlowe novel. Chandler's original outline reveals remarkable structural parallels between the script and the book:

> The crucial week in the life of a girl who decides to spend it in a tower suite in a hotel, under an assumed name, her identity thoroughly concealed with great care… During this week the frustrations and tragedies of her life are repeated in capsule form, so that it almost appears that she had brought her destiny with her, and that wherever she went the same sort of thing would happen to her… So Betty arrives at the hotel and her name is now, let us say, Elizabeth Mayfield.[20]

Discounting inevitable narrative details, the novel departs from the screenplay for the most part in scenery and in the endgame. The original is set in Vancouver, BC, with the investigation into Mitchell's death led by a *sympathique* Canadian lawman, Killaine, who falls for Betty after clearing her of blame. Like in Chandler novels, the script depicts a cross-section of society, from hyperbolic power figures to everyday Joes in everyday jobs. Coming into contact with all walks of life without being of any, Marlowe rubs shoulders with cabbies, hotel guests, tired cops, night guards, motel clerks, and other anonymous people who make up a town.

At the very least, then, beside the playback of Betty's troubles with the law and with the men in her life who end up with broken necks, the novel's title self-reflexively plays back the film screenplay from Chandler's glory days in Hollywood. Adding another layer of metatextual complexity, however, is the fact that the screenplay itself plays back some of Chandler's stories from his *Black Mask* period.

The older writer had no qualms cannibalizing his short fiction when the time came to compose the novels, and *Playback* is no exception, playing back themes, motifs, and even entire passages from "Guns at Cyrano's" (1936) and "I'll be Waiting" (1939). From a sultry redhead beached in a California hotel to Marlowe's "I'll always be waiting" (749), such narrative playbacks up the ante on the intertextual game Chandler is playing with his readers. Once again testifying to the state of Chandler criticism, at least one critic complained in 1993 that he had not seen the link between "I'll Be Waiting" and *Playback* noted anywhere, although it is mentioned in Marling's 1986 study.[21]

It should be evident by now that the number of playbacks, allusions, and outright references smuggled in by way of the title is far greater than Parker's words might lead one to believe. Already in 1948 the title signified more than a simple mirror of events before and after Betty's flight, but by 1958 it was supercharged with double meanings by alluding to the movie script and to Chandler's own short fiction. With the title as the symbolic gatekeeper to the garden of forking interpretations, *Playback* cautions: look not for an old-fashioned hardboiled mystery lest you mistake a self-reflexive deconstruction of genre for a manqué Marlowe caper.

PIRANDELLO MINUS THE OBTRUSIVENESS

Even as it delivers the hardboiled goods, *Playback* demonstrates a flamboyantly self-reflexive attitude to the genre and its formulas.

As apparent from his 1950 correspondence to his New York literary agent Carl Brandt, Chandler was getting tired of the hardboiled shtick. "From now on I am going to write what I want to write as I want to write it. Some of it may flop. There are always going to be people who will say I have lost the pace I had once, that I take too long to say things now, and don't care enough about tight active plots. But I'm not writing for those people now. I am writing for the people who understand about writing as an art."[22]

He was indeed aiming at a new audience, bidding adieu in his last Marlowe novel to an entire literary school, albeit with a parodic wink and intertextual nudge. "I am not satisfied", he wrote with an air of defiance, that "a novel cannot be written which, ostensibly a mystery and keeping the spice of mystery, will actually be a novel of character and atmosphere with an over-tone of violence and fear".[23] Utterances like these reflect his ambition to transcend the formula by leaving a lasting emotional effect on the reader, where the mathematics of the plot combines with a poetic aura of the places and people described.

The Long Goodbye, Chandler's second-last and arguably best book, was already a far cry from the shoot-first, ask-questions-later clichés plied at that time with tremendous success by comic-book writers like Mickey Spillane. This suburban upper-class novel of manners, whose working title was *Summer in Idle Valley*, solidified Chandler's reputation in England as a novelist and stylist of the first caliber.[24] Even as its poignant, at times almost meditative, plot is punctuated by a double murder, it veers away from the murder mystery to deal with the trials of friendship, existential solitude, and middle-age compromises. All in all, an apt stage-setter for Chandler's next literary experiment, the perplexing pastiche of the entire hardboiled genre—*Playback*.

Having grafted psychological drama and character study onto crime mystery (or was it the other way round?), Chandler would apologize for his early stories which honored the genre by luxuriating in death. Not that he was ever as prone to violence as other Black Masketeers. Most of his prose seems muted, almost cerebral, next to that of his peers, starting with Hammett. Before *Red Harvest*, in the days of "House Dick" (working title: "Bodies Piled Up"), the Thin Man was wont to go right over the top:

> I stepped past the maid and tried the door. It was unlocked. I opened it. Slowly, rigidly, a man pitched out into my arms—pitched out backwards—and there was a six-inch slit down the back of his coat, and his coat was wet and sticky. That wasn't altogether a surprise: the blood on the floor had prepared me for something of the sort. But when another followed him—facing me, this one, with a dark, distorted face—I dropped the one I had caught and jumped back. And as I jumped a third man came tumbling out after the others.

Exit realism. Enter pulp fiction at its hyperbolic and hilarious best.

Even as it delivers the hardboiled goods, *Playback* demonstrates a flamboyantly self-reflexive attitude to the genre and its formulas. To begin, in a tribute as ironic as it is deferential, the novel swarms with allusions to

Hammett's *Red Harvest*. One of the most obvious is the squat and thickset Kansas Op, Goble, whose manners and mannerisms make him a dead ringer for the squat and thickset Continental Op. The operative from *Red Harvest* is, in Dinah Brand's *blazon*, "a fat, middle aged, hard-boiled, pig-headed guy".[25] The operative from *Playback* is "a middle sized fat man and the fat didn't look flabby". Dropping hints like glass slippers, Chandler is ready with another one. Asked whether Goble is a close friend of his, without batting an eye Marlowe shoots back: "The operative word is close."

In the context, the really funny part comes when Goble, the reincarnated Op from *Red Harvest*, gets beaten to a pulp by a red-haired goon, Richard "Red" Harvest. Red Harvest himself is a throwback to the Hammett-era bruisers with gorilla biceps and an IQ around the level of room temperature. In the same vein, Henry Cumberland, Betty's well-to-do and well-connected father-in-law, is a spitting image of Hammett's Elihu Willsson, both as irascible and as disdainful of the law in the cities they own.

The knockout redhead Betty Mayfield, alias Eleanor King, mirrors the red-haired knockout Brigid O'Shaughnessy, alias Miss Wonderly. A good girl gone bad, an icy manipulator with the hots for the hero, an arrant actress who plays men like pawns, a runaway whose past catches up with her, she is a carbon copy of Hammett's archetypal femme fatale. So is her penchant for lying, with her copycat lines a dead giveaway of Chandler's tribute to her prototype. "I am a liar", purrs Brigid, "I have always been a liar."[26] "All right, I'm a liar", shrugs Betty, "I've always been a liar."

Taking this self-reflexivity to its logical end is Henry Clarendon IV. Just as Hammett cameoed in *Red Harvest* as Dan Rolff, the thin man with tuberculosis, in *Playback* Chandler stages his own appearance as an aging hotel-lobby philosopher (after his wife's death in 1954, Chandler sold their house, staying in Southern Californian hotels).[27] The idea may have been reinforced in his mind by the 1950 collaboration with Hitchcock—who cameoed in all of his films—on the screenplay to Patricia Highsmith's *Strangers on a Train*. Of course, Henry Clarendon IV is also a playback of Roger Wade, Chandler's self-portrait as an alcoholic with a writer's block in *The Long Goodbye*.

Playfully irreverent, in *Playback* Chandler insinuates himself into Marlowe's investigation as a snobbish, cynical hotel patron. His hair neatly parted, hands in white gloves (in his later years Chandler wore gloves to hide a skin condition), his eye is sharp and enamored of the female form. A hardboiled Pirandello minus the obtrusiveness, the author even sits down with his own creation for a chat that brims with ironic innuendoes and self-reflexive intimations, a trope that would come into its own during the half-century since.

Image 4.2   Raymond Chandler's house in La Jolla, California. *"Just as Hammett cameoed in* Red Harvest *as Dan Rolff, the thin man with tuberculosis, in* Playback *Chandler stages his own appearance as an aging hotel-lobby philosopher (after his wife's death in 1954, Chandler sold their house, staying in Southern Californian hotels)."*

AT ODDS WITH THE CANON

A hardboiled mystery buff might be excused for thinking he opened the wrong book when, instead of a taut whodunit, he is detoured through a lecture in philosophy.

Defying critics who allege that it is, in effect, a book-long slip of an errant pen, *Playback* takes the simple art of murder to a different level with self-reflexive gusto. Marlowe runs into a smart-aleck cabbie who remonstrates that car-tailing is something from crime novels, mister. Before she sleeps with him, Helen Vermilyea mocks him as, ahem, Mr. Hard Guy. The hero himself ricochets from one throat-clearing moment to another, wisecracking about TV dicks who never take their hats off and always drive dark inconspicuous cars. With countless echoes of the hardboiled classics and clichés setting the tone, Chandler-as-Clarendon is only waiting to kick this self-reflexive mockery into an even higher gear.

With Hammett and *Red Harvest* lurking in the wings, he lectures Marlowe, ostensibly about a woman: "She had an overblown style and she looked just a little hardboiled." Or three lines down: "She tries too hard" (827). As even Freud conceded, a cigar is sometimes just a cigar, and this exchange between Chandler's fictive spokesmen, Clarendon and Marlowe, might be as innocent of doubles entendres as a doctoral dissertation on Longinus. But in the wake of so many instances of self-reflexivity, if not self-parody, it is hard to shake off the impression of another inside joke. A touch snide, perhaps, but who could argue with this lowdown on the *Black Mask* school—overblown, overboiled, and trying too hard to convince readers that style was a matter not of aesthetics, but body pile-ups?

But not even these exuberant multiplications of self-reflexive irony prepare the reader for what follows. In a scene at odds with the canon of hardboiled mystery, with startling emotional candor, Clarendon meditates on dying. His existential anguish only accentuated by his clinical detachment, the old man confesses to the horror of having no companions on his last journey, save the white-starched hospital staff. Yet no sooner is his exorcism over then, puckish to the end, he deflates it with a self-aimed wink: "I talk too much" (827). Seconds later, he brings down the theatrical fourth wall, chiding Marlowe with a straight face: "You should have come to me for information. But of course you couldn't know that."

By that time readers can rightly wonder whether they are reading Chandler or a postmodernist novelist like Oswaldo Soriano, whose *Triste, Solitario, y Final* (1973) features Philip Marlowe, John Wayne, and Laurel and Hardy in a pastiche equally brimming with sadness and eruptions of violence. Not surprisingly, Chandler's Marlowe humors the old hotel philosopher, just like he humored another old man with a penchant for self-deprecation and cynical detachment in *The Big Sleep*. But, even as the novel chalks up another playback, the author and his creation are not done yet.

A hardboiled mystery buff might be excused for thinking he opened the wrong book when, instead of a taut whodunit, he is detoured through a lecture in philosophy. What else to call Clarendon's seemingly disjointed, yet emotionally arresting ramble that takes him from the complex patterns on a strelitzia bud to the deity behind creation? "Is he omnipotent?" asks Chandler-as-Clarendon, echoing Epicurus's *reductio* of an omniscient and benevolent God and the ubiquity of evil. The ancient philosopher set this trilemma in four striking derivations: Is God willing to prevent evil, but not able? *Then he is not omnipotent.* Is he able, but not willing? *Then he is not benevolent.* Is he able and willing? *Then whence evil?* Is he neither able nor willing? *Then why call him God?*

Chandler's own theodicean calculus forms one of the most moving passages he ever put down on paper. "How could he be? There's so much suffering and almost always by the innocent. Why will a mother rabbit trapped in a burrow by a ferret put her babies behind and allow her throat to be torn out? Why? In two weeks more she would not even recognize them. Do you believe in God, young man?", the writer asks his detective. The mute howl gathers force:

> How can I imagine a hell in which a baby that died before baptism occupies the same degraded position as a hired killer or a Nazi death-camp commandant or a member of the Politburo? How strange it is that man's finest aspirations, dirty little animal that he is, his finest actions also, his great and unselfish heroism, his constant daily courage in a harsh world—how strange that these things should be so much finer than his fate on this earth. That has to be somehow made reasonable. Don't tell me that honor is merely a chemical reaction or that a man who deliberately gives his life for another is merely following a behavior pattern. Is God happy with a poisoned cat dying in convulsions behind a billboard? Is God happy that life is cruel and that only the fittest survive? (829–30)

If it is difficult to square this monologue with the stereotype of hardboiled pulps, it is as difficult to square it with *Playback* being nothing but a "pale imitation" of Chandler's early work.[28]

WISE MAN, WINK, WINK

> Imitation may be the highest form of flattery, but self-imitation is higher still.

Whatever else they do, Chandler's philosophical reflections prove that the concerns of genre literature can be as profound as those of highbrow art, even if expressed in a *sui generis* collection of narrative tropes. Chandler's ambitious design for *Playback* is no less apparent when he self-reflexively draws parallels between God and artist. An omniscient and omnipotent Creator, he observes, would not have bothered to make the universe at all. "There is no success where there is no possibility of failure, no art without the resistance of the medium" (830). Little wonder why, in this tête-à-tête with his own creator, Marlowe calls him a wise man, wink, wink.

Playback openly belies the assumption that only highbrow fiction is interested in—or, for that matter capable of—reflecting on transcendence, be it couched in aesthetic, religious, or anthropological terms. Nobrow in its eclecticism, Chandler's swan song is *both* a crime caper and a serious study of social disintegration by an artist on a quest for a novel type of decorum. Theodicy and eschatology, the sociobiology of the soul, the role of Art in negotiating a truce with thermodynamic chaos: *Playback* offers enough intellectual content to upturn the picture of genre fiction as lite entertainment—and to befuddle aficionados of hardboiled hijinks who, on cue, complained of missing in *Playback* "the climate of malevolence and danger, the exotic characterizations, the driving pace and the imaginative mayhem that made Chandler's earlier books masterpieces of that kind".[29]

For the artist, defections from readers expecting another installment of *Murder, He Wrote* may have been a small price to pay. It is difficult, he sighed, "to keep your characters and your story operating on a level which is understandable to the semi-literate public, and at the same time give them some intellectual and artistic overtones which the public does not seek or demand".[30] What the public sought and demanded was Marlowe at his hardboiled best. What Chandler was after had more to do with capping his career with a work that would measure up to his self-image as an artist.

In *Something More Than Night*, Peter Wolfe offered a draconian interpretation of the countless ironies, allusions, and self-reflexive turns that drive the novel's aesthetics. According to the critic, the playbacks from the hardboiled classics and from Chandler's own career are nothing more than anomalies and, just because there are so many of them, the novel is an artistic failure. No matter that the consistency and multiplicity of these "anomalies" are clue enough that a very different narrative game than a straight-laced mystery is afoot. The list of Chandler's playbacks, playbacks of playbacks, and playbacks of playbacks of playbacks goes on, after all, seemingly without end. Imitation may be the highest form of flattery, but self-imitation is higher still.

Like his first books, *Playback* opens with a missing persons case and reincarnates his arch scoundrel, the blackmailer. Like *Farewell, My Lovely, The Lady in the Lake*, and *The Long Goodbye*, it features a name-changing runaway. The see-no-evil, hear-no-evil attitude also gives *Playback* the aura of early Chandler, with Clark Brandon a stand-in for Eddie Mars from *The Big Sleep* and Laird Brunette from *Farewell, My Lovely*. Locations are also familiarly ironic: Rancho Descansado (Relaxo) is as fraught with strife as are the Stillwood Heights in *Farewell, My Lovely* and Idle Valley in *The Long Goodbye*. If Mitchell is killed by his victim, so was Lindsey Marriott of *Farewell, My Lovely*, Louis Vannier of *The High Window*, and Chris Lavery of *The Lady in the Lake*—the latter novel being itself a playback of Chandler's story "The Lady in the Lake".[31]

In *The Long Goodbye* Marlowe returns a $5000 bill meant to buy his complicity to Terry Lennox, a Gatsby-like figure whose association with the mob robs him of the decency that made Marlowe befriend him in the first place. *Playback* plays back an identical $5000 bribe from Betty; then plays back the playback when its twin is returned to Brandon. In *The Long Goodbye* Marlowe shares a night with Linda Loring who, at the end of *Playback*, resurfaces as his wife-to-be. Betty is accused of her husband's death in a playback of Mrs. Murdock's murder of her husband in *High Window*. Throw in the Hammett and *Red Harvest* connection, with Betty lip-synching Brigid and with Spade's lines behind some of Marlowe's, and you will be right to wonder what these playbacks are all about.[32]

Back in 1950, Hammett himself sounded the death knoll for the hard-boiled school, pointing out in an interview with the *Los Angeles Times* that the times were inexorably a-changing. "This hard-boiled stuff—it is a menace... It went all right in the Terrible 20s. The bootlegger days. The racketeering days. There are racketeers now, to be sure, but they are nice, refined people. They belong to country clubs."[33] Exit flashy and violent Bugsy Siegel of Beverly Hills. Enter subdued and semi-respectable Clark Brandon of Esmeralda.

Hammett was right, of course. The 1950s did mark the twilight of the hardboiled tradition that ruled the pulps in the 1920s, the bookstands in the 1930s, the marquees in the 1940s, and that was poised to morph into the police procedural in the hands of Ed McBain in the 1950s. The point is that, created in the twilight of the hardboiled tradition, *Playback* was designed to reflect that it was created in the twilight of the hardboiled tradition. Playing back Chandler's script from the halcyon days of film noir, playing back the classics of the hardboiled genre, playing back his own oeuvre, out of a farewell Marlowe book its author fashioned a farewell bookend to the tough-guy school in an intertextual gambit overlooked by fans and critics.

With the Prohibition, the Depression, and World War II already consigned to history books, with the hardboiled decades drawing to an end, cultural newcomers like James Bond and Dr. Strangelove made the lone gumshoe in a rumpled fedora look old hat. A half-nostalgic, half-ironic farewell would have appealed to an artist keen to reclaim the middle ground between literary pretentiousness and its lowbrow counterpart. The "mystery story as an art form has been so thoroughly explored", protested Chandler, "that the real problem for a writer now is to avoid writing a mystery story while appearing to do so".[34]

Far from a brainchild of a talent in decline, *Playback* is so far ahead of the pack that, coming full circle, it only seems to those looking back like it was lagging behind.

A WHODUNIT WITHOUT A DUNIT

> Although not unheard of, this particular break with the formula is exceedingly rare because, as Chandler himself noted, it defies the premise of the form, leaving a discordant effect not unlike an unresolved chord in music.

By the time of *Playback* Chandler was ready to buck conventions, some of them of his own making. In the Addenda to "Twelve Notes", he originally jotted: "Love interest nearly always weakens a mystery", and—assuming that Marlowe is a really good detective—"A really good detective never gets married."[35] How transgressive to see Marlowe pledge himself to marriage, and then live out that pledge in *The Poodle Springs Story*, a book that was to dwell on the highs and lows of his wedded life against the background of the commodification of Poodle Springs (real-life Palm Springs, which Chandler was fond of visiting in the last years of his life).

And yet, even as flouting expectations and defying formulas are said to be the hallmarks of art, critical opinion shrugs off this genre-busting denouement, chalking it up to Chandler's dotage. Writer gets old, writer gets maudlin, writer himself wants to get married, writer obliges character with a wife—simple enough if you buy into this type of biographical fallacy.

Correspondence attests, however, that it was Chandler' friend and fellow detective writer Maurice Guinness who lobbied for the marriage.[36] The picture of diminishing intellect and creeping sentimentality is even further contradicted by the author's doubts about the whole idea. "I think I may have misunderstood your desire that Marlowe should get married", he wrote to Guinness in 1959. "A fellow of Marlowe's type shouldn't get married."

Aware of what an unusual book he was crafting, Chandler confided in 1953 in mock exasperation: "I have 36,000 words of doodling and not yet a stiff. This is terrible."[37] In fact, *Playback* deviates from crime novel conventions in so many ways that it threatens to become an anti-mystery. Although there are plenty of guns around, nobody fires one. With Mitchell presumed dead, there is no formal inquest, and no one is brought to trial. The hero does not uphold the law by nabbing the bad guy. Worse, he does not even report his findings to the police. Justice is not meted out, either in the legal or even in the poetic sense. Someone, just maybe, gets away with murder.

Taking for granted that every crime mystery must have a murder, some literary critics lay Mitchell's disappearance on Brandon, others on Betty. Either way, of course, it would mean that Chandler breaks the rules of the game insofar as, either way, the presumed murderer goes free. Yet hardly anyone comments on the fact that, in an ultimate twist for a murder mystery, Chandler does not deliver a clear-cut case of murder, even though no less than three people—Betty's husband, Mitchell, and Chang—perish in questionable circumstances.

Although not unheard of, this particular break with the formula is exceedingly rare because, as Chandler himself noted, it defies the premise of the form, leaving a discordant effect not unlike an unresolved chord in music. What might have been a false note in a routine whodunit, however, makes perfect sense in a book that, although not a traditional parody, sets out to topple all the fundamental conventions of the genre just like *The Big Sleep* did.[38] Evidence of another playback, perhaps? Quite likely, insofar as *The Big Sleep* and *Playback* are the only books of his in which crime and punishment do not go hand in hand.

Everything hinges, of course, on what happens to Mitchell. Is Betty a double murderess, or a victim of bad luck? Is Brandon a killer, or only Betty's gallant savior? Did he have Mitchell taken care of, or did he only take care of the corpse? In the end, however, all this is a red herring since Brandon does not kill Mitchell. In a letter from 19 May 1958—that is, *after* completing *Playback*—Chandler is explicit on this point. The ex-gangster's only crimes are getting rid of Mitchell's body and hiring a gunman (Red Harvest), thus precluding even a scenario in which Brandon kills Mitchell inadvertently, as in the original movie script.[39]

There is no escaping the fact that *Playback* is an anti-mystery, a whodunit without a dunit. So, how did Mitchell get into Betty's balcony chair without crossing her room? Why did she report seeing no injuries on him? Does the corpse disappear from the terrace or was it not there in the first place? As speculation mounts, so does the sense that this interpretive limbo is not an accident. When Marlowe asks Betty whether she actually saw Mitchell dead or whether she made it all up, instead of providing the answer, the next line reads: "The road forked" (806).

Appropriately enough, the forking ambiguity will not be resolved. No one will actually see Mitchell or his mortal remains again. During the verbal showdown with Brandon, Marlowe's reconstruction will be purely circumstantial, validated by his authority as detective-cum-narrator alone. Mitchell's death may have been set in motion by drink, misstep, Betty, or a combination thereof. People do, after all, fall over balustrades sometimes. But the timing and the considerations of *cui prodest* are too convenient not to implicate her—or Brandon.

Interestingly, on the assumption that the death of the lounge lizard removes a blackmailer, Chang's death could signify a removal of a witness to the removal of the blackmailer's body. In other words, were Mitchell's accident of the premeditated variety, it would put a different spin on the rest of the plot, not least by casting a sinister shadow over Chang's death. Mitchell's drunken misstep, on the other hand, bolsters the odds on the watchman's overdose being self-inflicted. In the end, we will never know the causes of death of Larry Mitchell and Ceferino Chang. The more one searches for a solution, the more it is clear that, while Brandon's hands are clean, there is enough suspicion cast on him to provoke speculation among generations of readers and scholars.

THE GREAT WRONG PLACE

In many ways America's microcosm, California is where tier-one bandits like Brandon shop for social acceptance with the brazenness of a real-life Jay Gould or a fictional James Gatz.

Taking Auden's praise as a starting point, one can better appreciate what kind of books Chandler wrote at the end of his life by looking at what is wrong in his Great Wrong Place. Published toward the end of the 1950s, when every TV commercial implicitly reassured Americans that they lived in the best of countries and in the best of times, *Playback* is, nonetheless, closer in its sensibilities to the bootlegging and racketeering 1930s and the wartime materiel-scamming 1940s. Nobody is outraged by corruption and vice because they are so commonplace. With a fat wallet to buy friends in high places, every fat cat is sure to land on his silk-stockinged feet.

When Marlowe Y-sects the sleepy-dog suburban resort of Esmeralda—a fictionalized version of Chandler's La Jolla—he does it without fanfare or even indignation. After a lifetime of sifting through society's garbage, Chandler's hero has seen it all. His tired, almost complacent, view of evil is one sign that the line between high crime and high society is about as real as a lawyer's promise. In many ways America's microcosm, California is where tier-one bandits like Brandon shop for social acceptance with the brazenness of a real-life Jay Gould or a fictional James Gatz.

Chandler's gallery of crooked cops, corrupt judges, criminal (in both senses of the word) lawyers, untouchable racketeers, and business moguls big enough to operate outside the law sum up his view of the USA. In this climate, which has only gotten worse since the War on Drugs farce, the O.J. Simpson trial fiasco, the Rodney King flare-up, and the Homeland Security fix, it is small wonder that Chandler's cops and detectives nourish such a jaded attitude toward law enforcement. The real criminals never see their day in court because graft and corruption are everywhere. Power to the people means in practice power to the people who can afford to buy immunity from even the most tenacious investigators. Although Marlowe will usually get the man who pulls the trigger, there is nothing to cheer about. The corrupt system remains intact. In the last scene of "Smart-Alec Kill", Chandler's *Black Mask* story from 1934, the PI and a police captain go to celebrate after closing the case. "What'll we drink to?" asks the cop. "Let's just drink", replies the hero.

Playback lacks the type of sadistic cop that appeared regularly in Chandler's earlier novels. But the fact that Marlowe actually thanks the fuzz for not working him over is proof enough of the enmity between the public and the public servants on the other side of the blue line. The very presence of private detectives and private security personnel, who nowadays vastly outnumber uniformed police, is an implied censure of the latter's efficacy. With a mogul like Cumberland above the law because he owns the town in which the law is dispensed, and a former gangster like Brandon living it up like Howard Hughes instead of enjoying R&B with the Department of Corrections, who is to talk about justice? Whether Mitchell suffers a genuine or a planned accident, no one—not even Marlowe—can touch the former Kansas kingpin.

Although justice in *Playback* is as perverted and powerless as it is in Faulkner's *Sanctuary*, in many ways Chandler's novel situates itself closer to another American crime classic, *The Great Gatsby*.[40] To readers familiar with Chandler's essays, this is hardly a surprise: normally stingy with praise, on more than one occasion he referred to Fitzgerald's novel as a little pure art. A Midwestern Gatsby whose verbal tic, "old man", rings as phoney as his counterpart's "old sport", Brandon too is a former racketeer who buys respectability by the billfold. Acquiring lavish property, phasing out former cronies, throwing tainted dough around, like Gatsby he hopes to join the establishment of Esmeralda. The similarities hold up until the end, for the Kansas gangster's social success is as genuine as the one from New York. In Goble's inimitable words: "He's just a nigger to them" (815).

Like *The Great Gatsby*, *Playback* is at once cynical and idealistic, dramatic and melodramatic, a story of moral and social decay embedded in a story of blackmail and death. Browbeaten by the prestige of the canon, we like to forget that Fitzgerald's masterpiece is also a crime story set in the hard-drinking, hard-partying, hardnosed days of the speakeasies. The reason why it is not deprecated as a pre-RICO gangster fiction decked out in the jazz beat of the era is its uncompromising audit of America's soul for sale. But then it is hardly different from *Playback*, which tosses out its own audit of America's soul on the heap of plastic wrappers from TV dinners of the era.

ANYTOWN, USA

But as in the days when he wrote about the great big whore of Los Angeles, Chandler's top villain is the American urban sprawl rendered by means of his unvaryingly melancholy cityscapes.

As acerbic and understated as in his correspondence, Chandler wastes no opportunity in *Playback* to take potshots at guns and lawyers, two icons of the uneasy relationship between America and American justice. Guns, drawls Marlowe, "are just a fast curtain to a bad second act" (756). The third act is played out today in real time, punctuated with daily reports of firearm massacres in living rooms and schoolyards, not to mention full-blown riots following unlawful deaths of a Trayvon Martin or a Michael Brown or an Eric Garner.

In just one atrocity among hundreds, in December 2012 Adam Lanza shot dead twenty children and seven women, including his own mother. In response, in 2014 New York passed some of the toughest gun control laws in the country, including a partial ban on semi-automatic assault weapons, limits on high-capacity magazines, and means to keep guns from the hands of mentally ill individuals who make threats. In the rest of the USA, however, rifles and shotguns can be bought—and carried—without a permit or registration. In Arizona you can purchase a handgun with an instant background check and in some locations carry it without a permit. Only a handful of states restrict assault weapons after the 1994 ban lapsed at the end of Bush II's first term.

According to the United Nations Office on Drugs and Crime, even as self-reported gun ownership across the country appears to be dropping, gun murder rates in the USA remain greater by an order of magnitude than in any other developed country: thirty-two times greater than in Norway or England and sixteen times greater than in Australia or Germany. The only countries ahead of the USA are Latin and South American narco-nations like Honduras or Colombia, the latter of which made news in 2014 by releasing from jail John Jairo Velasquez (aka Popeye), top hitman of the late Colombian drug lord Pablo Escobar, who confessed to personally killing 300 people and having a hand in eliminating close to 3000.

Another target for Chandler's wrath is the judiciary system, tailored to profit lawyers at the expense of pretty much everyone else. Decades later, Nelson DeMille's protagonist, who happens to be a Wall Street tax lawyer, makes no bones about this legal runaway train:

> I honestly don't know how anyone functions in this society without a law degree. Even I, Harvard Law, class of '69, have trouble figuring out legal from illegal, as the laws pile up faster than garbage in the county dump. (194).

Not that the public is beyond reproof. The USA accounts for more than a third of global legal spending, with lawyers crawling under every rock and a hard place. In fact, if one is to believe one of the oddball cops in Joseph Wambaugh's police procedural *Glitter Dome*, these days the next word a child learns after "mom" is "sue". True to form, Betty makes no distinction between lawyers and blackmailers when advised that she may need a good attorney. "That's a contradiction in terms", she sneers. "If he was good, he wouldn't be a lawyer" (808).

But as in the days when he wrote about the great big whore of Los Angeles, Chandler's top villain is the American urban sprawl rendered by means of his unvaryingly melancholy cityscapes. Driving around, Marlowe witnesses the dismal reality of Anytown, USA: tawdry, littered, decked out with a parade of false fronts, giant billboards, smoky poolrooms, street toughs, and fast food joints serving paper food on paper plates. Endless miles of intercity "divided six-lane superhighway dotted at intervals with the carcasses of wrecked, striped and abandoned cars tossed against the high bank to rust" (800), belch him out in Esmeralda, where postcard-pretty storefronts hide "broken crates, piles of cartons, trash drums, dusty parking spaces, the backyard of elegance" (834).

All this is a fitting prelude to Chapter 20—reminiscent of Faulkner's historical interpolations in *Requiem for a Nun*—where the plot languishes on the back burner while an inconsequential motel owner by the name of Fred Pope broods over Esmeralda's drift from a lifeless village to a soulless resort in the hands of a second-generation robber baroness. This type of social tableau, rare in a genre typically driven by murder mystery, is not so rare in a writer who has always deemed plots superfluous to the spirit of urban realism. Chandler's chapter-long dramatic monologue conjures up the decline in social cohesion, the splintering of communities, and the rise of the me-first and money-first ethic he observed as a nearly decade-long resident of La Jolla. "They'll take your last dollar from you between your teeth and look at you like you stole it from them", drawls Fred Pope.[41]

Pictures of roadside wreckage, urban blight, and human poverty are Marlowe's retinue as he makes his way through the sunlit resort's dark side to Chang's crack den. Before *Needle Park* and *Gridlock'd*, before dope became a middle-class problem, this is one of Chandler's most squalid and forlorn postcards from the edge. The kitchen, where the garage watchman ODs before ending strung up on an electric wire, has lino worn through to the boards. A single window jammed shut, a light bulb hangs from the cracked and leak-stained ceiling for illumination. Not fit for a pig, the junk pad is exactly what Marlowe says it is: a rich man's improvement on a rich man's property—a one-room slum.

Nor are the divisions between the haves and the have-nots that much different from the divisions between men and women. Scrutinizing Betty's photo, Marlowe remarks the absence of a wedding ring. The small print is glaring: in her late twenties, a girl ought to have a husband, or else there's something wrong with her—wrong enough to cue the investigator. Later, in the house of Helen Vermilyea, the hero states flatly: "You've been married, of course." Reflecting the precariousness of women's economics, the syllogism is simple. Since she owns property, and property is acquired by men, the house must be from her husband, a conjecture confirmed in the next line.

These days we figure on social commentary in crime novels—in fact, we frequently read them for precisely that reason. Urban proceduralists like Ed McBain or his Swedish admirers, Maj Shöwall and Per Wahlöö, or the heirs of the private eye tradition like Ross Macdonald or Walter Mosley routinely instruct readers on how much (or how little) the urban zoo has changed since Chandler's times. But all learned their social chops from this classics-trained Californian, who, with the zest of a modern-day Michael Moore, never hesitates to tell us where we took the wrong turn.

With a Technicolor eye for image and a Panasonic ear for language, Chandler follows losers in life, drifters, grifters, drunks, washouts, lonely people coming together for a brief moment of sex or love during which even their togetherness is tinged with the certainty of solitude. People who saw too much of the wrong side of life, cynical people who lost their ideals, so that even their dreams are dreamed only in black and white. Who is to say that *Playback* is not as fresh and topical today as it was in the days when we liked Ike? Who is to say—William Marling excepted—that it lacks social dimension?

I Cannot Work or Sleep Till I Have Finished It

The only question worth debating is how much the mature artist was in control of his medium.

Is Chandler's farewell novel art? As always in the case of genre literature, the answer is complicated by ingrained prejudice. In "Chandler and the Reviewers" (1995), J.K. Van Dover distilled a quarter century of heat-of-the-moment commentary into the following appraisal:

He was defiantly proud of his commitment to the detective story and of his achievement in transforming it to serve his artistic vision, but ironically, public recognition of that achievement evidently depended upon denying its basis. (20)

The reviews themselves document how even friendly critics felt obliged to justify Chandler's predilection for hardboiled fiction. Deploring a waste of talent, they beseeched him to leave his gumshoes in the foyer as a price of entering the literary salons.

Knocking genre art for lack of literary mettle is, of course, a bit like knocking a diamond for being only a compact lump of carbon. Chandler himself did not harbor any illusions. "Once in a long while a detective story writer is treated as a writer, but very seldom", he growled to a crime fiction critic on the *New York Herald Tribune*.[42] However expertly he writes a mystery story, "it will be treated in one paragraph, while a column and a half of respectful attention will be given to any fourth-rate, ill-constructed, mock-serious account of the life of a bunch of cotton pickers in the deep south".

Today Chandler is recognized for his hardboiled lyricism, arguably unequaled in his mastery of the metaphor and simile since the days of the metaphysical poets. But he deserves equal recognition as a social observer and a local regionalist. Fraught with dramatic potential, his genre-bending experiments, such as the marriage of a hardcore bachelor, dovetail with other unconventional elements of this most unconventional mystery: cross-genre adaptations, intertextual borrowings, metafictional references, playfully deconstructive clichés, self-reflexive asides, authorial intrusions, and ironic wordplay, to say nothing of pages of sociological and existential discourse. As a parodic retrospective on Chandler's own career and on the hardboiled tradition, his genreflecting and self-reflecting novel is the best proof of what he called "the strong element of burlesque in my kind of writing".[43]

In the end, *Playback* corroborates Chandler's claim that the artistic differences between the canon and the best of popular art are hardly measurable compared with the gap between the serious novel and any representative piece of Attic literature from the fourth century BC.[44] For the same reason, even though his hero has come to define the hardboiled decades, his roots belong to the literary tradition stretching from Cooper's Natty Bumppo to Twain's Huck Finn. Poor, marginalized, distrustful of phoney intellectualism, armed with fistfuls of common sense, a flair for the vernacular, and a heart of gold, he is a literary representative of his genre and of his entire race—an American.

Whether Chandler's hardboiled classics are art depends ultimately on one's definition of art. In some ways it is difficult to call *Playback* a masterpiece. Time and again, it spits out lines that ring phoney and forced. It cranks out jack-in-the-box characters who pop into the story only to pop out without a trace. It shows stitches in the plot, some as conspicuous as the helicopter said to spirit Mitchell's cadaver away. Not that this is news to any Chandler fan, or indeed to the author himself. "I'm a poor plotter, bad at construction", he conceded on more than one occasion, pleading greater interest in the scene, dialogue, and character.[45]

In the face of these flaws in the diamond, Jerry Speir's eulogy for Chandler and *Playback*—it is "obviously the product of age and hard work rather than of the facility of youthful talent" (79)—sounds suspiciously like an apology. No one disputes that the novel was composed by a mature artist. The only question worth debating is how much the mature artist was in control of his medium. Put more bluntly, the question is not how hard Chandler worked to whip his screenplay into a self-deconstructing novel, but rather to what effect and with what degree of success.

On balance evidence suggests that, not content merely to relive past glories, the old master was playing for very different stakes. The proof is on the page. Look for social commentary, transcendent themes, self-parody, and aesthetic irony, and you will find them aplenty. Look for the criminal jungle, hardboiled attitudes, fast blondes, and hired snoopers, and you will find them too. But if the latter is all you look for, you'll go home let down by this quintessentially nobrow neither-fish-nor-fowl. This is, indeed, why *Playback* slipped through the fingers of Chandler loyalists and antagonists alike, starting with highbrows like Fiedler who went slumming to confirm his bias.

He should have listened to Auden who, perhaps with Chandler in mind, confessed: "I must be careful not to get hold of a detective story for, once I begin one, I cannot work or sleep till I have finished it."[46]

NOTES

1. See Hubin's bibliographical study; thoroughly revised, parts of this research are based on Swirski (2005), Chap. 5.
2. See Fowler.
3. Swirski (2005), Chap. 4.

4. Contemporary studies foreground the diversity and malleability of the genre; for example, Mullen and O'Beirne.
5. Auden, 408.
6. Hiney, 277.
7. 1957 letter to Helga Greene, in Gardiner and Walker, 94; see also 1945 letter to Charles W. Morton, 74.
8. *The Big Sleep* 1:589 (when possible, I refer to the Library of America edition by volume: page); Chandler frequently commented on Marlowe's romantic or sentimental nature; see, 2:1038–9. In "Rats" (especially page 131), Rabinowitz discusses the symbolism of knight moves in *The Big Sleep*.
9. 2:651; below, *Poodle Springs*, 208.
10. *Poodle Springs*, 8; *Playback*, 799; all subsequent references are to *Playback* (Library of America edition) unless indicated otherwise.
11. Cumberland is Lee Kinsolving in the British edition; see Chandler's letter from 4 October 1958, in Gardiner and Walker, 242.
12. Marling (1995) 147, 150, 151; for other dismissals, see Van Dover, 35–7; Babener, 147; Peter Wolfe, 235.
13. Page 150.
14. Page 152; Webb praises "Chandler's brilliantly suggestive reporting of the seedy side of California", 6.
15. In Gardiner and Walker, 220.
16. Speir, 78; see also Skenazy, 6.
17. Gardiner and Walker, 68; on deception and artifice, see Babener.
18. À propos Mitchell's body removal problem, Peter Wolfe declares that no rope (sic!) or person is capable of lowering a man's dead weight down 120 feet.
19. Brewer, 267, echoed by James Pepper in the preface to the first US edition; for Chandler's hatred of it, see Hiney. Ironically, it remains the only Chandler novel never to become a feature film; even *Poodle Springs* is now a ho-hum HBO feature, starring James Caan.
20. MacShane (1976), 143; see also 1953 letter to H.N. Swanson, in Gardiger and Walker, 235. The screenplay is available as *Raymond Chandler's Unknown Thriller*; in 2013 it was turned into a graphic novel.
21. Tate, 122; Marling, 147.
22. In Gardiner and Walker, 90–91.
23. In Gardiner and Walker, 56.
24. Letter to Hillary Waugh, 1955, in Gardiner and Walker, 62.
25. Page 85; following quotes from *Playback*: 762; 817.
26. Page 88; next quote, *Playback*, 807.
27. On Chandler-Clarendon, see Speir, 81–3; Tate, 106–10; Peter Wolfe, 234–5.

28. Freeman, 240.
29. Charles Rolo in the *Atlantic Monthly*, quoted in Van Dover, 35.
30. In Gardiner and Walker, 61.
31. Published in 1939 in *Dime Detective Monthly*, a reference to Sergeant Green may be another pun, given Chandler's then engagement to Helga Greene.
32. See Tate for several conjectural examples of allusion and wordplay.
33. In Diane Johnson, 229.
34. In Gardiner and Walker, 48.
35. See also letter to Maurice Guinness, 1959, in Gardiner and Walker, 249.
36. In Gardiner and Walker, 247; following quotes on 248, 249. Guinness was a cousin of Helga Greene.
37. In Gardiner and Walker, 236.
38. See Peter Rabinowitz, 129.
39. See Gardiner and Walker, 241.
40. In "The Turn", Rabinowitz traces links between Chandler and Conrad, especially in their narrators.
41. Page 842; see Chandler's letters from 1939 and 1956 (in Hiney and MacShane, 18–19; 222–223), 1949 (in Gardiner and Walker, 27).
42. In Gardiner and Walker, 48.
43. In Gardiner and Walker, 53.
44. In Gardiner and Walker, 58.
45. In Gardiner and Walker, 216.
46. Auden, 406.

CHAPTER 5

The Urban Procedural: Ed McBain

BIG LIGHTS, BIG CITY

There is no escaping the fact that the history of the USA is urban history.

In *The Age of Reform* (1956) Richard Hofstadter distilled 400 years of American history to the observation that the USA was born in the country and moved to the city. These days more than ever, American cities, these beehives of habitation crisscrossed by tendrils of traffic-bearing arteries, *are* America. Their values and problems define not only what the USA is, but also what other nations perceive the USA to be. As business hubs and social pressure cookers, they set the pace for the rest of the country, if not for the world at large.

Whether in the Americas, Eurasia, or Australasia, cities of today crawl with millions of human ants, drawn or driven there by reasons of lifestyle, employment, or internal and external immigration. Sprawling across conurbations, some already house teens of millions. A few—even before the advent of cities of the future, exemplified by the architectural and social blueprints for Tokyo's one *kilometer*-high Sky Cities—tens of millions. Little wonder that behind the downtown façades of concrete, steel, and quartz, many of today's cities look and act like they were spat out from giant trash compactors.

Back in the year 1800, only 6% of Americans dwelled in cities. Reflecting the era when agriculture was king, population density

© The Editor(s) (if applicable) and The Author(s) 2016
P. Swirski, *American Crime Fiction*,
DOI 10.1007/978-3-319-30108-2_5

inconsequential, and the Jeffersonian ideal of countrified gentry living in happy mediocrity still in the air, cities were defined as settlements of at least 8000 people. Since then, testifying to the triumph of the urban ethos even in rural communities, they have dwindled in the eyes of the Census Bureau to agglomerations of just 2500 or more. Even more to the point, the percentage of Americans dwelling in them has crept past ninety.

There is no escaping the fact that the history of the United States is urban history. As centers of economic enterprise, political power, and cultural diversity, cities have traditionally occupied a foremost place in America's vision of itself. Yet Thomas Wolfe's haunting lines from *The Web and the Rock* (1939) perfectly capture the ambivalence that many Americans have felt toward the tangle of social upheavals that go by the name of urbanization:

> It was a cruel city, but it was a lovely one; a savage city, yet it had such tenderness; a bitter, harsh, and violent catacomb of stone an steel and tunneled rock, slashed savagely with light, and roaring, fighting a constant ceaseless warfare of men and of machinery; and yet it was so sweetly and so delicately pulsed, as full of warmth, of passion, and of love, as it was full of hate. (473)

Barely a generation later, with America at its geopolitical zenith and Manhattan proud home to the United Nations, industrial designer Raymond F. Loewy rhapsodized about New York being "the conclusive proof that there is an American civilization".[1] Little could he know that just a decade later Big Apple would hit rock bottom, as proclaimed by the 30 October 1975 *Daily News* headline: "Ford to City: Drop Dead". Boom or bust, however, it has never lost its dual character. Today, as ever, it continues to combine the glamor of *Big Lights, Big City* with the wretchedness of *Big Bad City*. It continues to pull in newcomers in search of a better life, trapping them in snarled traffic and in snarling contests with the newcomers next door.

In contrast to Robert Moses, who often saw New York's bustling immigrant communities merely as traffic impediments to his building authorities, today's city planners work to turn streets into a pedestrian-friendly glue that binds city blocks and 'hoods from within. Be that as it may, the chronic and acute ills that have bedeviled New York and other American urban centers during the industrial and then post-industrial ages are now commonplace around the world. Like it or not, American-style cities and American city lifestyle are by now a global phenomenon.

Globalization means more than watching Hollywood remakes of French movies on Chinese bootleg DVDs, watching Nigerian footballers sporting Taiwanese-made Nikes compete in European football leagues, or watching Algerian auto-racers use Bosch tools to fix Subarus stalled in the middle of the Sahel. It means that the unstoppable concentration of business and human capital in cities is to be found everywhere, from São Paulo to Surat to Singapore to Sydney. Australia, in fact, is the best case in point, with just five cities (Sydney, Melbourne, Brisbane, Perth, and Adelaide) housing 60 % of the population of the continent.

It is no different in Asia, home to the largest number of people living in the country, but also the largest number of people living in the city. China alone underlies the global hegemony of the urban lifestyle. As Jared Diamond reports in *Collapse: How Societies Choose to Fail or Succeed*, in the second half of the twentieth century China's population only doubled, whereas its urban population tripled, yielding more than half a billion Chinese city-zens. During the same period the number of cities in China swelled by 500 %, while the existing ones exploded in size.

The flip side of worldwide urbanization is that, for all its regional accents, the global village today looks more and more like an American city. Just take the suburban train from Narita to Tokyo. Drive through the Pudong district in Shanghai. Take a minibus from Lai Chi Kok to Kowloon Bay in Hong Kong. Hit the highway from exurban Linkou to Taipei. Drearily, you will see the same rows of concrete boxes housing the same chains of fast food joints, convenience stores, coffee shops, and shopping malls. Luring global villagers to local franchises with the neon homogeneity of American brands, with each day rush-hour Asia looks more and more like mall-o-centric USA.

With the McDonaldization of global culture, with Hollywood and American television beamed 24/7 around the planet, with Levittowns and inner-city ghettoes sprouting all over the world map, it is hardly surprising that American cities today evoke a set of globally recognizable images. On the one hand there is the glitter of CBD office towers, high-society shopping emporiums, and iphone-toting affluence. On the other there are armies of the homeless, rock stars (drug addicts in street lingo), and trigger-happy gangs. Both epitomize the American urban experience as much as *it* is epitomized by New York City.

SALVATORE ALBERT LOMBINO

An Italian immigrant who, like Salvatore Lombino, changes his name and makes good as an artist in New York in a quintessentially American experience.

Born Salvatore Albert Lombino before changing his name in 1952, Evan Hunter was a genre artist par excellence.[2] Writing under the pen name of Ed McBain, he won unswerving loyalty from generations of readers for his cycle of 87th Precinct police procedurals, with sales receipts to prove it: more than 100 million copies worldwide. This is not counting his other cycle of legal procedurals written as Evan Hunter and starring Matthew Hope, attorney at law, or a steady trickle of standalone books, such as *Candyland: A Novel in Two Parts*—a psychological study and a crime story rolled into one and authored in 2001 by Evan Hunter *and* Ed McBain.

Fellow bestsellers like Nelson DeMille freely praise McBain as a dedicated and prolific writer who often took chances with his non-Eighty-Seventh Precinct novels. "He was very versatile and could have written in most genres and been comfortable with any plot, character, or setting."[3] Yet even critics of the apocalyptic ilk would find it hard to dismiss McBain as a generic crowd-pleaser. Over half a century of writing the world's longest running crime series, his fifty-six-book opus about a fictional New York police precinct has elicited praise from just about everyone, including the tastemakers. The *New York Times Book Review*, for one, could not decide whether his prose was dazzling or formidable, the usually reticent *Guardian* dubbed him a virtuoso, and *Publishers Weekly* summed up the consensus with: "McBain is so good he ought to be arrested."

Criminal and forensic investigations lie at the heart of every 87th Precinct novel and, true to form, McBain's heroes are a squad of police detectives who process crime scenes as routinely as they pronounce on the American way of life. But his principal character is as remarkable as the ending of Hitchcock's *The Birds*, for which he wrote the screenplay. It is not a person, although he personifies "her" in every novel. It is a place, a synecdoche, and a state of mind. It is a habitat overrun by millions, where fortunes and lives can be made or lost overnight. It is, as in the eponymous title of his 1999 bestseller, *The Big Bad City*.

While leaving zero doubt as to its real-life counterpart, McBain never names the metropolis he portrays with so much passion. Instead, tongue-in-cheek pointing to his narrative debt to *Dragnet*, he prefaces every 87th novel with a disclaimer: "The city in these pages is imaginary. The people, the places are all fictitious. Only the police routine is based on established investigatory technique." It is the same city he portrayed as Evan Hunter in *Streets of Gold* (1974), an intensely personal memoir of an Italian immigrant who, like Salvatore Lombino, changes his name and makes good as an artist in New York in a quintessentially American experience.

Image 5.1   Evan Hunter in 2001 at a book signing in New Paltz, New York. *"It is the same city he portrayed as Evan Hunter in* Streets of Gold *(1974), an intensely personal memoir of an Italian immigrant who, like Salvatore Lombino, changes his name and makes good as an artist in New York in a quintessentially American experience."*

As literary anthropology of the American city, McBain's series is as good as it gets, but all good things must come to an end. The author's death in July 2005 put an effective end to the 87th Precinct, unless—as with Chandler—a lesser talent is hired to take over the reins, something the master vowed never to let happen. With this in mind, he intended to tie up all narrative loose ends in the final installment of the series, to be called *Exit*. Instead, readers have to make do with the posthumously released *Fiddlers* (2005).

One way or another, the tenth anniversary of McBain's own exit invites a fresh look at the artistic legacy of a proceduralist who for half a century held the greatest and the baddest American metropolis under a literary microscope. Inventing the police procedural, only to reinvent it as the urban procedural, he transformed his fictional Gotham into the touchstone of the American urban experience and his nobrow *policiers* into essential reading for anyone wishing to understand the people who live, work, commit crime, and conduct business in America today.

With Hammett and Cain swept away by the postwar boom, with Chandler retooling the tough-guy act in his pensive *The Long Goodbye* and self-reflexively parodic *Playback*, the 1950s were fertile ground for a novel brand of detective fiction. Mickey Spillane and his lantern-jawed anti-Communist vigilante Mike Hammer notwithstanding, gone were the days of a solitary sleuth with a Webley .455 for hire. The law-and-order business was now the provenance of a graduate of police academy, a career member of a civic bureaucracy, a specialized cog in a well-greased investigative machine. After the Mafia syndication and the federal failure to control the controlled substance business, crime became too organized to leave it to a bunch of rumpled loners, no matter how lethal their side-of-mouth drawl.

Enter McBain and the police procedural with its emphasis on the realism of the investigative technique and the workaday mundanity of police bureaucracy. Nowadays with former police detectives like Joseph Wambaugh, criminal-court reporters like John Katzenbach, or forensic anthropologists like Kathy Reichs harnessing their expertise to the task of storytelling, realism in literary crime is a given. "Have you ever seen Mike Hammer or Sam Spade spend their days poring over statements like old bloody book-worms?", mutters a jaded Chief Inspector in *The Hatchet Man*, a 1976 police procedural by William Marshall. A reply from a tired detective sums up a revolution in worldview. "They weren't cops. They were private eyes" (137).

It was the hardboiled penslingers who took crime out of a British draw-ing room and dumped it in the middle of the American backstreet. But it was McBain who tossed it in the back of a city police cruiser on a pile of lurid tabloids, junk food litter, crack spoons, economic avarice, me-first mentality, and racial prejudice. Riding shotgun with the blues to absorb their workaday MO and that curious Babel of bureaucratese, slang, and underworld idiolect that makes up copspeak, he was one of the first to direct the narrative spotlight on the men and women in blue. Celebrated for their trademark realism and pitch-perfect dialogue, his novels would even inspire arguably the most successful—and the most realistically low-key—television police show *Hill Street Blues*.

GRAPHIC AND PHOTOGRAPHIC

McBain's factographic aesthetic, with its visual feel of the municipal machine, is felt far outside his American imitators.

McBain is a nobrow master of dialogue of people of all walks of life and ethnic backgrounds. He is a master of description of their lives, whether rich and affluent, materially and culturally destitute, or driven and riven by crime. And behind them always loom the crowded city blocks and busy city streets, where the eye glides past little Italian bakeries and coffee shops humming with chitchat, past old redbrick theater buildings and gentrified modeling agency boutiques, past ghettos and slums, to the cramped, ratty, coffee and urine-smelling rooms of the station house.

With his urban procedurals forming an anatomy in fifty-six parts of the environmental niche occupied by nine out of ten Americans, New York provides the parabolic cityscape. Immortalized in prose from Lawrence Sanders to Colin Harrison and from Thomas Wolfe and Tom Wolfe, McBain's metropolis is a thing of beauty frequently described in lyrical terms that recall the opening of Woody Allen's *Manhattan*. Even so, the gritty canons of the police procedural—the genre he established almost single-handedly in 1956 with *Cop Hater*—always lead him back to the city morgue and to the rotting core of today's Headline News America.

This love-and-hate, night-and-day, Jekyll-and-Hyde portrait of the urban sprawl is quintessentially McBain (though not Evan Hunter). His literary and sociological élan belies conservatives for whom genre fiction belongs, in Harold Bloom's notorious body slam, on the compost heap of popular culture. Charting the rugged and drugged life stories on the twentieth-century metropolitan frontier, time and again his police procedurals cross over into the domain of urban procedurals, to take their place next to *The Quaker City*, *The Jungle*, *An American Dream*, and *The Bonfire of the Vanities*.

Book after book, the 87th rounds up the daily docket of the City's celebrity highfliers and criminal lowlifes blowing each other kisses while being whisked away on the gravy train, or just blowing each other away with sawed-offs. Among unputdownable thrills, chills, and kills, it takes time to document the detritus of life in an overpopulated human zoo. Indeed, famous as it is for nail-biting pacing, the series is no less famous for its graphic and photographic reproductions of half a century of urban collage.

Book after book, it recreates topographical sketches, street signs, traffic signs, license plates, ferry schedules, airline schedules, business cards, phone-book listings, address book pages, bank passbook entries, utility bills, telephone bills, credit card bills, personal checks, letters from the editor, handwritten notes, personal letters, prescription drug labels, photographs, modeling portfolios, advertising photos, tabloid clippings, media headlines, architectural blueprints, theater programs, stage diagrams, music concert ads, police cruisers, batons, shields, and hats, handcuffs, walkie-talkies, wanted flyers, incident report forms, human ears, merchandising stickers, Christmas cards, party invitation cards, and even a facsimile of the front page of Folger's Folio edition of Shakespeare's plays.

The 87th may be set elliptically in New York, but corruption and vice, political bigotry and ethnic strife, and pathological loneliness and pathological violence are facts of life in any modern metropolis. This is one reason why McBain's factographic aesthetic, with its visual feel of the municipal machine, is felt far outside his American imitators. Fans of Britain's Inspector Morse—between 1987 and 2000 an acclaimed TV series—will not fail to notice how Colin Dexter packs his cycle with the same litter of everyday life in the city that has come to define the 87th Precinct.[4]

Handwritten notes, news columns, obituaries, last will, posters, notices, hotel receipts, a *Police Gazette* puzzle, a diploma, wall plaque, sundry drawings, Medical Examiner's forensic report, letter franking chops, a vehicle license plate—all of them garnish just the last book in the series, *The Remorseful Day*. Just as in McBain, the Morse procedurals function as urban *vademecums* to posh parklands, tawdry tenements, and everything else in between. And, just as in McBain, they employ the visual inserts as markers on the map of the city coalescing before the reader's eyes.

Visitors to the Hong Kong from William Marshall's Yellowthread Street cycle of procedurals find themselves in equally familiar territory. *The Hatchet Man*, to take only one example, reproduces a postmortem report, lab report, ballistics report, consular report, transcript of victim interview, Public Relations Department press release, police bulletin, eyewitness statement, and even the lid of an ammunition box. No less a pointer to McBain is the disclaimer that ushers in every installment of Detective Chief Inspector Harry Feiffer and his squad: "The Hong Bay district of Hong Kong is fictitious, as are the people who, for one reason or another, inhabit it."

There is also the Swedish common-law wife-and-husband team, Maj Sjöwall and Per Wahlöö, celebrated for the ten-book cycle of police procedurals starring homicide Detective First Grade (later Inspector) Martin Beck and his squad. Absent are the visuals, but the series, which includes their international bestseller *The Laughing Policeman* (1969), openly positions itself in the tradition of the American master.[5] Among others, McBain's Tweedledum-and-Tweedledee homicide dicks Monroe and Monoghan are reincarnated as the equally lazy, inseparable, and dimwit Stockholm patrolmen Kvant and Kristiansson—both alliterative pairs priceless in their comic-relief cameos.[6]

In keeping with McBain's documentary aesthetic, the Swedish authors also harnessed their procedurals to more than a cat-and-mouse game of cops and robbers—or, these days, narcs and dealers. As they programmatically put it in their manifesto, in the Beck decalogue they set out to "use the crime novel as a scalpel cutting open the belly of the ideological pauperized and morally debatable so-called welfare state of the bourgeois type".[7] Declarations of this nature belie highbrow critics' condemnations of genre bestsellers as subliterature. Do they, however, validate police procedurals as sociological and ideological barometers of the contemporary city?

THE WORST IN CHRISTENDOM

From students robbing graves to supply teaching hospitals with cadavers to the inundation of waterfront violence, to regular Blacks v. Irish riots (following the latter's rapid takeover of the domestic service market), New York City set the pace for the transformation of old-time homogenous townships into modern municipalities.

Colossal both in absolute terms and relative to highbrow fiction, sales figures for crime mysteries set in relief the fantastic appeal of fictional cops and killers. Inevitably, they also beg the question: Whence the allure of what is, after all, a singularly dirty and thankless profession? Whence the seemingly unquenchable thirst for heroic cops rather than heroic garbagemen or proctologists? As you may have guessed, a rough and ready answer is to be found in the 87th Precinct which, with each page-turning episode of *On the Case*, smuggles in whole pages from the Big Book of Bad City civics.

The rise of homegrown crime literature is often traced through generalizations about American history and heritage of armed violence, frontier mentality, and vigilante justice. While true in their own right, their role in the genesis of what is universally recognized as the first modern detective story, Poe's "The Murders in the Rue Morgue" (1841), is arbitrary at best. Violence, the frontier mindset, and vigilantism have been part of life in America long before Poe without producing modern crime literature. A more prosaic but more accurate explanation is that the rise and the character of American crime fiction paralleled the rise and the character of modern cities, modern crime, and modern police.

Right into the early nineteenth century, the means of upholding law and order in cities remained essentially unchanged from the days of Shakespeare. Court-appointed constables, armed with powers of arrest and charged with occasional detective duties, oversaw city commerce in daytime, while unpaid civilian watchmen patrolled select parishes and precincts at night. Although the 1731 Montgomerie Charter obligated all male New Yorkers to serve on such patrols, the middle class routinely relegated the duty to ill-paid irregulars, even as cities and crime swelled beyond control.

With mushrooming populations crowding in unlit and unheated tenements, with law enforcement capricious at best and nonexistent at worst, urban centers bred poverty, vice, unpaved streets, and sewage-filled open gutters faster than you could say "American Dream". In 1800 there were only six American cities with a population of 8000 or more. In 1900 there were almost five hundred. Record levels of mostly East and South European immigrants—nine million between 1880 and 1900 alone—queued up in snaking lines to get into the promised land. But, unlike the earlier boatloads, rather than heeding Horace Greeley and heading out west, many chose to stay put in the Big Bad City.

In this they were joined by masses of native refugees from New England where rural communities suffered a catastrophic decline. Even though during that time New England's population rose by 20 % overall, almost 1000 out of her 1500 townships shrank.[8] To counter the chaos and strife in the five boroughs, newly passed zoning laws began to segregate Wall Streets, residential areas, and shopping districts from industrial parks, tenement slums, and ubiquitous inner-city ghettos for blacks, Italians, Greeks, Turks, Poles, Russians, and all others who did not fit the White Anglo-Saxon Protestant mold.

From students robbing graves to supply teaching hospitals with cadavers to the inundation of waterfront violence, to regular blacks versus Irish riots (following the latter's rapid takeover of the domestic service market), New York City set the pace for the transformation of old-time homogenous townships into modern municipalities. But with the national economy forever see-sawing between its manic and depressive phases, and with unemployment in the millions during frequent and protracted recessions, other cities hardly fared better. Shuddered Rudyard Kipling after visiting Chicago at the century's turn: "I desire urgently never to see it again. It is inhabited by savages."[9]

In the 1820s, having got an early taste of urbanization, Thomas Jefferson famously branded American cities ulcers on the body politic. Reviving Jefferson's revulsion at the asphalt jungle, in 1901 celebrated columnist Percy Grant reminded his readers in *Everybody's Magazine* of that denunciation before proceeding with an anatomy of urban "filth, poverty and vice".[10] Andrew D. White, President of Cornell University, publicly concurred: "With very few exceptions, the city governments in the United States are the worst in Christendom."

All the same, when Britain established its London Metropolitan Police Service in 1829 (detective division 1842), it was amidst profound unease that it could be turned into a standing army or other apparatus of sociopolitical repression. Even as it recognized the need for a modern police force, the USA was even more susceptible to such fears. Combined with a widespread hostility to regulation—especially among immigrants who equated it with the Old World—were also specifically American factors such as suspicion of a British institution, a tradition of vigilante justice, large itinerant population, decentralized legislative authority, absence of ingrained notions of social decorum, and not least deep-seated ethnic and racial divisions.

It is hardly surprising that when the first police department was created in New York in 1845, followed by Chicago in 1854, no heed was paid to the mental or physical fitness of these as-yet uniformless cops. Funding was so scarce that, in a city of 600,000, only 9 men comprised the entirety of Chicago daytime police (to put this in perspective, today's NYPD instead of almost 40,000 would be fielding a force of 120). Patrolmen were not even permitted to carry firearms, so acute was the dread of potential insubordination. Only in the 1880s did Philadelphia and Boston arm their men, and New York a decade later.

Exacerbated by political bosses who ran police departments like private fiefdoms, corruption and mismanagement rotted the system in no time at all. Just twenty-two years after the birth of the NYPD, the State Legislature fired all of New York's cops, declaring the city "too corrupt to govern itself".[11] It was no different with detective squads, founded in Boston (1846), New York City (1857), Philadelphia (1859), and Chicago (1861), when coppers on the beat proved to be insufficient deterrent. Underpaid and overworked, investigators proved no more resilient to the temptation of the easy sleazy.

COLONEL MUSTARD AND LADY BUXOM

The history of police and crime in the USA shaped the crime story—shaping it, like the western, into an archetypal American genre.

All this helps explain why the America of that era saw the appearance of the first licensed private detectives and of the first modern detective stories. Most PIs were ex-constables who lost work when cities began to set up police departments. The need for law enforcement was so high that in St. Louis, Baltimore, and Philadelphia private detective agencies sprang up before police departments did. In Chicago Allan Pinkerton opened shop in 1851, cashing in on the lack of results in suppressing crime due to the rank unprofessionalism of the regular police.

Pinkerton's Agency actually offered to take over policing Chicago at two-thirds of the price tag with a guarantee that the citizens would actually be protected.[12] Tellingly, their offer was declined. Things were, if anything, even worse in the Big Apple. In 1887 George Walling detailed his professional career in *Recollections of a New York Chief of*

Police: an official record of thirty-eight years as a patrolman, detective, captain, inspector and chief of the New York Police. His summation of the Big Bad City was unflinching: "in New York there is less liberty and protection of property than in almost any city of Europe, Russian cities not excepted" (600).

The rising tide of crime and inadequate policing were felt acutely enough to mobilize parts of society to create wholesome citizens by dint of moral reform. Even more indicative than the state of Maine, which, in a harbinger of the Prohibition, legislated itself legally dry as early as 1846, were the New York Society for the Suppression of Vice and the New York Society for the Prevention of Crime. Both campaigned to eradicate crime by bringing the social controls of small-town America to the chaos of the modern metropolis. Both echoed the Founding Fathers who, during the 1774 Continental Congress, disapproved and discouraged every Species of Extravagance and Dissipation, such as horse racing, gaming, cock fighting, shows and theater plays, and other Diversions and Entertainments.

Among other initiatives, the Vice Societies proceeded to improve mores by suppressing and even banning crime fiction, citing examples of youths who allegedly ran afoul of the law after reading story papers and dime novels. In a campaign to abolish crime by abolishing it from the printed page, they even cornered the Massachusetts legislature into a different kind of prohibition. In a measure reprised during the anti-comic book hysteria during the 1950s and the Senate hearings on art content in the 1980s, Massachusetts politicians banned sales to minors of books or magazines containing police reports or accounts of criminal deeds (unwittingly testifying to their popularity).[13]

Meanwhile, fed by immigration, collapse of rural communities, and competition for industry jobs, cities continued to grow. Between 1880 and 1900 New York City mushroomed from under two million to three and a half. The zoning laws passed to bring a semblance of order to this formless expansion began to segregate neighborhoods from one another. In one notorious example, virtually without police supervision, some 300,000 Italians formed a city within a city, ruled by the increasingly organized Cosa Nostra. With homicide rates more than double those in the equally industrialized and urban England, violent crime was spinning out of control.

Laying bare the rot in Tammany Hall, the turn-of-the-century Lexow Investigations pinpointed NYPD as one of the chief culprits. Cops were involved in wholesale election fraud in return for sinecures from pols. Patrolmen and officers bought their promotions as a matter of course and, to recoup expenses, ran city-wide extortion rackets from brothels, saloons, and gambling houses. As before, the malaise was not confined to New York. When the Denver Police and Fire Board openly refused to enforce the law, the Governor attempted to remove them, only to find out that they refused to be fired, fighting pitched battles with the state militia until President Cleveland sent in federal troops to stop further bloodshed.[14]

Not accidentally, it was around that time that American crime literature began to acquire its distinctive character. Its hard edge and penchant for topical realism owed to the grim reality of crime in the city and to the fact that many writers were journalists or editors employed by the slicks. Heir to investigative journalism, the American crime story was contemporary in tone and narrated against the backdrop of current events and urban realism, not to say naturalism.

Muckraking exposés replaced the timetables needed to crack the alibis of Colonel Mustard and Lady Buxom. Eschewing the Victorian diction and decorum, the style became geared toward precision and parsimony of expression. The hero was no longer an armchair ace *à la* Mycroft Holmes or Hercule Poirot but a hardnosed investigator with an attitude and his sleeves rolled. The crime was no longer a geographically and socially isolated event to be investigated at leisure, but an open-ended violation in a corrupt social system requiring urgent and active response.

Even the titles revealed parallels between what muckrakers were up to in the real world and what PIs faced in fiction. Melville D. Post's *The Powers That Prey* was a fit companion to Arthur B. Reeve's "The Campaign Grafter" and Samuel H. Adams's "The One Best Bet", in which the detective goes after hinky politicians. The biggest difference between these early modern crime stories and the procedurals of today, however, lies in their lasting optimism. Crime, no matter how villainous or ubiquitous, is not yet seen as a threat to the American way of life. Underneath the temporary and localized aberrations, imply the writers, lies a healthy society. It would take Hammett's dog-eat-dog cynicism, Chandler's desolate odes to corruption, and McBain's urban grit to put things in a different light.

All this is to say that domestic crime fiction did not come into its own until it came to terms with American social and urban geography. Instead of a static, homogenous, small-town setting, it had to deal with a sprawling urban nightmare. Instead of ratiocinating a logical proof of crime, the detective had to mingle with people from all walks of life, including the underworld. Only after gaining their confidence could he get them to spill enough dirt that might lead him to the solution of the homicide in the hostile city.

The history of police and crime in the USA shaped the crime story—shaping it, like the western, into an archetypal American genre. Where Zane Grey, Louis L'Amour, and Larry McMurtry wrote Westerns, McBain wrote "Easterns" about heroic thin-blue-liners who brought a semblance of order to the chaos of the lawless streets, keeping outlaws and miscreants at bay. Unmasking corruption in high places, tracking vice in the police ranks, reporting realistic crime in realistic language, like the hardboiled noir the modern police procedural was both a literary convention and a direct response to the twentieth-century metropolis, exposing the tension between the public and the bureaucracy supposed to protect it. At the end of the day, American crime writers did not have to invent the genre in which they worked. They wrote about what they saw around them—the mean streets of the naked city.[15]

M*E*T*R*O*P*O*L*I*S*

She is no longer a player making her moves against the backdrop of the big bad city. She is the Big Bad City.

"Among the mystery writers who first influenced me were Raymond Chandler, and Dashiell Hammett and James M. Cain", revealed McBain in a 2000 interview.[16] He could hardly have selected better models: a literary aesthete, a former detective, and a court reporter. Hammett, at one point a Pinkerton Op himself, broke new ground by creating a one-man law enforcement force. By hook or by crook, the Continental Op would cleanse Poisonville of corrupt politicos, crooked power brokers, less than licit lawyers, gangster bosses, and other organized and loose-cannon offenders.

In sheer doggedness, McBain's hero, Detective Second Grade Steve Carella, is a blood relative of the Op, even though by Carella's time the lone-wolf methods and lifestyle have gone out of style. Where Hammett's shamus worked alone, for the boys on the squad their significant other is their partner. Where the tough guys celebrated busting a few skulls with a Scotch in one hand and a fast femme in the other, the bulls shun alcohol when on duty, assiduously Mirandize their suspects, and file reports in tedious triplicate. Where private eyes' private lives were so private that they hardly mattered at all, many of the 87th Precinct cops rush home in tatty sedans to their families and wives.

Old habits die hard, however, and in the 2003 introduction to his early 87th novel *Killer's Payoff* (1958) McBain recalled his first publisher's demands for a more sexy characterization of one member of the squad. To his credit, he continued, he stuck to his guns and resisted the pressure to turn Cotton Hawes "into a goddamn private eye" (xvii). So thorough was McBain's transformation of the hardboiled template, in fact, that Carella, the 87th leading man, was actually pooh-poohed by the same Pocket Books executive for being not a hero but a married man.

Complementing McBain's overhaul of the hardboiled formulas was the debut of equally unglamorous lawbreakers. The larger-than-life Elihu Willsson and king-size Casper Gutman gave way to ordinary career felons, so much so that the first four novels in the series—*Cop Hater, The Mugger, The Pusher, The Con Man*—were all titled after the common variety of a crook a real-life policeman might encounter, in keeping with McBain's goal of developing "a realistic look at a squad room of cops who, when put together, would form a conglomerate hero in a mythical city".[17] Yet none of these transformations is as striking as the makeover of the femme fatale.

Hot on the trail of a Dinah Brand or Brigid O'Shaughnessy, a genre connoisseur will look in vain in all the obvious places, from red-light show girls and Hollywood madams to executive escorts and other free enterprise gold-diggers chasing a buck in the postwar decades. This is because, like other mainstays from the hardboiled matrix, in McBain's hands the femme fatale would undergo a dramatic facelift. Seductive and ubiquitous, she is still as constant a fixture on his narrative horizon as she was when tough mugs rode into the sunset, rods blazing from getaway flivvers' running boards. Ritzy and glitzy one moment, cheap and sleazy the next, she makes herself available to all while belonging to none. Only now she is no longer a player making her moves against the backdrop of the big bad city. She *is* the Big Bad City.

Most hardboiled novels, including those of Hemingway, McCoy, Cain, and Chandler, seldom deviate in their narrative tenor from a gruff and melancholy monotone. In contrast, McBain's narrator experiments with a rainbow of voices and points of view. He can be as gritty as car park cement or pulsing with still-life lyricism reminiscent of Pablo Neruda, a melange of street argot and prose poetry that endows his metropolis with her own voice.

But by far the most consequential departure from the hardboiled matrix is in the role played by the City. In most private eye mysteries the metropolitan sprawl is either an ominous backdrop or a panoramic stage on which taciturn players act out their violence-, greed-, and sex-fuelled fantasies. In contrast, McBain's Gotham is the ultimate femme fatale. Female killers, seductresses, lovers, and grifters still strut their stuff in the streets of the City, but the most bewitching of them by a long shot is the City itself, her stilettos high-rise steel and her heart bulletproof glass.

From a myriad clues strewn over the years, no one will have any difficulty identifying her as New York. Who needs more than this dead giveaway? "The city for which these men worked was divided into five geographical sections. The center of the city, Isola, was an island, hence its name: 'isola' *means* 'island' in Italian. In actual practice, however, the *entire* city was casually referred to as Isola."[18] Lest there be no mistake, the typography in *Kiss* (1992) drives home that we are talking about New York State's only M*E*T*R*O*P*O*L*I*S*! The cover of *Cop Hater*, the novel that inaugurated the series, depicts bullet holes, spent cartridges, a tattered police shield, typewritten forms, and blood spatter, all pointing to the police procedural. In 1999, symbolizing the evolution into the *urban* procedural, the cover of *Big Bad City* depicts the gateway to New York: the Brooklyn Bridge.

All the same, in the 1999 introduction to the new edition of *Cop Hater*, McBain cautioned his readers against transposing Isola straight onto Manhattan. "It is next to impossible to overlay a map of my city on a map of New York", he pointed out, for reasons equally pragmatic and aesthetic in nature.[19] On the one hand, even when assisted by a fulltime researcher, it proved too difficult to verify every aspect of the real city before committing it to the page. On the other, it was just too much fun to create a fictional metropolis based on the one towering around him. Decoupled from its real-life twin, while sharing its geographical markers, the city, then, became a character.

Image 5.2 Midtown Manhattan as viewed from Weehawken, New Jersey/ Lower Manhattan as viewed from Exchange Place, Jersey City, New Jersey. *"On the one hand, even when assisted by a fulltime researcher, it proved too difficult to verify every aspect of the real city before committing it to the page. On the other, it was just too much fun to create a fictional metropolis based on the one towering around him. Decoupled from its real-life twin, while sharing its geographical markers, the city, then, became a character."*

NOTHING BUT A WOMAN

Scattered over nearly fifty years and more than fifty books, these lyrical refrains accentuate the prosaic reality of homicide that does not let up any day or month of the year.

And what a character she is. Her majesty and radiance are in evidence from the very first scene on the first page of the first 87th novel. "From the river bounding the city on the north, you saw only the magnificent skyline. You stared up at it in something like awe, and sometimes you caught your breath because the view was one of majestic splendor.... And at night, coming down the River Highway, you were caught in a dazzling galaxy of brilliant suns, a web of lights strung out from the river and then south to capture the city in a brilliant display of electrical wizardry."[20]

Released just a few months later, the second book in the series *The Mugger* (1956) opens with a flat avowal: "The city could be nothing but a woman", before continuing in an extended prose lyric—or, if you like, panegyric:

> You know her tossed head in the auburn crowns of moulting autumn foliage, Riverhead, and the park. You know the ripe curve of her breast where the River Dix moulds it with a flashing bolt of blue silk. Her navel winks at you from the harbour in Bethtown, and you have been intimate with the twin loins of Calm's Point and Majesta. She is a woman, and she is your woman, and in the fall she wears a perfume of mingled wood smoke and carbon dioxide, a musky, musty smell bred of her streets and of her machines and of her people.
>
> You have known her fresh from sleep, clean and uncluttered. You have seen her naked streets, have heard the sullen murmur of the wind in the concrete canyons of Isola, have watched her come awake, alive, alive. You have seen her dressed for work, and you have seen her dressed for play, and you have seen her sleek and smooth as a jungle panther at night, her coat glistening with the pin-point jewels of reflected harbor light. You have known her sultry, and petulant, and loving and hating, and defiant, and meek, and cruel and unjust, and sweet, and poignant. You know all of her moods and all of her ways.
>
> She is big and sprawling and dirty sometimes, and sometimes she shrieks in pain, and sometimes she moans in ecstasy.
>
> But she could be nothing but a woman. (1)

McBain's personification of the city as femme fatale is as fervent as it is frequent. Glancing between the covers of *Give The Boys a Great Big Hand* (1960), you will be excused for a doing double take and a double-check whether you opened *The Mugger* by mistake. The city is a woman, it could be nothing but a woman, declares the narrator, before carrying on: "And, like a woman, the city generates love and hate, respect and disesteem, passion and indifference. She is always the same city, always the same woman, but oh the faces she wears, oh the magic guile of this strutting bitch" (142).

Scattered over nearly fifty years and more than fifty books, these lyrical refrains accentuate the prosaic reality of homicide that does not let up any day or month of the year. Only the Big Bad City always takes on a new hue. In the December of *Mischief* (1993), she is "a dazzling snow princess in silver and white" (295). In the April of *The Heckler* (1960), she *is* April, "a delicate thing who walked into the city with the wide-eyed innocence of a maiden, and you wanted to hold her in your arms because she seemed alone and frightened in this geometric maze of strangers, intimidated by the streets and buildings" (1).

All serial narratives need to maintain continuity over time lapses between installments which, in the case of the 87th Precinct, have been as long as two years and as short as two months. From the second book to the last, therefore, the series is interlaced with set pieces designed to refresh readers' memory, such as the stroke-of-a-pen miniatures of the station house's prime movers and shakers. Steve Carella, Meyer Meyer, Bert Kling, Artie Brown, Hal Willis, Cotton Hawes, Andy Parker, Ollie Weeks (from the Eighty-Eighth), and quite a few members of the supporting cast have their blurbs reprinted almost verbatim from one book to the next.

Fixing Carella's athletic looks, Meyer's bald pate, Kling's boyish charm, Brown's hulking size, Willis's short stature, Hawes's streak of white hair, and Ollie's commanding girth in the mind's eye, continuity is also cultivated via a bevy of subplots—from Kling's hapless romantic entanglements to the vicious killing of Carella's father—which straddle successive episodes. In fact, only Chandler in *Playback* stands on a par with McBain's penchant for self-allusions, references, and quotes that challenge literary detectives with their flamboyant, if never obtrusive, barrage of self-referentiality.[21]

As in Chandler, not even titles are immune to wordplay. Coming right on the heels of *Money, Money, Money* (2001), in *Fat Ollie's Book* (2002) Carella is heard to mutter: "Money, money, *money*" (51). Things get curiouser still when Carella seeks succor from a Florida attorney, Matthew Hope. The brief phone chat with the hero of McBain's *other* series leaves both with the impression of, ahem, a special bond between them. McBain's characters even go to see movies based on the 87th novels. In *The Last Dance* (2000), the picture in question is part of a Kurosawa retrospective. "It was titled *High and Low*, and it was based on a novel by an American who wrote cheap mysteries" (38). Quite so.[22]

At the end of the day, the number of these intertextual links far exceeds the needs of a sequential narrative, even one diffused over half a century. It is entirely consistent, on the other hand, with the evolution of the police procedural into the urban procedural and the consequent reversal of the relation between people and places. Stories are customarily driven by agents projected against a more or less static background. Foregrounding character continuity and turning Carella's squad into fixed points on the story grid, McBain refashions them in effect into a permanent backdrop on which to project his most complex character—the City. After all, as he remarks in *Killer's Payoff*, "a city is only a collection of people and people are timeless" (1–2).

The 87th Precinct sits at the heart of a modern metropolis which, all hard concrete and realism on the one hand, is all personification and literary metaphor on the other. You may hate her for her project slums and poverty but, like with the femme fatale, you cannot stay indifferent to her charms. She will turn your head with her knockout skylines and boutique opulence, but she will make you hurry your steps past black ghettos like Diamondback, so full of roaches and crack vials that even burglars do not bother it any more.

McBain's imagery frames a chiaroscuro in social contrast. With overworked cops grinding out their shifts under the city's neon eyes, the 87th pays equal tribute to her chic and chicanery, both of them writ large and All-American. One moment it is a suburban backyard filled with domestic bliss in the form of crisp laundry hung out to dry. The next it is back to the rat race in the overcrowded rat cage filled with aggression, fear, and feces. As glitz and glamor vie with garbage and gore, the daily struggle for survival in the big bad city drives McBain's brand of artertainment: a rhapsody in police blue.

MISCHIEF

The author chronicles the days in the life of that globally ascendant genus, the city dweller, condensing a full course in urban civics into a single novel like *Mischief*.

In a 2000 interview, McBain stated: "I see the city in the 87th Precinct as being a metaphor for the entire world."[23] It is in this context that one must interpret the historical asides—from the Dutch traders, who in 1619 dumped the first cargo of slaves onto Jamestown, to the mostly Saudi raiders, who in 2001 obliterated the World Trade Center—that pepper the pages of the 87th saga. The crown jewel of urban USA is a stand-in not only for metropolitan North America but also for every global city of the global village.

Looming larger than even its real-life correlative, McBain's Big Apple is a living superbeing caught up in the daily drama of living on the edge of survival. From the ecological standpoint, of course, modern metropolitan sprawls are catastrophic aberrations rather than optimal habitats for *Homo sapiens*. Armed to the teeth, overcrowded worse than the municipal zoo, overrun by bipedal predators high on adrenalin and testosterone, American cities of today resemble nothing so much as a mad scientist's experiments in urban sociology.

Measuring out five decades of postwar American experience, like milestone McBain's procedurals track the wax and wane of New York City, measuring out its greatness by the distance from the Upper East Side penthouse to the project basement. In between *Cop Hater* and *Fiddlers*, with the investigative journalist's eye for detail, the author chronicles the days in the life of that globally ascendant genus, the city dweller, condensing a full course in urban civics into a single novel like *Mischief*:

> the city had cut its hospital budget by thirty-five percent last year and the Chancery was a city hospital. It was now working with a skeleton staff more appropriate to a clinic in Zagreb than to a hospital in one of the world's largest and most influential cities. (44)

> Four out of five American families were caring at home for their sick or elderly parents. Women constituted seventy-five percent of these caretakers. (46)

> There were four million Alzheimer's sufferers in the United States of America. This number was expected to triple within the next twenty-five years. (47)

> One out of every four blacks in this city was foreign-born. (85)

> Nowadays, the immigrants you got from Latin America and the Caribbean preferred remaining citizens of their native lands, shuttling back and forth like diplomats between countries, supporting nuclear families here and extended families in their homelands. (86)

> Actually, nothing sold on the street was every *truly* pure; the more the drug was stepped on, the more profit there was for everyone down the line. But the new stuff was decidedly more potent than what the city's estimated 200,000 heroin addicts were used to. (91)

> Crim Mis One was defined as: *With intent to do so and having no right to do so nor any reasonable ground to believe that one has such right, damaging property of another: 1. In an amount exceeding $1,500; OR 2. by means of an explosive.* (127)[24]

> targeting a doctor who performed abortions, telephoning him and screaming the word "Murderer!" into his ear was considered a crime in most states of the union. In this state, it was called Aggravated Harassment, and it was a

Class-A misdemeanor, punishable by the same year in prison and/or thousand dollar fine a graffiti writer could get for vandalizing a building. (131)

simple Harassment, as opposed to the *aggravated* kind.... was defined as "engaging in a course of conduct or repeatedly committing acts which alarm or seriously annoy another person and which serve no legitimate purpose". (132)

In this city, some twenty to thirty police officers were shot every year. (202)

in the month of January... the precinct had dispatched Charlie Two to the [homeless men's] shelter a total of eight times, three of those times to investigate reported assaults, five of them to investigate emergencies that subsequently required hospitalization for rat bites and/or drug overdoses. (227)

In this city, killing someone wasn't such a big deal. In the first quarter of the year, for example, five hundred and forty-six murders were committed... Sixty-one percent of all the murders in this city were committed by firearms... in *eight* percent of this city's murders feet or fists were the weapons. (259)

Murder in the Second Degree, a Class-A felony defined in §125.15 with the words "A person is guilty of murder in the second degree when, under circumstances evincing a depraved indifference to human life, he recklessly engages in conduct which creates a grave risk of death to another person, and thereby causes the death of another person...." Manslaughter in the Second Degree was defined in §125.15 as "Recklessly causing the death of another person". (349)

When the sound of gunfire in *The Big Bad City* is said to be as common as the sound of salsa, it might seem like a pulp-fiction conceit. But any notion of hyperbole or artistic license is dispelled by facts. Our space-age cities are notorious breeding grounds for every class of wrong conceivable. From murder to forcible rape to motor vehicle theft, no one is safe, not even with a cop for every 370 people in the country, not counting rent-a-cops who far outnumber the blues. These days the demand for auxiliary security personnel is so overwhelming, in fact, and their already prodigious numbers swelling so rapidly, that the line between private and public policing is getting distinctly fuzzy, giving a new twist to the old street slang: the fuzz.

THE *N* WORD

McBain's procedurals make no bones that racial wars are fought today with the same desperation as in the post-emancipation decades in which Negroes were sold down the river of Yankee capitalism.

While privatization of law enforcement (not to mention penitentiaries) continues to make headways across the USA, it is business as usual in the crime business. The 2013 edition of *City Crime Rankings: Crime in Metropolitan America* makes no statistical bones about the accuracy of McBain's Big Bad City. A major crime occurs in the USA on average every two seconds, to a total of almost fourteen million *reported* offenses. Of this gigantic number, two million are violent crimes. Put differently, a homicide, forcible rape, robbery or aggravated assault take place every eighteen seconds somewhere in the country.

Predictably enough, the two urban heavyweights are blighted the most. The baddest city in the country is Los Angeles with a grand total of more than half a million reported crimes, followed by New York with almost half a million, and Detroit a distant third with a quarter million (rounded down). Not that this is news to anyone. The swelling tide of crime in America was memorably highlighted by J. Edgar Hoover in his 1964 public report *Crime in the United States*. Since 1958, wrote the FBI director, "crime has increased five times faster than our population growth" (3). Presumably he did not include in his statistics his own bureau's illegal activities conducted in documented disregard for its own charter, not to mention the US legal codes.[25]

A half century later, fuelled by the decline in the socioeconomic conditions, the dispersal of capital and manufacturing base across the globe, and the steady erosion of the middle class, violent crime rates (though, notably, not homicides) are five times higher than when Hoover went public with his warning. This is only one of the consequences of the migration of "the other half" into inner-city cores, and the hemorrhaging of affluence into the suburban and exurban rings. Both are fuelling that iconic twentieth- and twenty-first-century phenomenon: a metropolis with an empty heart patrolled by the increasingly defeasible metro police. As McBain would often put it, this city *anything* could happen.

Speaking of vice and men, book by book McBain points out that, while the police may win some battles, they are losing the war, unable to stem the groundswell of crime rooted in social and economic neglect too acute for any precinct or even department to deal with. Nor is he shy to figure racism, ill-masked by a veneer of political correctness, as the reason why tens of millions Americans cannot extricate themselves from the quicksand of poverty. The lack of integration boils up to the surface every time citizens are treated as Americans in name only—or not even, especially when their ethnic heritage does not conform to the WASP cookie cutter (Lombino's own name change a case in point).

What's in a name? Like in real-life New York, the fictive ghettoes and slums of the 87th are better known by their ethnic monikers than the whitewashed names tacked on by developers. In the same way, as McBain's cops never tire of pointing out, the proliferation of ethnically hyphenated Americans is a constant reminder of the mental apartheid that permeates the nation. These days, with differences between black Democrats and black Republicans as great as those between white members of either faction, and as intransigent, the political disfranchisement of poor Blacks and Hispanics is greater than ever. The realpolitik of party allegiance means that, even though the Republicans know that millions of poor will not vote for their neocon policies, they will not court them anyway for fear of alienating the business and the retirees' vote. Since the Democrats know it too, the dispossessed lose all political leverage.

McBain's procedurals make no bones that racial wars are fought today with the same desperation as in the post-emancipation decades in which Negroes were sold down the river of Yankee capitalism. They make it equally clear that, in this game of racial chess, every move by the White is countered by the Black. In the streets of *The Big Bad City*, there is little pretense of harmony. "They don't *say* nigger anymore, but they still *think* nigger. Same as up here. The *N* word is forbidden, but that doesn't stop the white man from thinking it. The only reason he doesn't say it out loud is he knows it can get him killed" (197).

All part of his crash course in urban civics, McBain's dollops of ethnic realism make even more sense when set in the context of who is working and who not. Even during Clinton's economic expansion in the 1990s, with national unemployment whittled down to 4 % and twenty-two million jobs created—more than under Reagan and Bush I combined—the numbers masked serious disparities. Among blacks sixteen- to nineteen years old, that is, the age group most likely to strike out in all senses of the word, more than one in four was jobless.[26] Not that this qualifies as news any more. For every decade of the twentieth- and twenty-first-century unemployment rates for black men and women have dwarfed those of whites.

At the end of the day, the 87th procedurals make clear that, even if it is true that every crime has a price, it is always bargain season in the city. McBain is, of course, too seasoned an artist to turn his cycle into a monotonous and monochromatic litany of America's social ills. Good fiction is more than a social document, no matter how pointed its facts of life. Even as he dispenses urban verisimilitude with both fists, the author never allows it to jack the story out of the bullet-fast lane. Chronicling the quotidian rhythms of the City, he refines the procedural into the nobrow recipe of knockout suspense and a survival manual for urban dwellers.

Be that as it may, any one of McBain's novels, multiplied over millions of copies in circulation, is likely to weigh heavier in the reader's mind than promo flyers from NYC's Tourist Board. Thanks to an almost Spartan parsimony of expression, he can boil down the spirit of any neighborhood in the city to a paragraph or two. F. Scott Fitzgerald and Nelson DeMille needed full-scale novels, *The Great Gatsby* and *The Gold Coast*, respectively, to mete out literary justice to the Long Island aristocracy. In *The Big Bad City* McBain time-lapses it into a snapshot of the housing and social development of his fictional Sand's Spit. As for Manhattan, *Kiss* says it all:

> This was a city in decline. The cabbie knew it because he drove all over this city and saw every part of it. Saw the strewn garbage and the torn mattresses and the plastic debris littering the grassy slopes of every highway, saw the bomb-crater potholes on distant streets, saw public phone booths without phones, saw public parks without benches, their slats torn up and carried away to burn, heard the homeless ranting or pleading or crying for mercy, heard the ambulance sirens and the police sirens day and night but never when you needed one, heard it all, and saw it all, and knew it all, and just rode on by (147–148).

BEHIND THE THIN BLUE LINE

> If realism is the name of the game, McBain goes one better again by visually integrating all manner of police accessories into his procedurals.

John Douglas, legendary FBI profiler and author, thinks he knows why readers continue to be spellbound by police procedurals. Blow-by-blow crime plots offer them a window onto a world they know little about, including the investigative technique of detectives, be they FBI agents, state troopers, or investigative journalists. Indeed, Martin Cruz Smith, Jeffery Deaver, Michael Connelly, and other practitioners of the genre lace their plots with the minutiae of police science and bureaucracy. No longer Chandleresque knights, their case detectives and lab techs follow the same procedural rulebook that gets star billing on nonfiction hit shows such as *Medical Detectives, The FBI Files, The New Detectives, America's Most Wanted, Exhibit A, Cold Case Files, Solved, On the Case, American Justice, Homicide Hunter*, and dozens of others.

In the same spirit of literary realism, Douglas identifies his own procedurals (coauthored with Mark Olshaker) as vehicles for educating the public. "One of the things which I think we tried to do in *Journey Into Darkness* and then again to some extent in *Obsession*", he argues, was "to make children into profilers themselves".[27] His reasoning? If children are to avoid becoming victims, they need to understand what options are available to them. If a child is lost in a shopping mall, that child has to become a profiler and ask: Who can I trust? Merely to tell a kid not to talk to strangers is not going to be helpful, argues Douglas. "In fact, it's going to be very detrimental. If a kid gets lost in a shopping mall, he's got nobody to talk to but strangers."

But if realism is the name of the game, McBain goes one better again by visually integrating all manner of police accessories into his procedurals. From teletype messages, missing person's reports, crime scene sketches, fingerprint files, case reports, autopsy reports, scene-of-crime reports, lab reports, surveillance reports, complaint reports, rap sheets, search warrants, evidence tags, age and gender tables, bomb diagrams, bullet casings, pistol licenses, duty grids, toxicology charts—right down to search warrant applications, interrogation transcripts, and sections of the penal code, generations of readers get to *see* what lies behind the thin blue line.

If McBain's early procedurals laid down the ground rules of the then novel genre, faithfully representing and reproducing the quotidian grind of the homicide investigative machine, as time went on, however, the ambitious writer began to bend the very rules he had put in place. Not surprisingly, once again they brought art closer to the street. It is not even a question of the 87th cops looking to jumpstart a case that is getting cold faster than a body in a meat locker by turning to a psychic. It is a matter of violating perhaps the most sacrosanct genre convention and letting the killer go free.

Not to look too far, McBain's parting shot *Fiddlers* introduces a not unsympathetic serial killer bent on exacting revenge from a group of people who traumatically "fiddled" with his life. His murders will out but, although apprehended in the end, the killer will not be brought to court in a dramatic denouement: the wheels of justice grind far too slowly to convict a man who is dying of cancer and has only weeks to live. In fact, although only once in a blue moon, the 87th detectives do fail to nail their suspects just as their real-life counterparts, who know all too well that only about two-thirds of homicides are ever cleared, let alone brought to court.

McBain's gradual remaking of the genre is accompanied by self-irony with which he distances himself from numerous copycats. Most often it surfaces in the playful "catch-me-if-you-can" asides aimed at the attentive reader. Thus Fat Ollie Weeks, top-notch crime buster and top-notch bigot, writes a perfectly awful book about cops known as Fat Ollie's book in *Fat Ollie's Book*. "The trouble was he was trying too much to sound like all those pissant writers out there who were not cops but who were writing what they called 'police procedurals'" (24), winks his creator.

McBain's verisimilitude extends to his cops who span the gamut from good to bad to ugly. Some are chronically overworked family men, some lazy nine-to-fivers, and some, like Fat Ollie, not only first-grade detectives and Detectives First Grade but first-grade jerks to boot. In *The Big Bad City* the big bad cop wastes no time proving it as soon as he hops into a taxi. "The first thing Ollie always did with a Pakistani cab driver—or for that matter, any cab driver who looked like a fucking foreigner, which was only every other cab driver in the city—was show his shield. This was so there'd be no heated arguments later on; some of these fuckin camel jockeys were very sensitive" (266).

Even though McBain aims for mimetic fidelity, he is the first to concede that his core group of 87th detectives might be difficult to find on New York City's payroll. "I know that all cops are not sterling characters. But you have to have someone to root for. I balance it with rotten cops who will take a bribe, who will beat somebody up."[28] Art, in this latter case, imitates life imitates art. Like Mark Fuhrman of the O.J. Simpson's murder-trial ill fame, Fat Ollie is a dedicated cop and a flaming racist who embodies the attitudes of many sworn officers of the law.

In return, the attitudes of the public are embodied in the endless variety of "pig" jokes and other epithets hurled at the men and women supposed to protect them. In *The Big Bad City* Carella sets Brown straight: "People don't like cops, is what it is. We remind them of storm troopers" (66). Regularly thrust into the limelight by the likes of Louis Eppolito and Stephen Caracappa and the scandals synonymous with their names, they will never become media darlings unless they overcome the image of incompetence, brutality, and abuse of power conjured up almost daily on the 11 o'clock news.

All too often seen as donut-scarfing caricatures at best, corrupt and trigger-happy brutes at worst, policemen and whole departments have been sued for their real and imagined failures. Unfortunately, instead of improving protection and making cops more accountable, it only closes the ranks and makes covering one's ass that much more of a priority. The fact that the police wield so much power, enforced by firearms, nightsticks, stun guns, Kevlar vests, and a code of silence grimmer than the omerta, is disconcerting. With powerful arguments both on the prosecution and defense's sides, there is no hiding, however, that even as the public distrusts the cops, it calls them to the frontline the second the bonds of civility start to slip.

CRIME AND THE CITY

A fifty-plus fugue opus on the life and death in the city, the 87th is held together by its author's view of crime fiction as realistic literature and of literary realism as sound sociology.

No discussion of McBain's procedurals would be complete without the discussion of women in blue. Of the numerous female protagonists that over the years enter and exit the series' inner core, Sharyn Cooke in particular underscores the difficulties women face with advancement in a male-dominated force. She first joins the cast in *Mischief* as a surgeon operating on a shot cop—another policewoman. She then lands a bigger role in *Romance* as Kling's girlfriend. By the time of *Last Dance* (1999) Chief Cooke's personal history has become as familiar as Kling's, and her relationship with him as fraught with interracial epiphany.

The unconventional spelling of Sharyn's first name is due to the simple fact that, at the time of the baby's birth, her thirteen-year-old mother did not know how to spell Sharon. In an experience familiar to generations of underaged, unwed, and uneducated mothers, writes the narrator, she later put her daughter through college and then medical school on money earned scrubbing floors in white men's offices after dark. "Sharyn Cooke was black, the first woman of color ever appointed to the job she now held" (156).

How does McBain's fiction stack up against real life? Historically women were barred from the force until Alice Wells, the first American policewoman, joined the LAPD in 1910. Although by 1917 some thirty US cities employed women cops, they were for the most part entrusted only with desk duties and low-echelon public relations posts. Giving credence to John Lennon when he sang that "Woman Is the Nigger of the World", it was not until the Civil Rights Act (1964) and the Equal Employment Opportunity Act (1972) that women and minorities began to assume a more active profile in policing.

Rome was not, however, built in a day—or even in a century, as apparent from the pages of the *Encyclopedia of Women and Crime*. In most police departments today, activities associated with femininity continue to be perceived as lower in status and further removed from real police work than those traditionally associated with manly prowess. Thus "the informal world of the street, clean money, normal violence, and routine lying are linked to masculinity and the police occupation. The academy and assorted 'inside' jobs involving secretarial and administrative tasks are perceived as feminine."[29] Nearly 80 % of police units in the USA still have no women of color in executive ranks, although some have risen to the level of deputy commissioner and commander (in Pittsburgh, DC, New York City, Philadelphia, Miami-Dade, and Detroit).

In an earlier study, "Police Organizations, Municipal and State", Michelle Meloy concluded that, even when women successfully enter law enforcement, their upward mobility is likely to be curtailed insofar as the token status of policewomen subjects them to gender stereotyping, increased job performance pressure, and isolation from male officers.[30] Be that as it may, according to the US Department of Justice in the year 2000, of 800,000 fulltime law enforcement officers in the country, almost 100,000 were women. Twelve percent does not sound like much, especially next to Britain's eighteen, but in the light of the historical record, it is not to be shrugged off lightly either.

"I consider the 87th Precinct a continuing novel about crime and punishment in our times, and each separate novel is like a chapter in a long, long novel", acknowledged McBain in 1983.[31] Approached as one monumental life book, like in the case of Julio Cortazar's *Hopscotch*, the cycle becomes an interactive whole whose chapters can be ordered and reordered to produce a shape-shifting kaleidoscope of antecedents and descendants, precursors, and epigones. A fifty-plus fugue opus on the life and death in the city, the 87th is held together by its author's view of crime fiction as realistic literature and of literary realism as sound sociology.

Today violent crime, gangland streets, chronic unemployment, downtown ghettoization, snagged traffic, racial tension, graft, and red tape remain the reasons why what is left of middle-class America leaves the *urbs* in droves for the suburbs. And because all these faces of urban blight regularly cameo in McBain's procedurals, for those who want to keep their hands on the literary pulse of the megalopolitan sprawl his mysteries remain their best bet. And the fact that so many turn to it with a devotion which baffles pulp-fiction critics is one more reason for according it the literary respect it deserves. For, even as they entertain, just like Grisham's legal procedurals, McBain's urban procedurals form, inform, and transform the perceptions of tens of millions of readers.

Far from being an escapist and violent mass-market product, in McBain's hands the crime-and-vice procedural is a modern incarnation of naturalism in American letters, with Crane's *Maggie: A Girl of the Streets* and Dreiser's *Sister Carrie* at its roots. On the other side of this equation, even as postmodern aesthetics downplays reality as a simulacrum and realism as passé, in McBain's hands popular art meets head-on the challenge of meting out poetic justice to the environment that houses nine out of ten Americans. With an ethnographic acumen second to none, he steals the show from other litterateurs whose prose—of which Paul Auster's *New York Trilogy* may be the best known—is long on self-deconstruction but short on crime and the city.

From the fact that McBain's procedurals are perfect beachbooks for intellectuals, it does not follow that they are minor literature. And from the fact that they are fiction, it does not follow that they are not to be taken as serious chronicles of America and its city blights. Today's urban habitat is historically the most complex and the most challenging since the birth of the modern city, and McBain's procedurals are some of the best (not to say most readable) commentaries on its stresses and excesses. But don't take my word for it. Grab any one of his books and settle the matter for yourself, at the risk of finding that McBain's City is like the sole of your shoe—once you get going, it will follow you everywhere.

NOTES

1. See http://www.epodunk.com/quotes/ny1.html; thoroughly revised, parts of this research are based on Swirski (2007), Chap. 3.
2. The name probably comes from Hunter College which he attended after the war; in 1981, citing outstanding professional achievement, the College inducted him into its Hall of Fame.
3. 2015 Interview with Peter Swirski; below, Zalesky, 54.
4. Inspector Morse was played by the late John Thaw in the hit TV series; Dexter put Morse to rest in *The Remorseful Day*, the last novel of the cycle.

A similar argument could be developed, for example, for the Edinburgh of Ian Rankin's Inspector Rebus series.

5. Also a 1973 movie with Walther Matthau, which retains little more than the title.

6. After Kvant's death in the fourth-last novel, he is replaced by a narrative clone, Kvastmo.

7. Liukkonen.

8. Blum, 474.

9. *American Notes*, 207.

10. Page 555; following quote in Blum, 470.

11. In Panek, 4.

12. In Panek, 5.

13. See Rasula for a superb analysis of the comics wars in the 1950s.

14. See Swirski and Wong (2006), and Panek (1990) for background.

15. The roots of these factual fictions go back to the days before novels; see Davis, J. Paul Hunter; on modern urban environments, see Mike Davis; Heise.

16. Raab, 13.

17. *Killer's Payoff*, xv.

18. *Mischief*, 248.

19. Both quotes in this paragraph from *Cop Hater*, xiv.

20. *Cop Hater*, 1–2.

21. In contrast to the ostentatious self-reflexivity of Auster's New York Trilogy.

22. The film is based on *King's Ransom* (1959); McBain also wrote the script.

23. Raab, 13; see http://users.bestweb.net/~foosie/mcbain.htm.

24. Crim Mis: Criminal Mischief.

25. Swirski, *Ars Americana*, Chap. 1.

26. Page 82; see also table: "Unemployment Rates for Selected Groups in the Labour Force: 1947–1998" in Kurian, 86.

27. In Reichs.

28. Raab, 13.

29. Hunt, 174.

30. Meloy, 172.

31. Cited in Carr, 15.

CHAPTER 6

Take Two: Nelson DeMille and F. Scott Fitzgerald

EPPOLITO AND CARACAPPA

Like the mythical Hydra the mafia reared its head to reveal how much this supposedly washed out organization continued to control both America's finest city and the city's finest.

In April 2006, just as the final season of *The Sopranos* was drawing to its enigmatic finish, two former NYPD detectives were convicted of extortion, racketeering, and obstruction of justice. By itself, this was not exactly news in the city and in the police force still haunted by the ghost of Frank Serpico. But this time around there was a new twist to the old tale of greed, crime, and duplicity. While going through the motions of solving murders in the daytime, the two homicide cops had been moonlighting as killers-for-hire for the mob.

As the prosecutors assiduously documented in court, between 1986 and 1990 the two police, Louis Eppolito and Stephen Caracappa, killed at least eight victims for one of New York's major crime families. In a made-for-Hollywood script, the henchmen got their assignments at prearranged Long Island highway gas stations or alternatively—dim the spots and cue the rain machine—at a Staten Island graveyard. Testifying to how valuable this inside connection was to the Lucchese family, after the deeds the dirty cops would collect their thirty pieces of silver directly from the underboss "Gaspipe" Casso.[1]

© The Editor(s) (if applicable) and The Author(s) 2016
P. Swirski, *American Crime Fiction*,
DOI 10.1007/978-3-319-30108-2_6

But what really transfixed the public were not even their crimes or, once caught, hand-over-the-heart protestations about being railroaded by the big bad city. It was the backstory, ready-made for Hollywood and then some. Caracappa, it quickly came to light, stole a page from Poe's detective classic "The Purloined Letter" about hiding in plain sight. While working out of organized crime homicide unit, he actually had a hand in setting up a mafia murder-probe office. Eppolito, on the other hand, had two-timed the city hall on his application to the force about being a son of a Gambino crime family member (his uncle and cousin were also Gambino wiseguys).

The Hollywood screenplay kicked into an even higher gear when it emerged that Eppolito had had a walk-on part in Martin Scorcese's mafia blockbuster *Goodfellas*, based on the criminal career of another associate of the Lucchese family, Henry Hill (portrayed by Ray Liotta, alongside Joe Pesci and Robert De Niro). The renegade cop, who in 1992 authored a self-serving book *Mafia Cop: The Story of an Honest Cop Whose Family Was the Mob*, also appeared in several other movies and even tried his hand at scriptwriting for Hollywood, albeit without much success.

News about the mafia has not exactly been news since at least Joe Valachi, whose own underworld career was filmed as *The Valachi Papers* (1972), starring Charles Bronson. In 1963 Valachi, soldier in the Genovese family, broke *omertà* to become the first made guy to publicly admit the existence and the power of the mob. His revelations to the Congressional Hearing on Organized Crime, broadcast on radio and television and run by every paper in the country, were costly to the organization already reeling from the 1957 Apalachin exposure, when New York state troopers flushed out a meeting of a hundred mafia bosses from around the continent.

But while the Italian crime syndicate stretching across the country was no longer flying under the radar, few citizens gave a second thought to how its extensive underground economy and political influence fit into the postwar decades. A middle-aged Italian writer in conjunction with a young Italian filmmaker would change that. Mario Puzo's runaway bestseller *The Godfather* (1969), adapted in 1972 and 1974 by Francis Ford Coppola into two eponymous "epictures", did for mobsters what it did for Marlon Brando, Al Pacino, James Caan, and Robert Duvall: made them household names.

Since then, having established itself as a lucrative market niche, the mob story has drawn the most bankable names both in Hollywood and in publishing. On the one hand there was Scorsese, who built a signal career on shooting the gangs of New York and Las Vegas. On the other there was Richard Condon who, drawing no distinctions between organized politics and organized crime, reinvented himself in the 1980s with a succession of mafia bestsellers known as the Prizzi tetralogy. Underscoring their nobrow potential, in 1985 John Huston turned *Prizzi's Honor* into an Oscar and a box-office winner for himself, Jack Nicholson, and Angelica Houston.[2]

Late in the 1990s came the millennium-spanning *The Sopranos*, the biggest mafia hit with the audiences and the critics to date. But even more than the seemingly endless array of genre blockbusters—or, for that matter, genre spoofs from Puzo-era *The Gang That Couldn't Shoot Straight* to the Sopranos-era *Analyze This*—the vitality of mafia fiction showed in the way that mob slang had detached itself from the men who run the gauntlet of felony indictments and wormed itself into everyday American speech.

The boss, the underboss, and the *consigliere* are by now as common in this urban "indict-ionary" as is the slang for clipping, whacking, popping, wasting, burning, and otherwise getting your mark. Everyone is wise to the lingo for a crew (gang) of heavy (packing) muscle (soldiers), or for juicing (paying vig to) a shylock (loanshark), cutting points (percentage) to a fence (swag dealer), or greasing (paying off) the heat (uniformeds) or the bulls (detectives). Mob "tawk" pops up even in such improbable places as the Meg Ryan and Tom Hanks romantic comedy *You've Got Mail*, in which a neighborhood bookseller is urged to go to the mattresses over turf threat from a bookstore chain.

Few viewers today remember the original Enrico "Rico" Rossi from ABC's *The Untouchables*. Everyone, on the other hand, has heard of RICO, the Racketeer Influenced and Corrupt Organizations Act passed in 1970 to clamp down on organized crime (it has also been used to prosecute insider traders and even anti-abortion protesters). "Make your mark in New York and you are a made man", quipped Mark Twain in 1866, never suspecting the sinister undertones his words would acquire from the mobsters.[3] After all, together with pure Sicilian or Italian ancestry, nothing but a kill gets a donsky (wannabe wiseguy) made in the Cosa Nostra.

The historical roots of the old-style mafia are often traced back to the late thirteenth century. Following the French invasion of Sicily, which mobilized local landowners into resistance, this underground opposition became known as Morte alla Francia Italia Anela, or MAFIA. The birth of the modern criminal octopus dates, on the other hand, to the economic and social unrest that followed Italy's annexation of the island in 1860.

In a telling testimony to its enduring power, in August 2015 the entire coastal district of Ostia—the favorite recreational port and playground of Rome—became the largest Italian administrative unit to date to come under direct government control. The reason? Complete breakdown of the rule of law due to mob subversion.

In the USA the DA's Office, the NYPD, and the Feebs have declared the Cosa Nostra down and out in the wake of high-profile arrests of more than a thousand members and associates in the 1980s. In 1990 law enforcement capped this unprecedented cull by taking down even the teflon-coated boss of the Gambino family, the Dapper Don John Gotti. Now, with the homicide dicks Eppolito and Caracappa turning the phrase "murder cops" inside out, like the mythical Hydra the mafia reared its head to reveal how much this supposedly washed out organization continued to control both America's finest city and the city's finest.

JACK CANNON

His first book, published under the razzle-dazzle penname of Jack Cannon, was the 1974 potboiler called *The Sniper*, starring lone-wolf plainclothes NYPD Detective Sgt. Joe Ryker and his two shoulder- and ankle-holstered pals.

What might a recipe for the ultimate nobrow novel look like? First, take an intelligent genre classic like *The Godfather*: thirty-plus million copies sold, translations into all the major, many minor, and some languages that most people have never even heard of, and Hollywood adaptations so iconic that real-life mafiosi would reportedly imitate what they saw on the big screen. Then take a pedigreed but popular classic like *The Great Gatsby*, retooled and reinvented for every new generation, recently as a six-hour marathon stage performance hailed by the *New York Times* as the "most remarkable achievement in theater not only of this year but also of this decade".[4]

Put them together, run through the satyricomic blender, season to taste (late spring to early winter, in this case), and you have the makings of a perfect beachbooks for intellectuals, a literary analogue to a romantic date where style meets substance and *GQ* locks hands with IQ. Interestingly, such a book actually exists: a 1990 *New York Times* bestseller, a Book-of-the-Month Club main selection, and an all-round nobrow showpiece called *The Gold Coast*. No less interestingly, its author Nelson DeMille openly splits the difference between the highbrows and lowbrows, owning up to "commercial instincts and literary ambitions".[5]

Ambitious as he is, at least by the not terribly exacting standards of mafia fiction, DeMille's literary roots, in the best tradition of Hammett or McBain, sprout from the pulps. His first book, published under the razzle-dazzle penname of Jack Cannon, was the 1974 potboiler called *The Sniper*, starring lone-wolf plainclothes NYPD Detective Sgt. Joe Ryker and his two shoulder- and ankle-holstered pals. Within a year it was joined by five more procedurals, all competent but undistinguished tokens of the type. By then their author had already quit his day job as an insurance fraud investigator and never looked back.

Flouting the stereotype of a genre hack, DeMille shelved Ryker just as the series was starting to attract a fan base. Then within a year he put out three nonfiction titles—*Hitler's Children*, *Killer Sharks*, and *The Five-Million-Dollar Woman: Barbara Walters* as Kurt Ladner, Brad Matthews, and Ellen Kay, respectively. Whence the coyness? As he tells it, he always knew he could do better, so he preferred to hone his chops until he was ready to star in his own "write". That day came in 1978 with *By the Rivers of Babylon*, so much so that in the wake of *The Gold Coast* the *Denver Post* enthusiastically anointed him king of "the rarified world of the intelligent thriller".[6]

A decorated Vietnam war lieutenant, DeMille is a Hofstra graduate in political science and history and a longtime member of Mensa, who has notched up upward of thirty million book sales while picking up honorary doctorates in literature from Hofstra, Long Island University, and Dowling College. His home library in a Tudor mansion in Long Island's Garden City (actually a village) is stacked with Roman history, British literary classics, and twentieth-century American canon from Fitzgerald and Hemingway to Ayn Rand and Truman Capote. His favorite contemporaries, on the other hand, are Tom Clancy and Steven King.

Even as he turns his back on mob story formulas in *The Gold Coast*, DeMille admits to leaning on cliffhanger technique and a generally reader-friendly philosophy of composition, right down to "short sentences, short paragraphs and short chapters".[7] As for his vaunted historical accuracy—in 2012 he was even invited to contribute a foreword to a volume about Long Island's Gold Coast in the *Images of America* series—he prides himself on extensive library and online research, tons of face-to-face interviews, and field trips to locations ranging from the normally off-limits Plum Island to

Moscow, Belfast, and even postwar Vietnam. If *The Gold Coast* bucks the pattern, it is because its territory, both geographical and social, required a great deal less research. As DeMille told me, he wrote about what he knew and saw growing up on Long Island.

While the long announced film version of *The Gold Coast* has so far failed to materialize, in 2003 one of DeMille's earlier military investigative thrillers was made into a television movie with Don Johnson. Another, *The General's Daughter*, is a highly grossing 1999 Hollywood feature starring John Travolta and Madeleine Stowe. The author, who played no part in the adaptation, declares it terrific in every way save for the Hollywood ending. This has not stopped him, on the other hand, from tacking one on to the sequel to *The Gold Coast*, published eighteen years after the original under the title of *The Gate House*.

As for the original, even as it was riding the charts back in 1990, it drew, just like *The Great Gatsby* in its time, a scattershot mix of pans and panegyrics. For every *Publishers Weekly* blasting both barrels at a "bloated, unpersuasive thriller", there was a *New York Times Book Review* boosting "as keen a social satirist as Edith Wharton".[8] Indeed, even reviewers who remained neither shaken nor stirred by DeMille's brand of two-fisted, if every now and then ham-fisted, satire did not shy from comparing him to Tom Wolfe and Nick Dunne, not to mention Puzo and Fitzgerald.

A quarter century later it is ever more apparent that *The Gold Coast* is more than a standard-issue mafia thriller—not least because it scarcely even fits the thriller profile. To be sure, it places itself in the thick of mafia and lawyer fictions, what with the obligatory passages of mob lore and FBI surveillance on the one hand and legal shenanigans and courtroom drama on the other. But even as it is does so, it demands to be read as a modern *Satyricon*, so apt in its distillate of late twentieth-century American mores and manners that by the middle of the twenty-first, if not before, it might end up being read as a historical novel.

These days it is already taught in some classrooms as a companion piece to *The Great Gatsby*, waiting for the day when *The Godfather* makes required reading lists, with *The Gold Coast* again as a natural take two. All this is to say that, although *The Gold Coast* may not have won the Pulitzer, as mass-market artertainment it is tops in its class. Without pretensions to wow the eliterary establishment it amalgamates a satirical récit of regional history with a pulse-quickening face-off with the mafia, gilding it all with a bellyful of laughs (or at least audible snickers) and vindicating *The Boston Globe* when it calls DeMille "unusually ambitious for a genre writer".[9]

As for the author himself, when I pushed him about these nobrow ambitions, he shot back with his customary touch of humor:

Yes, I was aware I was writing my best work. Why? Well, it was a departure from my usual action/adventure, and also I chose to write it in first person, which I hadn't done with my previous novels and the effort was liberating—though my editor reminded me of the old publishing advice that only suicide notes should be written in the first person.[10]

TROUBLE BREWS IN HAPPY VALLEY

Right there you have a recipe for a delicious comedy of manners, in which High Society rubs elbows with the underworld while ethnic cultures and philosophies of life clash beyond any hope of rescue from Emily Post.

John Sutter is a successful Wall Street tax lawyer (is there any other kind?) whose blue-blood family roots stretch back to the pilgrims who crawled off the *Mayflower* and, on the other side, to the Long Island Whitmans of *Leaves of Grass* lineage. He has everything a forty-something American-style aristocrat might wish for, beginning with a couple of flown-the-coop kids and an oversexed wife, heiress to a grand estate on Long Island's Gold Coast—the very same immortalized in *The Great Gatsby*. Add to this a Mensa brain, killer looks, and a wit to match, and you get as close to a superhero without dressing him up in a cape.

The palatial estate comprises a white elephant of a fifty-room beaux arts mansion (up for sale) and a modest fifteen-room guesthouse occupied by John and Susan. There is also a six-room gate house deeded for life to Ethel and George Allard, former estate managers who, now in their dotage, take care of gardening and other light chores as, in effect, family retainers. Besides all that there are stables with horses, a cushy annual allowance for Susan, a cozy trust fund for the kids, and ritzy invitation-only clubs where *noblesse* can drink and socialize without much regard for *oblige*. Living in America has never been without its premiums.

But behind this manicured façade trouble brews in Happy Valley. Gripped by middle-life crisis, John develops a distaste for his profession, a taste for contretemps with his spouse, and an allergy to his social peers. By his own admission he flails around looking for a challenge. But be careful what you wish for. Enter the antagonist, Frank Bellarosa, boss of the most powerful New York mafia family. Tired of Brooklyn, he moves into a posh residence called the Alhambra next door to the Sutters—this in a manner of speaking, what with the estates being bigger even than the egos of the robber barons and Jazz Age tycoons who built them.

From the get-go Frank goes out of his way to befriend his neighbor or, when that founders on a few social icebergs, make him beholden to his Italian benefactor. As it later turns out, Frank is about to be indicted for a murder he claims he did not commit and is shopping for what he can't buy in his own circles: a clean lawyer. Once he has the Social Register attorney in his debt and halfway in his pocket—a far-fetched conjunction of John's boneheaded tax evasion and Frank's shady connect in the IRS—Frank "The Bishop" Bellarosa will play him like a pawn against a cartoonishly power-hungry DA. Or at least this is the plan.

Meanwhile, like moths John and his wife are drawn to the fire, soon flirting with it recklessly, he for the sake of asserting his manhood, she for the sake of pleasing her womanhood. One thing leads to another and soon the Godfather makes the WASP lawyer an offer he can't refuse: represent me in court or represent me in court. John has no illusions what defending the head of a mafia family will do to his career, to say nothing of finding himself permanently in the rearview mirror of his Gold Coast peers. But he has his own reasons for playing the patsy, and so an upstanding councillor becomes *consigliere* to a John Gotti lookalike.

Right there you have a recipe for a delicious comedy of manners, in which High Society rubs elbows with the underworld while ethnic cultures and philosophies of life clash beyond any hope of rescue from Emily Post. With narrative frisson provided by the charismatic and unpredictable Don Bellarosa, the result is a page-turning drawing-room comedy, hands down the most entertaining and artertaining of the kind. "My artistic intentions", recapped the author during our interviews,

> was on one level to show a clash of cultures, followed by each man recognizing some common ground, common problems, and human bonding… My other intention was to show that America was changing, as it has always changed, and that some changes are good, and some are not. Sutter and Bellarosa obviously represent two dying worlds.[11]

DeMille's design can be calibrated not only by the chances he takes in positioning his novel in the wake of *The Great Gatsby*, but also by the chances he takes by denying easy identification with the key players. Look more closely, and you could easily mistake his hero for a serpentine lawyer and a social snob, whose only redeeming graces are his love for his loopy wife and a knack for sardonic repartees. Undoubtedly, it is difficult not to like him as he smartasses the wiseguys or flips the bird to a team of mob assassins while staring into the business end of their shotguns. On the other hand, even as his first-person point of view works in terms of setting the mise-en-scène, his narrative voice is so undifferentiated that it gets difficult to tell at times who is talking and who is listening.

This has to do with the fact that, aside from being a Wall Street blue blood, Sutter is a character type that fronts most of DeMille's bestsellers. Refurbished as John Corey and Paul Brenner, two leads in their own series, he shares with them pretty much everything except the street address and the tailor.[12] Same build, same looks, and same cocksureness make Sutter less of a literary creation than he ought to have been as a variation on a theme by Fitzgerald. He and his two clones even share the same taste in jokes, most of which are, admittedly, good enough to keep interest from flagging when believability and fatigue with the uppity rich threaten to become a problem.

Where Sutter is snotty, his wife is only snooty, a forty-year-old going on fourteen in everything from libido to lifestyle. Although not as ditzy as Daisy Buchanan, she is as sheltered from real life outside the boutiquey hamlets that litter Long Island between the Gold Coast and the Hamptons. Disdaining to get a job or even read a newspaper, like Daisy she is not only painfully naïve about how America really works, but could not care less. As for the last element of the love triangle, Frank Bellarosa may have Gatsby's affability and a penchant for conspicuous consumption, but he is no less a gangster and a *persona non grata* in this enclave of old money privilege.

Even more than in the principal characters, Fitzgerald's presence is detectable in the structural parallels, some of which, to DeMille's credit, do not become apparent until the denouement. All the same, before the plot resolves itself in a surprising albeit Gatsby-intimated reversal of fortune, somebody will be snubbed, somebody seduced, somebody two-timed, and somebody shot dead by a jilted lover. And like Nick Carraway, on the last pages somebody will leave town trying in vain not to look back on the story of double-dealing and love born of human frailty, passion, and greed.

More than anything else, however, the ubiquitous, if for the most part muted, undertow of *The Great Gatsby* is apparent in DeMille's resolve to set the mafia plot against a broad canvas of Long Island's history before and after the Jazz Age. Readers looking for a straight-ahead mob thriller are bound to be disappointed with what actually makes *The Gold Coast* a good novel: reams of regional history interlaced with upper-class satire of manners. Like *The Great* Gatsby, *The Gold Coast* is not only a love story and a mob story, but also a story about the empty space at the heart of the American Dream. "Like many of my peers, I've been all around the world", admits Sutter in one of his rare pensive moods, "but I've never been to America".[13]

ALL ITS WATCHES LIMP

For a quarter century after the Fitzgeralds had staggered home after their last binge, the stretch of land along the northern coast of Long Island stood frozen in time, its private roads and walled estates virtual fiefdoms of exclusive and reclusive money, as though all clocks and watches stopped at the sound of the closing bell on the evening of Black Tuesday.

Long Island's recorded history goes back to the 1600s when the Dutch and English settlers began to clear waterfront woodlands in order to build the first huts and villages. Many owed their survival to the local Indians, with whom they first traded and then fought for the right to expand their arable acreages, stitched by mushrooming networks of roads and settlements. By the end of the nineteenth century, long after the tribes had fallen to guns, germs, and steel, New York City consolidated the five boroughs, inundated them with immigrant masses, and drove the moneyed classes out into the relatively bucolic playgrounds of Long Island.

The turn of the century was a carnival of ostentation and arrogance. In spite of efforts to keep the New York Society to 400 persons of proper breeding, there were more than 4000 jockeying for status, and throngs of others clamoring to be enrolled in the fashionable set. The bidding for distinction was furious, with the tab for the notorious James Hazen Hyde ball reputed to be a hundred thousand dollars of 1899 vintage for just one evening. Making Gatsby look like a skinflint, parties would include presents for all invitees: gold watches, pearls, precious stones. Dinners would be served on plates of solid gold and guests, puffing on cigars wrapped in Franklin notes, would be put on horseback to cover more easily the expanse of tables.

Carried by the booming postwar demand for goods and services, the Jazz Age found America full of bustling industrial and commercial activity, convinced that its economy has at last found the philosopher's stone. From the perspective of the Great Depression, of course, the preceding decade would come to look like one manic Charleston danced out to the staccato of champagne corks popping on the party deck of the *Titanic*. The Thirties would replace the iconic image of febrile flappers doing the jig in a crowded speakeasy with the equally iconic image of an unending dance marathon, where sallow-looking contestants cling to one another for fear of wilting to the ground, never to get up again.

For a quarter century after the Fitzgeralds had staggered home after their last binge, the stretch of land along the northern coast of Long Island stood frozen in time, its private roads and walled estates virtual fiefdoms of exclusive and reclusive money, as though all clocks and watches stopped at the sound of the closing bell on the evening of Black Tuesday. Only after World War II, baby boomers began to spill out of Manhattan and Queen's into the Long Island farmlands and woodlands which, like the Indians of yore, stood little chance against the demand for track housing and planned communities like Levittown.

Today, as DeMille drolly and, other times, drily points out, there is little left of the Golden Age of the Gold Coast, that heady era immortalized by the excesses of real-life Jay Goulds and fictional Jay Gatsbys spanning the bull years of the robber barons and mafia bootleggers right up to the stock market meltdown of 1929. First the seemingly idle forests, then the still productive farms, finally the grandiose hundred-acre properties fell to bulldozers and wrecking balls under the complicit eye of zoning surveyors and real-estate developers.

Mass housing began to spill into and then overrun the region where at one time homegrown landed gentry inhabited residences of a hundred rooms or more, mounting equestrian parties that cantered the width of the island to take luncheon at exclusive establishments like the Seawanhaka Corinthian Yacht Club, which features notably in *The Gold Coast* and *The Gate House* (and where in 2008 DeMille married his third wife). The Gold Coast has never been a pastoral Jeffersonian democracy but an ecological niche for the rich.

As a satirist, DeMille is less a sniper than a high-volume, rapid-fire carpet bomber who likes to switch his targets as fast as a three-card Monte dealer likes to switch cards. As a local colorist, on the other hand, he is a thoughtful, even nostalgic witness to the historical transformation of real-life East Eggland from the bastion of plutocracy to today's mass democracy of tricked-out McChateaux and ever-multiplying subdivisions. Contrasting

Image 6.1   Oheka Castle, Long Island. *"Mass housing began to spill into and then overrun the region where at one time homegrown landed gentry inhabited residences of a hundred rooms or more, mounting equestrian parties that cantered the width of the island to take luncheon at exclusive establishments like the Seawanhaka Corinthian Yacht Club."*

old money and new, upper-crust hauteur and carpetbagging homogeneity, and ultimately the Jeffersonian and Hamiltonian visions of the country, he does for the Gold Coast what, across East River, Ed McBain did for the Big Bad City—bookmark it on the literary map of America.

Class structure is built on stratification, but money is too common in America to divide social classes by itself. For this you need money with pedigree, or at least money and pedigree. Rich as he is, Gatsby has neither and, although Daisy Buchanan is for sale, his bid is in the wrong currency. Ironically, while DeMille's Gold Coast residents look down their patrician noses on well-heeled upstarts like Bellarosa, they seldom pass a chance to scam their clients and the IRS, playing hardball with anything from stocks to securities to real estate. What sets them apart from the mobsters is not civic virtue but their Ivy League accents and lack of street muscle.

Oddly, both groups have more in common than they realize in that both struggle to adapt to the new post-industrial America, while idealizing their memories of the past. This nostalgia for the Golden Age that never was except in the mind's eye is one of the hallmarks of this unusual mafia thriller, whose sense of place, be it the imaginary East Egg or real-life Gold Coast, is matched only by a sense of displacement. Compounding the latter is the recognition that, a mere quarter century after publication, *The Gold Coast* itself looks more and more like a historical freeze-frame. With each passing year, its depiction of runaway suburban development from the year 1990 looks more and more like those blurry sepia-tinted daguerreotypes of sod-house settlers of the old West.

Today, as another crime writer Donald Westlake sighs in one of his gloomily comic Dortmunder capers, Long Island is another "Daliscape of concrete and ticky-tack, all its watches limp".[14] Indeed, both the Gold Coast and the southern section of the island, exemplified by the exclusive Hamptons, are under pressure from developers determined to obliterate the surviving estates and replace them with subdivisions tailored to yuppies and dinks swarming out of Manhattan offices. For their part, the latter increasingly hunt for city-style amenities in blissed-out beach country, all the better to enjoy their getaways from it all.

The symbol of these developments is the arrival of luxury condos, a commodity not usually identified with the Hamptons. For the aging baby boomers they are the flavor-of-the-moment alternative to shingled faux-chateaux that have been so in demand in the past. Now of retirement age, they look for Manhattan on the beach—country life without having to fret about details like security or upkeep. The net result are high-end condo or townhouse projects that tower over villages like Sag Harbor or Water Mill, right in the heart of the Hamptons, where the word condominium used to be the punch line to a bad joke.

As might be expected, the civic sentiment among local officials and longtime residents is akin to that of the mafia going to the mattresses. But even as the two social tides battle it out, with the suburbanites' demands running against the old guard, the simple historical truth is that there is no putting capitalism back in the bottle. As DeMille points out time and again, you stand a better chance of pushing back tectonic plates than of reversing the fate of the Gold Coast where a twenty-acre estate, let alone a hundred, is already getting to be as distant a memory as the silent pictures of Pola Negri and Rudolf Valentino.

All that remains today is nostalgia for houses, estates, and people as big as the myths about them, including the most enduring literary myth to which DeMille and his narrator return time and time again:

> When I walk this beach and look across to Sands Point, I think of F. Scott Fitzgerald's Jay Gatsby, the location of whose mythical house is the subject of some local theories and literary essays... And on the other side of the bay, up the beach on the next point of land, there is a big white colonial house which still stands and which I am certain is that of Gatsby's lost love, Daisy Buchanan. (192)

BRING ME THE HEAD OF ALFREDO GARCIA

> In his pre-executive days, in a grisly playback of *Bring Me the Head of Alfredo Garcia*, Gotti hacked off the head of one of his victims and lugged it around in a box for a week, displaying it to everyone who cared to look.

In fiction, and even more so in crime fiction, the protagonist is built on the back of the antagonist. The megalomaniacal Minister D— or the diabolical Professor Moriarty are cast as criminal masterminds quite simply because there is nothing heroic about defeating a village idiot. Both are precursors to later geniuses of fictional crime, such as McBain's the Deaf Man, whose nefarious plots are refreshingly foiled not so much by the bulls as by bad luck. But no matter how crafty and calculating they may be, the bad guys are narratively foredoomed to failure and thus fatally constrained in terms of character development.

It is against this background that DeMille shows his skill by creating a character out of what could easily have become a parody of a mafia boss. There is no hiding that Frank Bellarosa is in many ways a dead ringer for John Gotti. Gotti did two years in the slammer. Ditto Bellarosa. Gotti had three sons. Ditto Bellarosa. Gotti kept his blood family away from crime, save for his youngest son. Ditto Bellarosa. Gotti Junior was made and in the bidness by his late teens, eventually stepping into his father's shoes. Ditto Bellarosa Junior.

Both Gotti and Bellarosa have seats on the mafia commission. Both live by the motto of keeping their friends close and their enemies—in

Frank's case, the man whose wife he is fucking—closer. Thanks to jury tampering and witness intimidation both beat high-profile trials in the 1980s, earning a reputation for being untouchable. Gotti's greatest hit was the 1985 whacking of his boss, the head of the Gambino family Paul Castellano, which cleared the path for his hostile takeover. Even as *The Gold Coast* mentions this magnitude-ten earthquake on the mafia scale, it identifies Bellarosa as the top mafia boss in New York, which at that time would make him the head of the Gambinos.

Most of all, both are natty dressers, so much so that their sobriquets are dead giveaways to how closely DeMille's fiction rides coattails on fact: Dapper Don (Gotti) and Dandy Don (Bellarosa). Intriguingly, the connection between the two kingpins of the New York underworld runs not only from literature to history but also back. Young Gotti used to be thick with Carlo Gambino, boss of all bosses and real-life prototype for the patriarch of the Corleone family in Puzo's *The Godfather*, fleshed out in the film by jowl-padded Brando.

For all this biographical detail, *The Gold Coast* is not a *roman á clef* or even less a mafia exposé like Roberto Saviano's celebrated *Gomorrah*. The latter, an insider's account of the Neapolitan mafia, the Camorra, was so damaging in its revelations that its author had to go into hiding under twenty-four-hour police protection. But for the millions of DeMille's readers who have never sat across the table from a wiseguy or from a Little Italy spread, his novel is a priceless primer on the mob subculture and *paisano* culture (DeMille's mother was Italian so he grew up with the cuisine he dwells on so much in the novel).

For the same reasons, even as Bellarosa is modeled closely on Gotti he is far from a doppelgangster. For one, Frank is an educated history buff who can discourse with equal ease on Niccolò Machiavelli and St. Jerome. For two, once he buys up into the Gold Coast, he takes less after the real-life godfather than after an even more famous fictional parvenu with social ambitions. "Frank Bellarosa knew how to throw a party", concedes Sutter. "And I had a feeling that he did so in a manner that was in unconscious imitation of a Gatsby party, with everything a guest could want except the host, who watched his party from a distance" (133).

It is part of American culture to romanticize the outlaw, whether it is the buccaneering Henry Morgan, the bootlegging Al Capone, or the Big Bad City's business-as-usual John Gotti. Ever the creation of the media age, Gotti took pains to project a genial public image, famously offering coffee to the FBI agents assigned to tail him. But the dapper façade of a Catholic family man concealed a brutal psychopath. In his pre-executive days, in a grisly playback of *Bring Me the Head of Alfredo Garcia*, Gotti hacked off the head of one of his victims and lugged it around in a box for a week, displaying it to everyone who cared to look.[15]

Psychopaths can sustain this mental compartmentalization between public and criminal life so well that some serial killers actually maintained married relationships and families. But while people like John Gotti, or for that matter Frank Bellarosa, may project an affable persona that does not easily suggest a crime honcho, they are incurably duplicitous and deceitful—and those are their good points. This two-brain pathology of career bad guys was brought to light in a dramatic fashion by a discovery made during a mafia raid of the decade, which on this occasion did not take place in New York, Vegas, or Chicago, but in the birthplace of the Cosa Nostra: Sicily.

In 2007, during the capture and arrest of Salvatore Lo Piccolo, the reputed new boss of the Sicilian mafia, the cops ransacking his hideout stumbled on a paper goldmine. Hidden in the house near Palermo, where the gangster was nabbed after spending more than two decades on the run, was a large collection of coded documents that dealt with the business and the organization of the mafia. Once cracked, the cache revealed details of companies with mob connections and the hierarchy of the organization, still the most powerful on the island (in mainland Italy the Calabrian 'Ndrangheta has edged ahead of the Cosa Nostra).

But the curiousest document turned out to be a typed sheet bearing the title "Rights and Duties". Quickly dubbed the Ten Commandments, it spelled out in a form that openly echoed the Christian Decalogue the code of conduct for the Sicilian mob. Remarkably, even as the first injunction stipulates absolute fealty to a cutthroat criminal syndicate, others endorse professional ethics (keeping appointments), prosocial precepts such as not stealing (though only from other goombahs), and even moral imperatives such as truthfulness (presumably vis-à-vis the bosses rather than the cops). In fact, in an ultimate expression of inner compartmentalization, this field guide to being a good mobster holds degenerate killers to good behavior and moral values.

Ten Commandments

King James version	Mafia version
1. Thou shalt have no other gods before me.	1. Always being available for Cosa Nostra is a duty—even if your wife's about to give birth.
2. Thou shalt not make unto thee any graven image.	2. Appointments must absolutely be respected.
3. Thou shalt not take the name of the Lord thy God in vain.	3. No-one can present himself directly to another of our friends.
4. Remember the Sabbath day, to keep it holy.	4. Do not frequent pubs and clubs.
5. Honour thy father and thy mother.	5. Wives must be treated with respect.
6. Thou shalt not murder.	6. Never be seen with cops.
7. Thou shalt not commit adultery.	7. Never look at the wives of friends.
8. Thou shalt not steal.	8. Money cannot be appropriated if it belongs to others or to other families.
9. Thou shalt not bear false witness against thy neighbour.	9. When asked for any information, the answer must be the truth.
10. Thou shalt not covet.	10. People who can't be part of Cosa Nostra: anyone who has a close relative in the police, anyone with a two-timing relative in the family, anyone who behaves badly and doesn't hold to moral values.

Reading between the lines, it is instructive that career wiseguys are in need of reminders not to disrespect the mothers of their children, to say nothing of avoiding barflying and clubbing, two-timing the *capos*, and getting cozy with the police. All in all, it is hard to avoid the impression that the quality of membership in this most exclusive club is slipping even in the heart of Cosa Nostra country. DeMille's fictive crime boss is realistic about it, ruing for the Gold Age of American mafia in words played back verbatim in the sequel: "The old code of silence is dead... We rat out everybody, and we're happy we got the chance to do it."[16]

All this rank unprofessionalism on the opposite team ought to play into the hands of America's police forces, at least those that combat crime rather than commit it. Unfortunately, even as major-crime levels go down all around the USA, the reputation of the men and women in blue—whose own code of *omertà* is more entrenched than that of the mafiosi—goes down with it. Sworn to serve and protect, some of them are apparently in as much need of a set of Ten Commandments as the outlaws they are paid to chase.

The Most Dangerous Country in the World

They were a different breed of gangster than the shoot-first-ask-no-questions-later bandits roaming the streets in search of a score.

"Today we stand together as a city to try and right those wrongs, and to bring this dark chapter of Chicago's history to a close."[17] With this pablum and a five-and-a-half million dollar sop to the plaintiffs, on 14 April 2015, Chicago mayor Rahm Emanuel tried to erase a record of systematic torture of suspects—most of them black—by the Chicago police during the 1970s and 1980s. The next day the city revealed it was paying another five million to avert a lawsuit from the family of a black teen gunned down by a cop the year before (the police refused to release the video of the shooting). Money talks, and in this case it tells a dark story: in the decade prior to the current abuses Chicago paid out half a billion dollars to the victims of the police.

With cops often seen and acting as another street gang, little seems to have changed from 1993 when Joe Biden, then Chair of Senate Judiciary Committee—which is charged with oversight of the leading crime-fighting federal agencies—pronounced the USA to be "the most dangerous country in the world".[18] America, he said, carried this dubious distinction insofar as no country in the world notched a higher per capita murder rate. Typical of the man and his profession, his speech was but another example of that enduring American genre of political fiction.

This is not to downplay America's appalling record of homicide next to other developed nations. In Canada, for example, murder rates are per capita almost seven times lower than south of the border, and in Japan a whopping hundred times lower. But the statistical fact of the matter is that quite a few South American and African nations, to say nothing of Russia, report (and possibly underreport) rates double or even triple those in the States. More to the point, even prior to Biden's hyperbole violent crime in America began to crash. Indeed, over the last generation—roughly coeval with the publication of *The Gold Coast*—murder and manslaughter in the country plummeted to historically low levels.

There is no denying that in some hotspots, such as the notorious Sandtown-Winchester area of Baltimore—which is almost uniformly black and where more than half adults are jobless—homicide rates remain worse than in Honduras, the undisputed murder epicenter on Earth.[19] But more indicative of the nation at large are the perennial urban trend-setters, NYC and LA. In both of them homicides nosedived from about 2000 a year a generation ago to a quarter of that today. The USA may not be a kinder and gentler nation than under Bush I, but it is less homicidal.

America has come a long way, it seems, from the twentieth century during which it frequently appeared that land of opportunity and crime of opportunity were one and the same thing. At the beginning of the century, to take just one notorious example, William Devery became the head of NYPD after his conviction for extortion had been conveniently overturned. Or who could forget the city's Prohibition mayor John P. O'Brien who, when asked whom he would appoint as Police Commissioner, famously replied that they have not told him yet.

It was the Prohibition and the whale-sized profits to be made in its wake that impressed on crime bosses what the robber barons had figured long before, namely that market competition was not the American way.[20] All it did was bring bloodshed and bad publicity, driving the overhead up. The solution, analogous to industrial monopolies in banking, meatpacking, oil, steel, and railroads was collusion. The brainchild of Chicago mobster Papa Johnny Torio, it culminated in the historical 1927 sit-down of crime bosses known as the Group of Seven, which marked the dawn of syndicated crime.

The New York side was represented by Lucky Luciano, godfather of the Luciano (now Genovese) family; Mayer Lansky, prototype for Hyman Roth in *The Godfather*, who would go on to covertly finance the career of Richard Nixon; and Frank Costello, known as the prime minister of the underworld, who would be the model for Brando's Godfather. There were also delegates from Atlantic City, Philadelphia, Cleveland, and Detroit, and not least Kansas City's Tom Pendergast, who in 1935 would go on to elect a US Senator by the name of Harry S. Truman, who would eventually serve as the thirty-third President of the USA.[21]

They were a different breed of gangster than the shoot-first-ask-no-questions later bandits roaming the streets in search of a score. Their role model was Arnold Rothstein, fixer of the 1919 baseball world series—noted both in *The Great Gatsby* and in *The Gold Coast*—who sported toney suits, spoke cultivated English, mixed with celebrities, and wielded a significant amount of political clout behind the scenes. Meeting in the then gambling Mecca of Atlantic City, the Group of Seven divvied up turf, fixed dispute-resolution mechanisms, brainstormed how to diversify after the end of the Prohibition which was clearly marked for death (even President Harding was known to have a bootlegger), and even agreed to convince Al Capone to take the fall on a minor charge to get Chicago gangland violence off the front pages.

The symbol of this transformation from triggermen to businessmen was the idea of founding a gambling safe haven deep in the Nevada desert, where it would flourish as Las Vegas. The two-million city of today, which only in the last few years forfeited the crown of the gambling capital of the world to Macau, rose in the hard-baked sands in the 1940s as the emblem of the mafia's tactical quest for quasi-respectability. In another emblem, at the end of *The Godfather* Michael Corleone promises his wife that within five years all family businesses will be legit. The Corleones will retire from the life of crime—to the Gold Coast, perhaps—trading gunmen for Sutter-type lawyers.

Following *The Godfather*, the cultural mainstreaming of the mafia ratcheted up with Gay Talese's *Honor Thy Father* (1971), which attracted as much flak for its New Journalistic techniques as for drawing a straight line from the lives of the top mafiosi to the lives of ordinary citizens. The picture of organized criminals as hardworking Americans in pursuit of the trappings of the American Dream was so controversial that the media, led by *The New York Times*, lambasted it for apparently implying that "being a mobster is much the same as being a sportsman, film star or any other kind of public 'personality.'"[22]

None of that controversy hurt it with the paying public. Talese sold the paperback rights to Fawcett World Library for more than Fawcett had paid for the paperback rights to *The Godfather*, proving that the mafia had become a literarily valuable commodity. Now you could make as much off it as in it. To DeMille's credit, paying tribute to the trials and tribulations of running a criminal empire, he leaves no doubt that the bad guys are called bad guys because they *are* bad guys. On that subject, he told me,

> I was more personally familiar with the world of *The Godfather* than I was with the world of the monied residents of the Gold Coast. I could have written two books—New York Mafia and Gold Coast gentry—but each book would have lacked layers, perhaps, or some other element that would make it distinct... But by making Sutter an attorney I was also able to involve him in Frank Bellarosa's legal problems.[23]

Of course, for every John Sutter there was always a Frank Sinatra—recognizable in *The Godfather* as Johnny Fontane—who bluntly preferred hanging with the goombahs, going as far as to declare, "I'd rather be a don for the Mafia than President of the United States."[24] Vying for mafia roles in the movies, Sinatra always gladly headlined new mafia clubs and raised funds for all-out mob fronts like the Italian-American Civil Rights League, set up by the godfather of the Colombo family. The League's reach would prove strong enough to force the producers of *The Godfather* to remove the word *Mafia* from the original title.

TAKE TWO

> Like *The Godfather: Part III*, the whole adds up to less than the sum of the parts, be it leading, supporting, or just walk-in.

The Gold Coast had the ingredients of a good read: organized crime, cold-blooded murder, steamy sex, courtroom trickery, and not least, truckloads of humor. It also had the ingredients of a good book: Machiavellian plot, a couple of memorable antagonists, pointed social commentary, and deep sense of continuity with highbrow and genre classics of American litera-ture. Any doubts about the success of its nobrow recipe were dispelled eighteen years down the road by that clear sign of success in American culture: a sequel.

Despite Hollywood's unquenchable appetite for sequels, artistically speaking take two is nearly always a pale shadow of the original. As Gatsby himself found out, there are few second acts in America. The exceptions only confirm the rule, the most celebrated among them—indeed, many would argue the only one—being *The Godfather: Part II*. Viewed by hun-dreds of millions in and outside the USA, voted into top-ten American films ever, its depiction of Sicilian immigrants and their organized crime under-world is so potent that it in many people's minds it vies with historical truth.

Alas, take two on *The Gold Coast* is not one of these exceptions. You have to admire the audacity of writing a sequel to the novel that is itself a playback of Fitzgerald's—which itself plays back the material first used in his stories such as "Winter Dreams" (1922), "Dice, Brass Knuckles & Guitar" (1923), and "The 'Sensible Thing'" (1924).[25] But, even with-out going back that far, next to DeMille's own first take the sequel is an anticlimax. The plot is as thin as an Italian who eats away from home, the characters eloquent witnesses in the case against recycling, and the social satire all too often reduced to gags about tightwad in-laws.

It is not that *The Gate House* does not have its moments. Some of the humor is actually pretty good, such as when Sutter asks an old-school mobster for a business card, or when Bellarosa and his wife are socially snubbed as being formerly of Brooklyn. Some of the spousal banter rings up the best of Hammett's *Thin Man*, and the uppityness of the upper crust is always good for a putdown or two. But like *The Godfather: Part III*, the whole adds up to less than the sum of the parts, be it leading, supporting, or just walk-in.

What raises parts of *The Gate House* above the level of an enjoyable but ultimately forgettable laugh-a-minutethon is once again the characters' attempts to reconciliate the present with the past, personal and historical, individual and collective. "An individual life passes through a continuum of time and space, but now and then you enter a warp that sucks you back", contemplates Sutter, ten years older but not necessarily wiser or otherwise changed from *The Gold Coast*. "In fact, experience is just another word for baggage. And memory carries the bags."[26]

Memories of the past are always about the present, and this is as true in the sequel. Although not as fully integrated into the plot as in take one, historical asides and literary references abound, beginning with multiple nods to *The Godfather* (oddly absent from *The Gold Coast*). The changeover from the pre-World War II Social Register families to the new order, the settlement of Long Island in the 1600s, the mansions of the Gilded Age vintage, the local celebrities like John Philip Sousa, the peccadillos of the Vanderbilts and the Roosevelts—all these and other historical tidbits pop in and out of a family and *family* sitcom.

On an even larger canvas, just as in *The Gold Coast* the sequel draws pointed similarities between the fall of the Roman empire and the Bush-era USA. But most of all, history peeks from around every corner and through every keyhole through the lingering presence of Fitzgerald's greatest literary creation. The parallels go all the way back, in fact, to the composition of *The Great Gatsby* and *The Gold Coast*, both of which were consciously—even self-consciously—conceived as their authors' most ambitious and artistically integrated works.

Even as narratively Fitzgerald and DeMille look to the past, both accentuate it by constant foreshadowing. Fitzgerald's hints that race ahead of chronology have long been acclaimed as the building blocks of his tragic architecture. As in *Gatsby Rex*, DeMille's authorial intrusions leave a trail of narrative crumbs to hint at the tragic course of events in this otherwise comic novel. Of course, like with much else in nobrow fiction, in this case *tertium datur*. Even as foreshadowing hooks you in with intimations of

Image 6.2 Nelson DeMille in 2008/F. Scott Fitzgerald in 1921. *"The parallels go all the way back, in fact, to the composition of* The Great Gatsby *and* The Gold Coast, *both of which were consciously—even self-consciously—conceived as their authors' most ambitious and artistically integrated works."*

the entrapment and vendetta yet to come, it retards the climax with hundreds of pages of social comedy of manners.

The Gold Coast could have been twice as long, noted the author in our interviews, "but I self-edited as I wrote and kept in mind Fitzgerald's short but fully-realized *Gatsby*". Conservative gatekeepers may find in this explicit playback and implicit comparison to one of the masterpieces of American literature little more but misplaced chutzpah. And yet, as DeMille did not hesitate to point out, *Gatsby* "was not an instant classic and was considered by many critics and readers to be almost frivolous. But the passage of time ages a book and at some point the popular fiction becomes a 'classic'."

It is worth remembering that Fitzgerald died in near obscurity, in his darkest moments imagining himself being a failure even at being a failure. It was mainly thanks to the intervention of one literary critic that his star rose again. Edmund Wilson arranged for literary tributes to appear in

The New Republic, prepared an edition of *The Crack-Up*, and most of all edited Fitzgerald's unfinished last novel in one volume with his five best stories and the soon-to-be canonical *Gatsby*. Only time will tell whether *The Gold Coast* will follow in the footsteps of this slender Jazz Age novel also trashed in its time as a "dud" or as lacking even "one chemical trace of magic, life, irony, romance or mysticism".[27]

WE KEEP YOU CLEAN IN MUSCATINE

The greatness of *The Great Gatsby* lies precisely in the difficulty of separating the American dream of infinite social mobility from the chronic liar and front for the mobsters that is Gatsby.

The story of the Jazz Age prodigy and prodigal has been retold in so many biographies that, side by side with fourteen volumes of his collected works, they could fill a shelf even in Gatsby's sumptuous library. By 1908, when Scott entered St. Paul Academy, he was already convinced he wanted to be a writer, which in his eyes signified a Romantic man of action who lives his material first hand in order to write about it more intensely. Conceited to the point of being narcissistic, he fancied himself a foundling, transferring this alienation onto Gatsby, who lies about his parents being dead as part of his Platonic conception of himself.[28]

After charming his way into Princeton, Fitzgerald quickly fell afoul of his studies but in love with power and status, trusting that his keen eye for people and manners would eventually win him both. In November 1917 he was commissioned for officer's training in Kansas (the captain in charge was a baldy with a crumpled grin by the name of Ike Eisenhower). Every weekend at dances at the officer's club, surrounded by conversation, music, and rustling newspapers, he drafted his first novel. In Kansas he also met Zelda, who would have a decisive effect on his life and career.

The war over before he had seen combat, he went to New York and into advertising, registering a minor hit with a slogan for a steam laundry in Muscatine, Iowa: We Keep You Clean in Muscatine. A bit imaginative, his boss said, but you'll get the hang of it in time. After amassing well over a hundred rejections, he finally sold a story to the *Smart Set*, but it was too little and too late to stop Zelda from breaking off their engagement. At his wits' end, he again rewrote his first novel which, when it eventually came out in 1920, created a stir and made him a pot of money. That same month he married Zelda and together with the rest of America went on the gaudy alcohol-soaked spree known as the Roaring Twenties.

By October 1922 they were renting a house in Great Neck Estates on Long Island's Gold Coast, living up the American Dream. To shore up his finances, Fitzgerald wrote potboiler stories with the required jazz (upbeat) endings even as, deep down, he preferred to write about life's downs and disillusionments. In spring 1924, trying to get away from the high life and work on *Gatsby*, the family sailed for Europe. At that time Fitzgerald read a lot of Conrad, which may account for the brooding tones with which his narrator reconstructs the hero's downfall from the sidelines. It may also account for the oblique narration and broken chronology, which demand sifting through rumors and lies in search of a man behind the dream.[29]

The greatness of *The Great Gatsby* lies precisely in the difficulty of separating the American dream of infinite social mobility from the chronic liar and front for the mobsters that is Gatsby. Fitzgerald's deliberateness in personifying one of America's greatest themes in one of America's greatest literary creations is evident in his groping for the title. Less than a month before the April 1925 release, he frantically cabled his Scribner editor Max Perkins to rename the book *Under the Red White and Blue*.[30] Once it was out, he oddly fretted that women readers would not enjoy it because it had no important female character, and that critics would not because it dealt with the rich, instead of worker or farmer types.

The book objectifies his lifelong feeling that the upper classes were a race apart whose existence was more beautiful and intense than that of ordinary mortals. Interestingly, among the analyses of *Gatsby* as a great American novel, as a picture-perfect postcard from the Jazz Age (which he named), and as a love story for the ages, one rarely hears about it being a mob story. Yet the fact remains that, far from being a self-made man, Gatsby is made by the mob in about every way except being *made*. Behind his wealth and persona stands organized crime, from the thugs who pose as servants in his house to his handler Wolfsheim, based on Arnold Rothstein, the brain of the New York Jewish mafia (who returns in *The Gold Coast* as the mob shyster Weinstein).[31]

Gatsby dips deep into the cultural capital of the Black Masketeers, starting with the protagonist whose name rings in the hardboiled slang for "gun". Once you step back from high-society glitz, you find yourself in the chiaroscuro of mob fronts, bootleggers, and racketeers. Behind them lurk guns, murder and suicide, three dead bodies, casual brutality, police and political corruption, crooked bonds deals and hot securities, and even an offstage mafia-style rubout of Herman Rosenthal.[32] Gatsby's parties round up the picture with the usual suspects: bankers, senators, movie promoters, stock manipulators, and assorted celebrities, starlets, and moochers.

Undoubtedly, Fitzgerald was more personally invested in the class-crossed love story just because it was *his* story. "The whole idea of Gatsby is the unfairness of a poor young man not being able to marry a girl with money. This theme comes up again and again because I lived it", he wrote.[33] But he leapt on his editor's suggestion to flesh out Gatsby's criminal dealings, from incriminating phone calls to flat-out felonies, with the effect of turning his character from merely shadowy to downright shady. Jewish birth name, Gatz, cues an even more allegorical judgment of the crimes in that the Old Testament punishment for adultery or murder—as persistent rumors about him would have it—is death.

The narrator, who is also the moral compass of the story, concludes that Gatsby turned out all right in the end. The evil, he says, resided not in the man himself but in what preyed on Gatsby. The novel, however, shows Gatsby preying on everyone around him, notably Nick and Jordan, to get to the woman with a voice full of money. He discounts inconvenient lives such as Daisy's child's, trying to buy not only respectability but friendship. Most of all, he is a mob associate and a complicit criminal who, when the gloves come off during the standoff with Daisy's husband, shows himself to be as repellent as the men he works for.

In short, he is an all-out fraud, one symbol of which is his library—another elaborate prop for the con artist that is Gatsby. DeMille smoothly links him to *The Gold Coast* with an aside that the library in Bellarosa's mansion was imported wholesale in the 1920s. "There's five hundred feet of bookshelf. Books are ten bucks a foot. So that's five large" (258), boasts Frank. The mafia don and the mafia pawn have never looked more alike. In this light, it is fitting that the green light, which in both books symbolizes yearning for lost innocence, is also the color of the legal tender. I'm not sure what that green light meant to Jay Gatsby, shrugs DeMille's hero, "beyond the orgiastic future".[34]

American Dream

In a country whose legislators are committed to putting the tools of instant death in the hands of every citizen at all times, it is difficult to say which is more macabre.

In the ever-evolving world of crime fiction, the one ingredient that remains constant is violent crime itself. In broad outline, patters of urban homicide have not changed from at least as far back as the Middle Ages. Murder and manslaughter have always been predominantly the business of young men. Among them, the twenty- to twenty-four-year-old bracket is invariably the most lethal. The overwhelming majority of killers are from the bottom of society in terms of education and employment. As a rule, so are their victims. Although vastly more men kill then women, both sexes kill more men than women. Last but not least, the perpetrators almost always have prior run-ins with the law.

Violent crime in America conforms to these regularities. What sets it apart is the fact that so many of murder victims throughout the country are black men. They represent a shade above 5 % of the population but are killed at eight times the rate consistent with their population share. Statistically speaking, this translates into four out of ten homicide victims being black men. Equally troublesome, this rate has not budged during the last generation—the same during which in absolute numbers murder and manslaughter plummeted to levels not seen since half a century ago.[35]

The flip side of this picture is that homicide clearance rate has also fallen dramatically during the last half a century, from about 90 % in 1965 to a shade north of 60 % today. But before drawing any quick conclusions about the regression in murder investigations, it is interesting to note that cop killings are almost always solved at any time anywhere in the USA. Cynics will justifiably conclude that certain victims are evidently more equal than others. On the positive side, however, one could speculate that with the proper resources and motivation non-cop killings could presumably come to enjoy the same clearance rate.

Another statistical constant is that gun homicides, gun suicides, and mass shootings in America are vastly more numerous than in Europe. You might think that this would galvanize the country to tighten, if not restrict, access to firearms. But despite two-thirds of Americans being consistently in favor of gun control, many states are doing just the opposite. In 2015 alone Kansas legalized carrying a concealed handgun without the need for a license. Nevada ratcheted up legal protection for people who kill in self-defense from their cars. And Texas allowed civilians to carry handguns in the open.

In a country whose legislators are committed to putting the tools of instant death in the hands of every citizen at all times, it is difficult to say which is more macabre: the statistical rise in serial killings over the last half a century or the documented popularity of events such as the auction of goods belonging to Jeffrey Dahmer—serial killer, necrophiliac mutilator, and cannibal. But among all this fetishization of guns and fascination with violence the question looms even larger why exactly overall homicide rates in America should have dropped to half of what they were at their peak in 1991.

Criminology and social studies teem with theories about the sources of this mutation into a less murderous and felonious nation. Some tap the criminal justice system: mandatory and longer-term sentences, more cops and rent-a-cops, better algorithms for stats-crunching and profiling police strategies, right-to-carry-and-use gun laws, and the death penalty. Liberal-minded analysts single out social factors: aging population, legal abortion, less crack in the streets, less alcohol abuse, and even such tenuous links as less lead in gasoline (lead is a potent toxin, and gas-sniffing a cheap way to get high and out of hand). There is also the economy: more gated affluence, higher employment, lower inflation, and perhaps even such immeasurable factors as a periodic resurgence of confidence in the American way of life.

The truth is that nobody knows for sure, even as politicians take the credit for tougher stance on crime and relentless war on drugs. What is left out of their self-serving narratives is that crime is falling in Big Apple and the City of Angels, both of which are decriminalizing a number of offenses, starting with walking away from tossing every weed-puffer behind bars. Behind this progressivism stands pragmatism in the form of spiraling prison costs and overcrowding. With 5 % of world population, America houses a quarter of the world's prison population. This is even worse than Russia and more than six times worse than the country with which it shares well nigh everything except incarceration rates—Canada.

In raw numbers, almost two and a quarter million Americans are in the hole and another four and three-quarter million on probation or parole. With the total coming up to a staggering seven million, ironically, most prison terms are for minor and nonviolent drug offenses. Critics of the mandatory sentencing system include of late Barack Obama, who signaled his new position by commuting almost four dozen jailbirds and by visiting the El Reno federal penitentiary in Oklahoma, the first such by a sitting president. Having said that, 80 % of all inmates are jailed by states, where conditions are infinitely worse than in the federal pens.

The prohibition and criminalization of the drug trade, and thus lack of regulation and fiscal benefits through taxation, benefits only gangsters who exercise almost exclusive control over a global market worth a third of a trillion dollars annually. In 2014 the World Health Organization came out in favor of decriminalizing drugs. Most of Europe has already done so. More than half of Americans poll consistently in favor of decriminalizing pot, Earth's favorite controlled substance. To everyone except American legislators it is clear that, like during the prohibition on alcohol a century ago, the ban on federal participation in the manufacture and regulated sale of Schedule I and II controlled substances only fuels organized crime.

This is not to overlook the historical problems with the Jazz Age prohibition, such as the fact that the G-men frequently lacked jurisdiction to prosecute gangsters for murder and extortion, which were state crimes. Adding to the problem were the turf wars among the USA's law enforcement agencies, which fought crime almost as doggedly as they fought themselves (today there are roughly *fifty thousand* law enforcement agencies in the country). What the feds could do, however, was to go after the bad guys' tax returns. Wielded by the agents of the IRS, then and now form 1040 did more to put the mafiosi where they belonged than the police forces. It is a trick that gets a new coat of varnish from DeMille, insofar as in *The Gold Coast* it is the Mafia boss that sends the IRS after an upstanding citizen—if that's not a stretch to call a Wall Street lawyer.

In the second decade of the third millennium, even as homicide in America rides a low tide, crime at large rides high, still a shortcut to this or that dreamer's American Dream. Drug prohibition still funnels users toward dealers and still fuels death. In 2008 drug overdoses in the USA overtook car crashes as the main cause of accidental death. And if you get tired of statistics, there is always crime fiction waiting in the wings to satisfy the atavistic need coiled at the base of every reader's thalamus to vicariously experience the primal crime of passion, power, or revenge and to witness the dispensation of legal—or at least poetic—justice.

NOTES

[a] *The Telegraph* (2007); reordered to parallel the Christian Decalogue.
1. Trevelyan (2006).
2. Condon's screenplay adaptation of his own bestseller won the Writers Guild of America award and nominations for the Best Writing Oscar and the Golden Globe.
3. Twain, 176.
4. Brantley (2010).

5. In Finn, LI1.
6. Walker (2000).
7. BookBrowse (2000).
8. http://www.publishersweekly.com/978-0-446-51504-7, and back cover, 2008 edition, respectively.
9. Dyer, 49.
10. Email 6 June 2015.
11. July 2015.
12. Corey and Brenner both star in *The Panther* (2012).
13. 146; all references are to *The Gold Coast*, unless indicated otherwise.
14. Westlake, 12.
15. Maloney and Hoffman.
16. *The Gold Coast*, 726; *The Gate House*, 33.
17. *The Economist*, "Dark Days", 32.
18. Biden (1993); on American political fictions, see Swirski (2015), *Ars Americana*, and (2011).
19. *The Economist*, "Fixing", 8.
20. Until the 1930s, the 1890 Sherman Anti-Trust Act ended up being used mainly against labor unions.
21. On Lansky and Pendergast, see Swirski (2010), Chap. 2.
22. MacInnes, BR2; see also Shepard, 52; for a cultural history of the mafia, see Dainotto.
23. Personal interview, July 2015.
24. In Summers and Swan, 183.
25. Another story "Absolution" (1924) comes from an early version of *Gatsby* called *Trimalchio*; see West.
26. *The Gate* House, 83–84.
27. *The Great Gatsby: The Authorized Text*, 202.
28. Chapter 6 in *Gatsby*; on Fitzgerald, see Turnbull; Bruccoli; Meyers.
29. When Nick gets drunk at Myrtle's party, the narrative breaks down with him; fragmentation is, of course, a typical modernistic device.
30. *The Great Gatsby: The Authorized Text*, 207.
31. On page 179 Wolsheim boasts that he "made" Gatsby; Maxwell Perkins's spelling of the gangster's name was Wolfsheim; (*The Great Gatsby: The Authorized Text*, 200); in the novel it is Wolfshiem. Incidentally, Fitzgerald's first publication was a crime detective story.
32. For discrepancy between the novel and historical facts, see Logan.
33. Turnbull, 150.
34. Page 193; Fitzgerald's word of choice, changed by Edmund Wilson in his influential reedition of *Gatsby*, was "orgastic".
35. Leovy.

BIBLIOGRAPHY

Abadinsky, Howard. 1990. *Organized Crime*, 3rd ed. Chicago: Nelson-Hall.
Adorno, Theodor. 1941. On Popular Music. *Studies in Philosophy and Social Sciences* 9: 17–8.
Amis, Kingsley. 1965. *The James Bond Dossier*. London: Cape.
Anderson, Richard L. 1990a. Popular Art and Aesthetic Theory: Why the Muse Is Unembarrassed. *Journal of Aesthetic Education* 24: 33–46.
Anderson, Richard L. 1990b. *Calliope's Sisters: A Comparative Study of Philosophies of Art*. Englewood Cliffs, NJ: Prentice Hall.
Arendt, Hannah. 1971. Society and Culture. In Rosenberg, Bernard, and David Manning White, eds. *Mass Culture Revisited*. New York: Van Nostrand Reinhold. 93–101.
Armstrong, Nancy. 1987. *Desire and Domestic Fiction: A Political History of the Novel*. Oxford: Oxford UP.
Ashley, Mike. 2002. *The Mammoth Encyclopedia of Modern Crime Fiction*. New York: Carroll & Graf.
Associated Press. 2001. Book Sales Edge up in US Market. *Edmonton Journal* 3 June: C6.
Associated Press. 2001. Stephen King's E-Novella Not Enough to Keep Mighty Words Solvent. *Edmonton Journal* 14 December: E1.
Athanasourelis, John Paul. 2012. *Raymond Chandler's Philip Marlowe: The Hard-Boiled Detective Transformed*. Jefferson, NC: MacFarland and Co.
Aubry, Timothy. 2011. *Reading as Therapy: What Contemporary Fiction Does for Middle-Class Americans*. Iowa City: University of Iowa Press.
Auden, W.H. 1948. The Guilty Vicarage. *Harper's Magazine* May: 406–12.

© The Editor(s) (if applicable) and The Author(s) 2016
P. Swirski, *American Crime Fiction*,
DOI 10.1007/978-3-319-30108-2

Australasian Council of Women and Policing Inc. 2002. 2002 Women and Policing Globally. http://www.aic.gov.au/events/aic%20upcoming%20events/2002/policewomen3.htm.

Avital, Tsion. 2003. *Art Versus Nonart: Art Out of Mind*. Cambridge: Cambridge University Press.

Babener, Liahna K. 1995. Raymond Chandler's City of Lies. In *Los Angeles in Fiction*, ed. David Fine, 127–49. Albuquerque: University of New Mexico Press.

Bacall, Lauren. 2006. *By Myself and Then Some*. New York: Harper.

Baker, Donald G. 1982. From Apartheid to Invisibility: Black Americans in Popular Fiction, 1900–60. *Midwest Quarterly* 13: 365–85.

Balzer, David. 2014. *Curationism: How Curating Took Over the Art World and Everything Else*. Toronto: Coach House Books.

Banzhaf, John. 2003. Excerpts from Successful Student Project: Make Agnew Pay, UPI [1/6/83]. 2 Feb. http://banzhaf.net/docs/agnew.

Barnes, Brooks. 2010. Hollywood Moves away from Middlebrow. *The New York Times*. 27 December. http://www.nytimes.com/2010/12/27/business/media/27movies.html?_r=0.

Barsch, Achim. 1997. Young People Reading Popular/Commercial Fiction. In Steven Tötösy de Zepetnek and Irene Sywenky, ed. *Systemic and Empirical Approach to Literature and Culture as Theory and Application*. Edmonton and Siegen: University of Alberta ricl-ccs and Siegen University. 371–83.

Bauer, Raymond A. 1964. The Communicator and His Audience. In *People, Society and Mass Communications*, ed. Lewis A. Dexter and David M. White, 125–40. New York: Free Press.

BBC News. 2007. Grisham Collects Lifetime Honour. 28 March. http://news.bbc.co.uk/2/hi/entertainment/6503689.stm.

BBC News. 2013. Huge Survey Reveals Seven Social Classes UK. 3 April. http://www.bbc.co.uk/news/uk-22007058.

BBC News. 2014. US Author John Grisham 'Sorry' for Child Porn Comments. 16 October. http://www.bbc.com/news/world-us-canada-29654291.

Beacon, Richard L. 2003. Let's Supersize It. *Time*, 9 June: 49–50.

Beekman, E.M. 1973. Raymond Chandler and an American Genre. *Massachusetts Review* 14: 149–73.

Bell, Clive. 2011. *Art*. CreateSpace. (Orig. 1913).

Bennett, Tony, ed. 1983. The Bond Phenomenon: Theorising a Popular Hero. *Southern Review* 16 July: 195–225.

Bennett, Tony. 1990. *Popular Fiction: Technology, Ideology, Production, Reading*. London: Routledge.

Bercovitch, Sacvan, ed. 2002. *The Cambridge History of American Literature. Volume Six: Prose Writing, 1910–1950*. Cambridge: Cambridge UP.

Berelson, Bernard. 1951. Who Reads What Books and Why? *Saturday Review of Literature*, 12 May: 7–8, 30–1.
Berger, Arthur Asa. 1992. *Popular Culture Genres*. Newbury Park, CA: Sage.
Biden, Joseph R. 1993. Combating Violence in America. Speech to the Rotary Club, Wilmington, Delaware 16 December. Printed in *Vital Speeches of the Day*, 1994.
Birch, M.J. 1987. The Popular Fiction Industry: Market, Formula, Ideology. *Journal of Popular Culture* 21: 79–102.
Blaha, F. G. 1996. Dashiell Hammett. *Beacham's Encyclopedia of Popular Fiction*, *Vol. V*. Ed. Kirk H. Beetz. Osprey, FL: Beacham's Publishing. 800–04.
Bleikasten, Andre. 1985. Terror and Nausea: Bodies in *Sanctuary*. *The Faulkner Journal* 1: 17–29.
Bloom, Allan. 1987. *The Closing of the American Mind*. New York: Simon and Schuster.
Bloom, Clive. 1996. *Cult Fiction: Popular Reading and Pulp Theory*. New York: St Martin's.
Bloom, Clive. 2002. *Bestsellers: Popular Fiction Since 1900*. Basingstoke: Palgrave.
Bloom, Harold. 2000. Can 35 Million Book Buyers be Wrong? Yes. *The Wall Street Journal* 11 July: A26.
Bloom, Harold. 2000. *How to Read and Why?* New York: Scribner.
Blotner, Joseph. 1964. *William Faulkner's Library: A Catalog*. Charlottesville: University Press of Virginia.
Blotner, Joseph. 1991. *Faulkner: A Biography*. New York: Vintage.
Blotner, Joseph. 1993. Editor's Note. In Faulkner, William. *Sanctuary (The Corrected Text)*. New York: Vintage.
Blotner, William. 1977. *Selected Letters of William Faulkner*. New York: Random.
Boas, George. 1940. The Mona Lisa in the History of Taste. *Journal of the History of Ideas Vol. I.* 2: 207–24.
Bonn, Thomas L. 1989. *Heavy Traffic and High Culture: New American Library as Literary Gatekeeper in the Paperback Revolution*. Carbondale: Southern Illinois University Press.
BookBrowse. 2000. An interview with Nelson DeMille. https://www.bookbrowse.com/author_interviews/full/index.cfm/author_number/228/nelson-demille.
Booker, Christopher. 2004. *The Seven Basic Plots: Why We Tell Stories*. New York: Continuum.
Bourdieu, Pierre. 1984. *Distinction: A Social Critique of the Judgment of Taste*. Cambridge: Harvard University Press.
Bourdieu, Pierre. 1986. The Aristocracy of Culture. In *Media, Culture and Society: A Critical Reader*, ed. Richard E. Collins, James Curran, Nicholas Garnham, Paddy Scannell, Philip Schlesinger, and Colin Sparks, 225–54. Beverly Hills: Sage.

Boyle, Thomas. 1988. *Black Swine in the Sewers of Hampstead: Beneath the Surface of Victorian Sensationalism*. New York: Viking.

Brandt, Deborah. 2001. *Literacy in American Lives*. Cambridge: Cambridge University Press.

Brantley, Ben. 2010. Hath Not a Year Highlights? Even This One?. *The New York Times* 16 December. http://www.nytimes.com/2010/12/19/theater/19brantley.html.

Brantlinger, Patrick. 1983. *Bread and Circuses: Theories of Mass Culture as Social Decay*. Ithaca: Cornell University Press.

Breu, Christopher. 2005. *Hard-Boiled Masculinities*. Minneapolis: University of Minnesota Press.

Brewer, Gay. 1995. Raymond Chandler without His Knight: Contracting Worlds in *The Blue Dahlia* and *Playback*. *Literature and Film Quarterly* 23(4): 273–8.

Briggs, Julia. 1977. *Night Visitors: The Rise and Fall of the English Ghost Story*. London: Faber.

Brogan, D.W. 1954. The Problem of High Culture and Mass Culture. *Diogenes* 5: 1–13.

Brooks, Cleanth. 1963a. Faulkner's *Sanctuary*: The Discovery of Evil. *Sewanee Review* 71: 1–24.

Brooks, Cleanth. 1963b. *William Faulkner: The Yoknapatawpha Country*. Yale University Press: Princeton.

Brooks, Cleanth. 1978. *William Faulkner: Toward Yoknapatawpha and Beyond*. Baton Rouge: Louisiana State University Press.

Brooks, Van Wyck. 1915. Highbrow and Lowbrow. *The Forum* April: 481–492.

Brown, Erica, and Mary Grover. 2011. *Middlebrow Literary Cultures: The Battle of the Brows, 1920–1960*. Basingstoke; New York: Palgrave Macmillan.

Browne, Ray B. 1981. Up from Elitism: The Aesthetics of Popular Fiction. *Studies in American Fiction* 9: 217–31.

Browne, Ray B. 1989. *Against Academia: The History of the Popular Culture Association/American Culture Association and the Popular Culture Movement, 1967–88*. Bowling Green: Popular Press.

Browne, Ray B. 1994. *Eye on the Future: Popular Culture Scholarship into the Twenty-First Century*. Bowling Green: Popular Press.

Bruccoli, Matthew J. 1976. Raymond Chandler and Hollywood. In Raymond Chandler, *The Blue Dahlia*. Carbondale, IL: Southern Illinois University Press.

Bruccoli, Matthew J., and Richard Layman (eds.). 2002. *Hardboiled Mystery Writers: Raymond Chandler, Dashiell Hammett, Ross Macdonald*. New York: Carroll and Graf.

Bruccoli, Matthew J. 2002. *Some Sort of Epic Grandeur*. Columbia, SC: South Carolina University Press.

Bunzel, Ruth. 1929. *The Pueblo Potter: A Study of Creative Imagination in Primitive Art*. New York: Columbia University Press.

Calinescu, Matei. 1976. The Benevolent Monster: Reflections on 'Kitsch' as an Aesthetic Concept. *Clio* 6(Fall): 3–21.

Camus, Albert. 1968. *Lyrical and Critical Essays*. New York: Knopf.

Canfield, John Douglas (ed.). 1982. *Twentieth Century Interpretations of Sanctuary: A Collection of Critical Essays*. Englewood Cliffs: Prentice-Hall.

Cantwell, Robert. 1958. Faulkner's Popeye. *Nation* 186: 140–1.

Čapek, Karel. 1951a. Holmesiana, or About Detective Stories. In *Praise of Newspapers, and Other Essays on the Margin of Literature*, 101–122. London, G. Allen.

Čapek, Karel. 1951b. Proletarian Art. In *Praise of Newspapers, and Other Essays on the Margin of Literature*, 123–32. London: G. Allen.

Čapek, Karel. 1951c. *In Praise of Newspapers, and Other Essays on the Margin of Literature*. London: G. Allen.

Čapek, Karel. 1994. In *Tales from Two Pockets*, ed. Norma Comrada. North Haven, CT: Catbird Press.

Čapek, Karel. 2002. *Wayside Crosses*. In English *Cross Roads*. Trans. Norma Comrada. Highland Park: Catbird Press.

Carey, John. 1990. Revolted by the Masses. *Times Literary Supplement*, 12–8 January: 34, 44–5.

Carr, John C. 1983. *The Craft of Crime: Conversations with Crime Writers*. Boston: Houghton Mifflin.

Carroll, Joseph. 2004. *Literary Darwinism: Evolution, Human Nature, and Literature*. New York: Routledge.

Carroll, Joseph. 2011. *Reading Human Nature: Literary Darwinism in Theory and Practice*. New York: SUNY Press.

Carroll, Nöel. 1992a. Mass Art, High Art, and the Avant-Garde: A Response to David Novitz. *Philosophic Exchange* 23: 51–62.

Carroll, Nöel. 1992b. The Nature of Mass Art. *Philosophic Exchange* 23: 5–37.

Cassuto, Leonard. 2008. *Hard-Boiled Sentimentality: The Secret History of American Crime Stories*. New York: Columbia University Press.

Cawelti, John. 1970. *The Six-Gun Mystique*. Bowling Green: Popular Press.

Cawelti, John. 1976. *Adventure, Mystery and Romance: Formula Stories as Art and Popular Culture*. Chicago: University of Chicago Press.

Chabon, Michel. 2008. *Maps and Legends: Reading and Writing along the Borderlands*. San Francisco: McSweeney's Books.

Chandler, Raymond, and Robert Parker. 1989. *Poodle Springs*. New York: Berkley Books.

Chandler, Raymond. 1971. Raymond Chandler Introduces *The Simple Art of Murder*. In *The Midnight Raymond Chandler*. Boston: Houghton Mifflin.

Chandler, Raymond. 1972. Introduction. In *Trouble Is My Business*. New York: Ballentine.

Chandler, Raymond. 1985. *Raymond Chandler's Unknown Thriller: The Screenplay of Playback*. New York: Mysterious Press.

Chandler, Raymond. 1995a. *Later Novels and Other Writings*. New York: Library of America.

Chandler, Raymond. 1995b. *Stories and Early Novels*. New York: Library of America.

Chandler, Raymond. 2000. In *The Raymond Chandler Papers: Selected Letters and Nonfiction, 1909–1959*, ed. Tom Honey and Frank MacShane. New York: Atlantic Monthly Press.

CNN. 1999. Grisham Ranks as Top-Selling Author of Decade. 31 December. *CNN.com Book News*. http://www.cnn.com/1999/books/news/12/31/1990.sellers/

Cohen, Philip. 1988. 'A Cheap Idea... Deliberately Conceived to Make Money': The Biographical Context of William Faulkner's Introduction to *Sanctuary*. *The Faulkner Journal* 3: 54–66.

Collins, Carvel. 1951. A Note on *Sanctuary*. *Harvard Advocate* 135: 16.

Collins, Jim. 2010. *Bring On the Books for Everybody: How Literary Culture Became Popular Culture*. Durham, NJ: Duke University Press.

Cominsky, Paul, and Jennings Bryant. 1982. Factors Involved in Generating Suspense. *Human Communications Research* 9(Fall): 49–58.

Conrad, Peter. 1978. The Private Dick as Dandy. *Times Literary Supplement*, 20 January: 60.

Conroy, Mark. 2004. *Muse in the Machine: American Fiction and Mass Publicity*. Columbus: Ohio State University Press.

Cox, Dianne Luce. 1986. A Measure of Innocence: *Sanctuary*'s Temple Drake. *Mississippi Quarterly* 39: 301–24.

Crawford, Robert. 2015. *Young Eliot: From St Louis to the Waste Land*. New York: Farrar, Straus, and Giroux.

Creighton, Joanne. 1977. *William Faulkner's Craft of Revision: The Snopes Trilogy, the Unvanquished and Go Down Moses*. Detroit: Wayne State University Press.

Dainotto, Roberto. 2015. *The Mafia: A Cultural History*. London: Reaktion.

Dalziel, Margaret. 1957. *Popular Fiction 100 Years Ago: An Unexplored Tract of Literary History*. London: Cohen and West.

Davidson, Cathy N. 1989. *Reading in America: Literature & Social History*. Baltimore: Johns Hopkins University Press.

Davies, Stephen. 1991. *Definitions of Art*. Ithaca, NY: Cornell.

Davis, Kenneth C. 1984. *Two-Bit Culture: The Paperbacking of America*. Boston: Houghton Mifflin.

Davis, Lennard. 1983. *Factual Fictions: The Origins of the English Novel*. New York: Columbia University Press.

Davis, Mike. 1999. *The Ecology of Fear: Los Angeles and the Imagination of Disaster.* New York: Vintage.

Delamater, Jerome H., and Ruth Prigozy. 1998. *The Detective in American Fiction, Film and Television.* Westport, CT: Greenwood.

DeMille, Nelson. 1990. *Gold Coast.* New York: Grand Central.

DeMille, Nelson. 1997. *Plum Island.* New York: Warner.

DeMille, Nelson. 2008. *The Gate House.* New York: Grand Central.

DeMille, Nelson. 2012. *The Panther.* New York: Grand Central.

Dennis, Everette E., Edward C. Pease, and Craig LaMay (eds.). 1997. *Publishing Books.* New Brunswick and London: Transaction Publishers.

Deresiewicz, William. 2012. Upper Middle Brow: The Culture of the Creative Class. *The American Scholar.* http://theamericanscholar.org/upper-middle-brow/#.UUkcp6Xavlo.

DeShong, Scott. 1995. Toward an Ethics of Reading Faulkner's *Sanctuary. Journal of Narrative Technique* 25: 238–57.

Dessauer, John P. 1974. Some Hard Facts about the Economics of Publishing. *Publishers Weekly,* 5 August: 22–5.

Dessauer, John P. 1999. *Book Publishing: The Basic Introduction. New Expanded Edition.* New York: Continuum.

Dettmar, Kevin J.H., and Stephen Watt. 1999. *Marketing Modernism: Self-Promotion, Canonization, Rereading.* Ann Arbor: The University of Michigan Press.

Dexter, Colin. 1999. *The Remorseful Day.* London: Pan

Diamond, Jared. 2005. *Collapse: How Societies Choose to Fail or Succeed.* London: Penguin.

Doherty, Thomas. 1988. Toward—and Away from—an Aesthetic of Popular Culture. *Journal of Aesthetic Education* 22(Winter): 31–43.

Donaldson, Scot. 1978. *By Force of Will: The Life and Art of Ernest Hemingway.* New York: Viking.

Donaldson, Scot. 2009. *Fitzgerald and Hemingway: Works and Days.* New York: Columbia University Press.

Dorfles, Gillo. 1969. *Kitsch: The World of Bad Taste.* New York: Universe Books.

Dorinson, Zahava K. 1977. Ross Macdonald: The Personal Paradigm and Popular Fiction. *Armchair Detective* 10(43–5): 87.

Dostoevsky, Fyodor. 1979. *Polnoe sobranie sochinenia,* vol. 19. Leningrad: Nauka.

Dove, George. 1974–75). The Complex Art of Raymond Chandler. *Armchair Detective* 8: 271–4.

Dove, George. 1989. *Suspense in the Formula Story.* Bowling Green: Popular Press.

Driscoll, Beth. 2014. *The New Literary Middlebrow.* New York: Palgrave Macmillan.

Druce, Robert. 1982. An Appetite for Vulgarity: *Jaws* and the Blockbuster Complex: The 'Bestseller' Business. *Dutch Quarterly Review of Anglo-American Letters* 12: 236–43.

Dubrow, Helen. 1982. *Genre*. London: Methuen.

Dunbar-Odom, Donna. 2007. *Defying the Odds: Class and the Pursuit of Higher Literacy*. Albany: State University of New York Press.

Dunleavy, Linda. 1996. *Sanctuary*, Sexual Difference, and the Problem of Rape. *Studies in American Fiction* 24: 171–91.

Dunlop, M.H. 1991. *Practicing Textual Theory and Teaching Formula Fiction*. Urbana: Council of Teachers of English.

Durham, Philip. 1963. *Down These Mean Streets a Man Must Go: Raymond Chandler's Knight*. Chapel Hill: University of North Carolina Press.

Dutscher, Alan. 1954. The Book Business in America. *Contemporary Issues* 5 April–May: 38–58.

Dutton, Denis. 2009. *The Art Instinct: Beauty, Pleasure, and Human Evolution*. New York: Bloomsbury.

Dyer, Richard. 1990. Suspense, Surprise and Irony in 'The Gold Coast.' *The Boston Globe* 20 June: 49.

Eco, Umberto. 1994. *Apocalypse Postponed*. Ed. Robert Lumley. Bloomington: Indiana University Press.

Eisner, Will. 1991. *Comics and Sequential Art*. Tamarac, FL: Poorhouse Press.

Eliot, T.S. 1949. *Notes Toward the Definition of Culture*. New York: Harcourt, Brace.

Eliot, T.S. 1950. Religion and Literature. In *Selected Essays*, 300. New York: Harcourt. (Orig. 1936).

Ellstrom, Karen Aubrey. 1988. Faulkner's Closing of the Doors in *Sanctuary*. *Notes on Mississippi Writers* 20: 63–73.

Engel, Howard. 2001. *Crimes of Passion: An Unblinking Look at Murderous Love*. Toronto: Key Porter Books.

English, James F., and John Frow. 2006. Literary Authorship and Celebrity Culture. In *A Concise Companion to Contemporary British Fiction*, ed. James F. English, 39–57. Oxford: Blackwell.

Enron. 2003. Official Website. 6 Apr. http://www.enron.com.

Escarpit, Robert. 1982. *Trends in Worldwide Book Development 1970–78*. New York: UNESCO.

Ewen, Stuart. 1976. *Captains of Consciousness: Advertising and the Social Roots of the Consumer Culture*. New York: McGraw-Hill.

Faulkner, William. 1932. *Introduction. Sanctuary*. New York: Modern Library.

Faulkner, William. 1950. *A Requiem for a Nun*. New York: Random House.

Faulkner, William. 1981. *Sanctuary: The Original Text*. Ed. Noel Polk. New York: Random.

Faulkner, William. 1993. *Sanctuary (The Corrected Text)*. New York: Vintage.

Fiedler, Leslie A. 1966. *Love and Death in the American Novel.* New York: Stein and Day.

Fiedler, Leslie A. 1979. *The Inadvertent Epic: From Uncle Tom's Cabin to Roots.* Toronto: Canadian Broadcasting Corporation.

Fiedler, Leslie A. 1982. *What Was Literature? Class Culture and Mass Society.* New York: Simon and Schuster.

Fiedler, Leslie. 1990. Pop Goes the Faulkner. In Doreen Fowler and Ann J. Abadie, ed. Quest of *Sanctuary. Faulkner and Popular Culture.* Jackson: Mississippi University Press. 75–92.

Fine, David (ed.). 1995. *Los Angeles in Fiction.* Albuquerque: U of New Mexico Press.

Finn, Robin. 2009. In His Home, a Reflection of His Career as a Novelist. *The New York Times* 11 January: LI1.

Fiske, John. 1987. *Television Culture.* London: Methuen.

Fitzgerald, F. Scott. 1995. *The Great Gatsby: The Authorized Text.* With notes and a preface by Matthew J. Bruccoli. New York: Scribner

Flynn, James R. 2010. *The Torchlight List: Around the World in 200 Books.* New Zealand: Awa Press.

Foreshaw, Barry. 2012. *Death in a Cold Climate: A Guide to Scandinavian Crime Fiction.* New York: Palgrave Macmillan.

Forter, Gregory. 1996. Faulkner's Black Holes: Vision and Vomit in *Sanctuary. Mississippi Quarterly* 49: 537–62.

Fowler, Alastair. 1982. *Kinds of Literature.* Cambridge, MA: Harvard University Press.

Fowler, Christopher. 2013. Invisible Ink: No 160—Ronald Knox. *The Independent* 17 February. http://www.independent.co.uk/arts-entertainment/books/features/invisible-ink-no-160--ronald-knox-8497999.html.

Frazier, David L. 1995. Gothicism in *Sanctuary*: The Black Pall and the Crap Table. In *Douze lectures de* Sanctuaire, ed. Andre Bleikasten and Nicole Moulinoux, 13–22. Rennes: Presses Universitaires de Rennes.

Freeman, Judith. 2008. *The Long Embrace: Raymond Chandler and the Woman He Loved.* New York: Vintage.

Friedman, Lawrence M. 2005. *A History of American Law.* New York: Touchstone.

Frow, John. 1995. *Cultural Studies and Cultural Value.* Oxford: Clarendon Press.

Frow, John. 2006. *Genre.* London, New York: Routledge.

Fruscione, Joseph. 2012. *Faulkner and Hemingway: Biography of a Literary Rivalry.* Columbus: Ohio State University Press.

Frye, Northrop. 1976. *The Secular Scripture: A Study of the Structure of Romance.* Cambridge: Harvard University Press.

Fulcher, James. 1983. American Conspiracy: Formula in Popular Fiction. *Midwest Quarterly* 24: 152–64.

Gans, Herbert J. 1974. *Popular Culture and High Culture: An Analysis and Evaluation of Taste*. New York: Basic Books.

Gardiner, Dorothy, and Kathrine Sorley Walker, eds. 1997. *Raymond Chandler Speaking*. Berkeley: University of California Press. (Orig. 1962).

Geherin, David. 1985. *The American Private Eye: The Image in Fiction*. New York: Ungar.

Gelder, Ken. 2004. *Popular Fiction: The Logics and Practices of a Literary Field*. New York, London: Routledge.

Glover, David. 1996. *Vampires, Mummies and Liberals: Bram Stoker and the Politics of Popular Fiction*. Durham, NC: Duke University Press.

Grant, Percy Stickney. 1901. Are the Rich Responsible for New York's Vice and Crime? *Everybody's Magazine* 5(27): 555–60.

Greenberg, Clement. 1969. *Art and Culture*. Boston: Beacon.

Greenberg, Clement. 1986. In *Clement Greenberg: The Collected Essays and Criticism*, ed. John O'Brian. Chicago: University of Chicago Press.

Greenwood, Alice. 1983. Language Stereotypes in Mass Market Romances. *Cunyforum: Papers in Linguistics* 9: 157–73.

Grisham, John. 1995. *The Rainmaker*. New York: Dell.

Gross, Miriam (ed.). 1978. *The World of Raymond Chandler*. New York: A and W Publishers.

Guerard, Albert J. 1976. The Misogynous Vision as High Art: Faulkner's *Sanctuary*. *Southern Review* 12: 215–31.

Gulledge, Jo. 1985. The Reentry Option: An Interview with Walker Percy. In *Conversations with Walker Percy*, ed. Lewis A. Lawson and Victor A. Kramer, 284–308. University Press of Mississippi: Jackson.

Habash, Gabe. 2012. How Much Does the Times Book Review Matter? *Publishers Weekly*, 9 July: 8–9. http://www.publisherweekly.com/pw/by-topic/industry-news/bookselling/article/52907-how-much-does-the-times-book-review-matter.html.

Habermehl, Lawrence. 1995. *The Counterfeit Wisdom of Shallow Minds: A Critique of Some Leading Offenders of the 1980's*. New York: Lang.

Hahn Rafter, Nicole. 2000. *Encyclopedia of Women and Crime*. Phoenix: Oryx Press.

Hamblin, Robert W., and Charles A. Peek (eds.). 1999. *A William Faulkner Encyclopedia*. Westport, CT: Greenwood Press.

Hammett, Dashiell. 1985. Bodies Piled Up. In *The Black Mask Boys: Masters in the Hard-Boiled School of Detective Fiction*, ed. William F. Nolan. New York: William Morrow. (Orig. 1923).

Hammett, Dashiell. 1992. *Red Harvest*. New York: Vintage Crime/Black Lizard. (Orig. 1929).

Hammett, Dashiell. 2001. *Selected Letters*. Ed. Layman, Richard, with Jullie M. Rivett. Washington, DC: Counterpoint.

Hammill, Faye. 2010. *Sophistication: A Literary and Cultural History.* Liverpool: Liverpool University Press.

Hawkins, Harriett. 1990. *Classics and Trash: Traditions and Taboos in High Literature and Popular Modern Genres.* Toronto: University of Toronto Press.

Hayes, Michael. 1993. *Popular Fiction and Middle-Brow Taste.* London: Longman.

Hayward, Keith J., and Mike Presdee (eds.). 2010. *Framing Crime: Cultural Criminology and the Image.* London: Routledge.

Hefferman, Nick. 1997. Law Crimes: The Legal Fictions of John Grisham and Scott Turow. *Criminal Proceedings: The Contemporary American Crime Novel.* Ed. Peter Messent. Chicago: Pluto Press.

Heise, Thomas. 2011. *Urban Underworlds: A Geography of Twentieth-Century of American Literature.* Piscataway, NJ: Rutgers University Press.

Heller, Terry. 1984. Terror and Empathy in Faulkner's *Sanctuary.* *Arizona Quarterly* 40: 344–64.

Heller, Terry. 1989. Mirrored Worlds and the Gothic in Faulkner's *Sanctuary.* *Mississippi Quarterly* 42: 247–59.

Hemingway, Ernest. 1994. *To Have and Have Not.* London: Arrow. Orig. 1937.

Henderson, Gerard. 2011. Literary Festivals and Prizes Champion Politics over Quality. *Sydney Morning Herald.* 30 August. http://ww.smh.com.au/federal-politics/political-opinion/literary-festival-and-prizes-champion-politics-over-quality-20110829-1jicf.html.

Herald, Diana Tixier. 1995. *Genreflecting: A Guide to Reading Interests in Genre Fiction.* Englewood, CO: Librarians Unlimited.

Herbert, David T., and Colin J. Thomas. 1990. *Cities in Space: City as Place.* London: David Fulton.

Hernadi, Paul (ed.). 1972. *Beyond Genre.* Ithaca: Cornell.

Hernadi, Paul. 1978. *What Is Literature.* Bloomington: Indiana University Press.

Highet, Gilbert. 1954. Kitsch. In *A Clerk of Oxenford.* New York: Oxford University Press.

Hiney, Tom. 1997. *Raymond Chandler: A Biography.* New York: Atlantic Monthly Press.

Hirsh, E.D. 1978. What Isn't Literature. In *What Is Literature*, ed. Paul Hernadi, 24–34. Bloomington, IN: Indiana University Press.

Hoffman, Frederick J., and Olga Vickery (eds.). 1960. *William Faulkner: Three Decades of Criticism.* East Lansing: Michigan State University Press.

Holden, Jonathan. 1979. The Case for Raymond Chandler's Fiction as Romance. *Kansas Quarterly* 10: 41–7.

Hoover, J. Edgar. 1965. *Crime in the United States: the Uniform Crime Report—1963.* Boston: Beacon.

Horkheimer, Max, and T.W. Adorno. 1990. *Dialectic of Enlightenment.* New York: Continuum. (Orig. 1947).

Horsley, Lee. 2001. *The Noir Thriller.* Houndmills: Palgrave Macmillan.

Horsley, Lee. 2005. *Twentieth-Century Crime Fiction*. Oxford: Oxford University Press.

Hotchner, A.E. 2005. *Hemingway: A Personal Memoir*. Cambridge, MA: Da Capo Press.

Hubin, Allen J. 1994. *Crime Fiction II: A Comprehensive Bibliography 1749–1900*. New York, London: Garland.

Hughes, Winifred. 1980. *The Maniac in the Cellar*. Princeton: Princeton University Press.

Humble, Nicola. 2001. *Te Feminine Middlebrow Novel, 1920s to 1950s: Class, Domesticity and Bohemianism*. Oxford: Oxford University Press.

Humm, Peter, Paul Stigant, and Peter Widdowson. 1986. *Popular Fictions: Essays in Literature and History*. London, New York: Methuen.

Hunt, Jennifer C. 2000. Police Subculture and Gender. In *Encyclopedia of Women and Crime*, ed. Hahn Rafter, Nicole. Phoenix: Oryx Press.

Hunter, Evan, and Ed McBain. 2001. *Candyland: A Novel in Two Parts*. New York: Simon and Schuster.

Hunter, Evan. 1974. *Streets of Gold*. New York: Harper and Row.

Hunter, J. Paul. 1990. *Before Novels: The Cultural Contexts of Eighteenth Century English Fiction*. New York: Norton.

Hurd, Myles. 1980. Faulkner's Horace Benbow: The Burden of Characterization and the Confusion of Meaning in *Sanctuary*. *CLA Journal* 23: 416–30.

Huyssen, Andreas. 1986. *After the Great Divide; Modernism, Mass Culture, Postmodernism*. Bloomington: Indiana University Press.

International Publishers Association. 2001. Annual Book Title Production. *International Publishers Association*, 10 April. http://www.ipa-uie.org.

Jacobson, Marcia. 1976. Popular Fiction and Henry James's Unpopular Bostonians. *Modern Philology* 73: 264–75.

Jacoby, Susan. 2008. *The Age of American Unreason*. New York: Pantheon.

Jameson, Fredric. 1970. On Raymond Chandler. *Southern Review* 6, 3 July: 624–50.

Jensen, Margaret Ann. 1984. *Love's Sweet Return: The Harlequin Story*. Bowling Green: Popular Press.

John Grisham: The Official Website. 2014. Bio. http://www.jgrisham.com/bio/.

Johnson, Diane. 1983. *Dashiell Hammett: A Life*. New York: Random House.

Johnston, David Cay. 2006. Corporate Wealth Share Rises for Top-Income Americans. *New York Times*, 29 Jan.: 1:22.

Jones, Anne Goodwyn. 1985. *Gone with the Wind and Others: Popular Fiction, 1920–50*. Baton Rouge: Louisiana State University Press.

Jones, Malcolm. 1999. Grisham's Gospel. *Newsweek* 15 February: 65–68.

Kahneman, Daniel, and Amos Tversky. 1996. Choices, Values, and Frames. *American Psychologist* 39: 341–50.

Kahneman, Daniel, and Amos Tversky. 2000. *Choices, Values, and Frames*. New York: Russell Sage Foundation; Cambridge, UK: Cambridge University Press.

Kahneman, Daniel, Paul Slovic, and Amos Tversky. 1982. *Judgment Under Uncertainty: Heuristics and Biases*. New York: Cambridge University Press.
Kahneman, Daniel. 1992. Reference Points, Anchors, Norms, and Mixed Feelings. *Organizational Behavior and Human Decision Process* 51: 296–312.
Kaplan, Abraham. 1966. The Aesthetics of the Popular Arts. *Journal of Aesthetics and Art Criticism* 24(Spring): 351–64.
Katz, Bill. 1995. *Dahl's History of the Book*. Metuchen and London: Scarecrow.
Kaye, Howard. 1975. Raymond Chandler's Sentimental Novel. *Western American Literature* 10: 135–45.
Keefer, T. Frederick. 1969. William Faulkner's *Sanctuary*: A Myth Examined. *Twentieth Century Literature* 15: 97–104.
Kerr, Elizabeth M. 1980. The Creative Evolution of *Sanctuary*. *Faulkner Studies: An Annual of Research, Criticism, & Reviews* 1: 14–28.
Kipling, Rudyard. 1930. *American Notes*. London, New York: Standard Book Company. (Orig. 1891).
Knight, Stephen. 1980. 'A Hard-Boiled Gentleman': Raymond Chandler's Hero. In *Form and Ideology in Crime Fiction*. Bloomington: Indiana University Press.
Knight, Stephen. 2010. *Crime Fiction since 1800: Detection, Death, Diversity*. New York: Palgrave Macmillan.
Knights, Pamela E. 1989. The Cost of Single-Mindedness: Consciousness in *Sanctuary*. *The Faulkner Journal* 5: 3–10.
Knoepflmacher, U.C. 1975. The Woman in White. In *Worlds of Victorian Fiction*, ed. Jerome H. Buckley, 351–70. Cambridge, MA: Harvard University Press.
Kronenberger, Louis. 1937. To Have and Have Not. *Nation* 145: 439–40.
Krystal, Arthur. 2012. Easy Writers: Guilty pleasures without guilt. *The New Yorker* 28 May. http://www.newyorker.com/magazine/2012/05/28/easy-writers
Kubie, Lawrence S. 1982. William Faulkner's *Sanctuary*: An Analysis. In *Twentieth Century Interpretations of* Sanctuary: *A Collection of Critical Essays*, ed. John Douglas Canfield, 25–31. Englewood Cliffs: Prentice-Hall.
Kurian, George Thomas (ed.). 2000. *Datapedia of the United States 1790–2005: America Year by Year*. Lanham, MD: Bernan Associates.
Lakoff, George, and Mark Turner. 1989. *More than Cool Reason: A Field Guide to Poetic Metaphor*. Chicago: University of Chicago Press.
LaLonde, Chris. 1996. 'In Other Words': Language, Indentity, and Ideology in William Faulkner's *Sanctuary*. *Chiba Review* 18: 24–42.
Lassner, Phyllis. 2011. Testing the Limits of the Middlebrow: The Holocaust for the Masses. *Modernist Cultures* 6(1): 178–95.
Law, Graham. 1988. 'Il s'agissait peut-etre d'un roman policier': Leblanc, Macdonald, and Robbe-Grillet. *Comparative Literature* 40(Fall): 335–57.
Leavis, F.R. 1930. *Mass Civilisation and Minority Culture*. Cambridge, UK: Minority Press.

Lehuu, Isabelle. 2000. *Carnival on the Page: Popular Print Media in Antebellum America*. Chapel Hill, NC: University of North Carolina Press.

Leopold, Todd. 2012. Famed Quotation Isn't Dead—and Could Even Prove Costly. *CNN* 111 November. http://edition.cnn.com/2012/11/06/showbiz/movies/faulkner-midnight-paris-allen-lawsuit/.

Leovy, Jill. 2015. *Ghettoside: A True Story of Murder in America*. New York: Spiegel and Grau.

Levin, Harry. 1937. To Have and Have Not. *Nation* 20 October: 482–3.

Levine, Lawrence. 1990a. *Highbrow/Lowbrow: The Emergence of Cultural Hierarchy in America*. Cambridge: Harvard University Press.

Levine, Michael. 1990b. *Deep Cover*. New York: Dell.

Liukkonen, Petri. 2000. Maj Sjöwall (1935-). http://web.archive.org/web/20140415211352/http://www.kirjasto.sci.fi/sjowall.htm.

Loewy, Raymond F. 2006. Quotes. http://www.epodunk.com/quotes/ny1.html.

Logan, Andy. 1970. *Against the Evidence: The Becker-Rosenthal Affair*. New York: McCall.

Lowenthal, Leo, and Marjorie Fiske. 1957. The Debate over Art and Popular Culture in Eighteenth-Century England. In *Common Frontiers of the Social Sciences*, ed. Mirra Komarovsky, 33–96. Glencoe: Free Press.

Lowenthal, Leo. 1961. *Literature, Popular Culture, and Society*. Englewood Cliffs, NJ: Prentice Hall.

Luhr, William. 1982. *Raymond Chandler and Film*. New York: Ungar.

Lyday, Lance. 1982. *Sanctuary:* Faulkner's Inferno. *Mississippi Quarterly* 35: 243–53.

Lynes, Russell. 1954. *The Taste-Makers*. New York: Harper and Brothers.

Lynes, Russell. 1976. Highbrow, Lowbrow, Middlebrow. *Wilson Quarterly* 1(1): 146–58.

Lynn, Kenneth Schuyler. 1987. *Hemingway*. Cambridge, MA: Harvard University Press.

Macdonald, Dwight. 1953. A Theory of Mass Culture. *Diogenes* 3(Summer): 1–17.

Macdonald, Dwight. 1962. *Against the Grain: Essays on the Effects of Mass Culture*. New York: Vintage Books.

Macdonald, Dwight. 1974. *Discriminations: Essays and Afterthoughts, 1938–74*. New York: Grossman.

MacInnes, Colin. 1971. Honor Thy Father. *The New York Times*. 31 October: BR2.

MacLeish, Archibald. 1961. His Mirror Was Danger. *Life* 14 July: 71–72.

MacRone, Michael, and Tom Lulevitch (illustrator). 1997. *Naughty Shakespeare: The Lascivious Lines, Offensive Oaths, and Politically Incorrect Notions from the Baddest Bard of Them All*. New York: Cader Books; Kansas City: Andrews and McMeel.

MacShane, Frank. 1976. *The Life of Raymond Chandler.* New York: Dutton.

MacShane, Frank. 1986. *The Selected Letters of Raymond Chandler.* New York: Columbia University Press.

Madden, David. 1973. The Necessity for an Aesthetics of Popular Culture. *Journal of Popular Culture* 7(Summer): 1–13.

Mailloux, Steven. 1982. *Interpretive Conventions.* Ithaca: Cornell University Press.

Malamud, Bernard. 1996. *Talking Horse. Bernard Malamud on Life and Work.* Ed. Alan Cheuse and Nicholas Delbanco. New York: Columbia University Press.

Maloney, Eddie, and William Hoffman. 1995. *Tough Guy.* New York: Pinnacle Books.

Malraux, André. 1933. Preface à *Sanctuaire de W. Faulkner. Nouvelle revue française* 1 November: 744–747.

Mangum, Tersa. 1998. *Married, Middlebrow, and Militant: Sarah Grand and the New Woman Novel.* Ann Arbor: University of Michigan Press.

Mardsen, Michael T. 1980. Television Viewing as Ritual. In *Rituals and Ceremonies in Popular Culture*, ed. Ray B. Browne. Bowling Green: Popular Press.

Margaret, Mary. 2011. John Grisham Reveals His Surprising Favorite Book. *Parade* 10 July. http://parade.condenast.com/94285/marymargaret/10-john-grisham/.

Margolies, Edward. 1982. *Which Way Did He Go? The Private Eye in Dashiell Hammett, Raymond Chandler, Chester Himes, and Ross Macdonald.* New York: Holmes and Meier.

Marling, William. 1983. *Raymond Chandler.* Boston: Twayne.

Marling, William. 1995. *The American Roman Noir: Hammett, Cain, and Chandler.* Athens: University of Georgia Press.

Marshall, William Leonard. 1976. *The Hatchet Man.* London: Hamish Hamilton.

Martindale, Colin. 1990. *The Clockwork Muse: The Predictability of Artistic Change.* New York: Basic.

Mason, Fran. 2002. *American Gangster Cinema: From "Little Caesar" to "Pulp Fiction".* New York: Palgrave Macmillan.

Mason, Fran. 2011. *Hollywood's Detectives: Crime Series in the 1930s and 1940s from the Whodunnit to Hard-boiled Noir.* New York: Palgrave Macmillan.

Mason, Robert L. 1967. A Defense of Faulkner's *Sanctuary. Georgia Review* 21. 430–8.

Matthews, John T. 1984. The Elliptical Nature of *Sanctuary. Novel–A Forum on Fiction* 17: 246–65.

McBain, Ed. 1992. *Kiss.* London: Mandarin.

McBain, Ed. 1996. *The Mugger.* New York: Warner, 1996. (Orig. 1956).

McBain, Ed. 1999. *Cop Hater.* New York: Warner (Orig. 1956).

McBain, Ed. 1999. *The Big Bad City.* New York: Pocket Books.

McBain, Ed. 2000. *The Last Dance.* New York: Pocket Books.

McBain, Ed. 2003. *Fat Ollie's Book*. New York: Pocket Books.

McBain, Ed. 2003. *Give the Boys a Great Big Hand*. New York: Pocket Books. (Orig. 1960).

McBain, Ed. 2003. *Killer's Payoff*. New York: Pocket Books. (Orig. 1958).

McBain, Ed. 2003. *Mischief*. New York: Pocket Books. (Orig. 1993).

McBain, Ed. 2003. *The Heckler*. New York: Pocket Books. (Orig. 1960).

McCaghy, Charles H. 1980. *Crime in American Society*. New York: Macmillan.

McCann, Sean. 2000. *Gumshoe America: Hard-Boiled Crime Fiction and the Rise and Fall of New Deal Liberalism*. Durham: Duke University Press.

Meisel, Perry. 2010. *The Myth of Popular Culture: From Dante to Dylan*. London: Wiley-Blackwell.

Meloy, Michelle L. 1981. Police Organizations, Municipal and State. In *Women and Crime*, eds. Satyanshu, K. Mukherjee, and Jocelynne A. Scutt. Sydney; Boston: Australian Institute of Technology, Allen & Unwin.

Menand, Louis. 2011. Browbeaten: Dwight Macdonald's War on Midcult. *The New Yorker*. http://www.newyorker.com/arts/critics/atlarge/2011/09/05/110905cart_atlarge_menand.

Meriwether, James B., and Micheal Millgate (eds.). 1968. *Lion in the Garden: Interviews with William Faulkner, 1926–1962*. New York: Random.

Meyers, Jeffrey. 1982. *Hemingway: The Critical Heritage*. London: Routledge and Kegal Paul.

Meyers, Jeffrey. 2013. *Scott Fitzgerald: A Biography*. New York: Harper Perennial.

Middleton, Christopher. 2010. Exclusive: Best-Selling Author John Grisham Explains Why He's Courting Children with His Latest Legal Thriller. *The Telegraph* 28 October. http://www.telegraph.co.uk/culture/books/authorinterviews/7770412/Exclusive-best-selling-author-John-Grisham-explains-why-hes-courting-children-with-his-latest-legal-thriller.html.

Millgate, Michael. 1991. Undue Process: William Faulkner's *Sanctuary*. *Rough Justice: Essays on Crime in Literature*. Ed. M.L. Friedland. Toronto: University of Toronto Press. 157–69.

Miner, Madonne M. 1984. *Insatiable Appetites: Twentieth-Century American Women's Bestsellers*. Westport, CT: Greenwood Press.

Minter, David. 1997. *William Faulkner: His Life and Work*. Baltimore: Johns Hopkins University Press.

Modleski, Tania. 1986. *Studies in Entertainment: Critical Approaches to Mass Culture*. Bloomington: Indiana University Press.

Monkkonen, Eric H. 1981. *Police in Urban America 1860–1920*. Cambridge: Cambridge University Press.

Mooney, William H. 2014. *Dashiell Hammett and the Movies*. New Brunswick: Rutgers University Press.

Moran. Joe. 2000. *Star Authors: Literary Celebrity in America*. London: Pluto Press.

Moreland, Richard C. 1990. *Faulkner and Modernism: Rereading and Rewriting.* Madison: University of Wisconsin Press.

Morson, Gary Saul. 1981. *The Boundaries of Genre.* Austin: University of Texas Press.

Mott, Frank Luther. 1947. *Golden Multitudes: The Story of Best Sellers in the United States.* New York: Macmillan.

Muhlenfeld, Elisabeth. 1986. Bewildered Witness: Temple Drake in *Sanctuary.* *The Faulkner Journal* 1: 43–55.

Mullen, Anne, and Emer O'Beirne, eds. 2000. *Crime Scenes: Detective Narratives in European Culture since 1945.* Amsterdam/Atlanta, GA: Editions Rodopi.

National Center for Health Statistics. 2004 Health, United States, 2004. http://www.cdc.gov/nchs/products/pubs/pubd/hus/metro.htm#healthcare.

Neale, Catherine. 1993. Desperate Remedies: The Merits and Demerits of Popular Fiction. *Critical Survey* 5: 117–22.

Nelson, Polly. 1994. *Defending the Devil.* New York: William Morrow and Co.

Nemoianu, Vergil, and Robert Royal. 1991. *The Hospitable Canon: Essays on Literary Play, Scholarly Choice, and Popular Pressures.* Philadelphia: J. Benjamins.

Nicola, Allen, and David Simmons (eds.). 2014. *Reassessing the Twentieth-Century Canon.* New York: Palgrave Macmillan.

Nishiyama, Tamotsu. 1966. What Really Happens in *Sanctuary? Studies in English Literature* 42: 235–43.

Novitz, David. 1992. Nöel Carroll's Theory of Mass Art. *Philosophic Exchange* 23: 39–49.

Nussbaum, Martha. 1991. The Literary Imagination of Public Life. *New Literary History* 22: 876–910.

Nye, Russell B. 1970. *The Unembarrassed Muse: The Popular Arts in America.* New York: Dial Press.

O'Brian, Geoffrey. 1981. *Hardboiled America: The Lurid Years of Paperbacks.* New York: Van Nostrand Reinhold.

O'Leary Morgan, Kathleen. 2013. *City Crime Rankings: Crime in Metropolitan America.* Washington: CQ Press.

Olcott, Anthony. 2002. *Russian Pulp: The "Detektiv" and the Way of Russian Crime.* New York: Rowman & Littlefield.

Oliker, Michael A., and Walter P. Królikowski (eds.). 2001. *Images of Youth: Popular Culture as Educational Ideology.* New York: Peter Lang.

Olsen, Stein Haugom. 2001. The Canon and Artistic Failure. *British Journal of Aesthetics* 41(3): 261–78.

Palmer, Jerry. 1991. *Potboilers: Methods, Concepts and Case Studies in Popular Fiction.* London: Routledge.

Panek, Leroy Lad. 1990. *Probable Cause: Crime Fiction in America.* Bowling Green, OH: Popular Press.

Panek, Leroy Lad. 2000. *New Hard-Boiled Writers 1970s–1990s*. Bowling Green, OH: Popular Press.

Parker, Robert B. 1985. Introduction to *Playback*. In *Unknown Thriller: The Screenplay of Playback*, ed. Raymond Chandler's, xi–xxi. New York: Mysterious Press.

Parker, Robert B. 1991. *Perchance to Dream*. New York: Berkley.

Partridge, Ralph. 1958. Detection and Thrillers. *The New Statesman and Nation*, 30 August: 254.

Pawling, Christopher (ed.). 1984. *Popular Fiction and Social Change*. New York: St Martin's.

People. 2000. Worst of Pages. 25 December: 46. http://www.people.com/people/archive/article/0,,20133298,00.html.

Percy, Walker. 1987. *The Thanatos Syndrome*. New York: Ivy Books.

Pérez-Reverte, Arturo. 1998. *The Club Dumas*. New York: Vintage. Trans. Sonia Soto.

Pettey, Homer B. 1987. Reading and Raping in *Sanctuary*. *The Faulkner Journal* 3: 71–84.

Philips, Chuck. 1993. Rap Defense Doesn't Stop Death Penalty. *Los Angeles Times* 15 July. http://www.latimes.com/local/la-me-tupactxverdict15jul1593-story.html#page=1.

Philips, Deborah, and Alan Tomlinson. 1992. *Homeward Bound: Leisure, Popular Culture and Consumer Capitalism*. London: Routledge.

Phy, Allene Stuart. 1985. *The Bible and American Popular Culture: An Overview and Introduction*. Philadelphia: Fortress Scholars.

Piper, Henry Dan. 1970. The Fuller-McGee Case. In *Fitzgerald's "The Great Gatsby"*. New York: Scribner's.

Plimpton, George. 1954. Ernest Hemingway, The Art of Fiction No. 21. *The Paris Review*. http://www.theparisreview.org/interviews/4825/the-art-of-fiction-no-21-ernest-hemingway.

Plunket, Robert. 2000. Jailhouse Crock. *Advocate* 28 Mar.: 89.

Polchin, James. 1996. Selling a Novel: Faulkner's *Sanctuary* as a Psychosexual Text. In *Faulkner and Gender: Faulkner and Yoknapatawpha, 1994*, ed. Donald M. Kartiganer and Ann J. Abadie, 145–59. Jackson: Mississippi University Press.

Polk, Noel. 1981. Afterword. In Faulkner, William. *Sanctuary: The Original Text*. Ed. Noel Polk. New York: Random.

Porter, Dennis. 1981. *The Pursuit of Crime: Art and Ideology in Detective Fiction*. New Haven: Yale University Press.

Posner, Richard. 1997. Against Ethical Criticism. *Philosophy and Literature* 21: 1–27.

Powell, Steven (ed.). 2012. *100 American Crime Writers*. New York: Palgrave Macmillan.

Pringle, Mary Beth. 1997. *John Grisham: A Critical Companion*. Connecticut: Greenwood.

Raab, Selwyn. 2000. Interview: Writing Under an Assumed Name. *New York Times* Jan. 30: section 7: 13.

Rabinowitz, Paula. 2014. *American Pulp: How Paperbacks Brought Modernism to Main Street*. Princeton: Princeton University Press.

Rabinowitz, Paula. 2002. *Black and White and Noir: America's Pulp Modernism*. New York: Columbia University Press.

Rabinowitz, Peter J. 1979. Rats behind the Wainscoting: Politics, Convention and Chandler: *The Big Sleep*. *Studies in American Literature* 7(2): 175–89.

Rabinowitz, Peter J. 1979. The Click of the Spring: The Detective Story as Parallel Structure in Dostoyevsky and Faulkner. *Modern Philology* 76 May: 355–69.

Rabinowitz, Peter J. 1985. The Turn of the Glass Key: Popular Fiction as Reading Strategy. *Critical Inquiry* 11 March: 418–31.

Radway, Janice A. 1984. *Reading the Romance: Women, Patriarchy, and Popular Literature*. Chapel Hill: University of North Carolina Press.

Radway, Janice A. 1997. *A Feeling for Books: The Book-of-the-Month Club, Literary Taste, and Middle-Class Desire*. Chapel Hill: University of North Carolina Press.

Rainey, Lawrence S. 1988. *The Institutions of Modernism: Literary Elites and Public Culture*. New Haven: Yale University Press.

Rampton, David. 2008. *William Faulkner: A Literary Life*. New York: Palgrave Macmillan.

Rasula, Jed. 1990. Nietzsche in the Nursery: Naive Classics and Surrogate Parents in Postwar American Cultural Debates. *Representations* 29(Winter): 50–77.

Raub, Patricia. 1994. *Yesterday's Stories: Popular Women's Fiction of the Twenties and Thirties*. Westport, CT: Greenwood.

Rayner, Richard. 2009. 'The Associate' by John Grisham. 23 January. http://articles.latimes.com/2009/jan/23/entertainment/et-book23.

Reck, Thomas. 1975. Raymond Chandler's Los Angeles. *The Nation* 20 December: 661–3.

Regier, C.C. 1932. *The Era of the Muckrakers*. Chapel Hill: University of North Carolina.

Reichs, Kathy. 2005. Kathy and John Discuss their Work. http://www.kathy-reichs.com/mybooks.htm. See also: http://www.fanforum.com/f218/kathy-reichs-appreciation-1-because-without-her-bones-would-never-exist-62762836/index3.html.

Restaino, Katherine M. 1998. Miller's Crossing: The Poetics of Dashiell Hammett. In *The Detective in American Fiction, Film, and Television*, ed. Jerome H. Delamater and Ruth Prigozy. Wesport, CT: Hofstra University Press.

Reynolds, Michel S. 1981. *Hemingway's Reading, 1910–1940: An Inventory*. Princeton: Princeton University Press.

Roberts, Diane. 1988. Ravished Belles: Stories of Rape and Resistance in *Flags in the Dust* and *Sanctuary. The Faulkner Journal* 4: 21–35.

Roberts, Thomas J. 1990. *An Aesthetics of Junk Fiction.* Athens: University of Georgia Press.

Roberts, Thomas J. 1993. Popular Fiction in the Old Dispensation and the New. *Literature: Literature Interpretation Theory* 4: 245–59.

Rooney, Kathleen. 2005. *Reading with Oprah: The Book Club That Changed America.* Fayetteville: University of Arkansas Press.

Rose, Suzanna. 1985. Is Romance Dysfunctional? *International Journal of Women's Studies* 8 May/June: 250–65.

Rosenberg, Bernard, and David Manning White (eds.). 1957. *Mass Culture: The Popular Arts in America.* Glencoe: Free Press.

Rosenberg, Bernard, and David Manning White (eds.). 1971. *Mass Culture Revisited.* New York: Van Nostrand Reinhold.

Rosenberg, Bernard. 1971. Mass Culture Revisited 1. In *Mass Culture Revisited,* eds. Bernard Rosenberg and David Manning White, 3–12. New York: Van Nostrand Reinhold

Rosmarin, Adena. 1985. *The Power of Genre.* Minneapolis: University of Minnesota Press.

Ross, Malcolm. 1984. *The Aesthetic Impulse.* New York: Pergamon.

Rossky, William. 1995. The Pattern of Nightmare in *Sanctuary:* Or, Miss Reba's Dogs. In *Douze lectures de* Sanctuaire, ed. Andre Bleikasten and Nicole Moulinoux, 23–34. Rennes: Presses Universitaires de Rennes.

Rubin, Joan Shelley. 1992. *The Making of Middlebrow Culture.* Chapel Hill: University of North Carolina Press.

Rubinstein, Jonathan. 1980. *City Police.* New York: Farrar, Straus, and Giroux.

Sarland, Charles. 1991. *Young People Reading: Culture and Response.* Philadelphia: Open University Press.

Saviano, Roberto. 2008. *Gomorrah: A Personal Journey into the Violent International Empire of Naples' Organized Crime System.* New York: Picador. Trans. Virginia Jewiss.

Schafer, William J. 1991. Faulkner's *Sanctuary:* The Blackness of Fairytale. *Durham University Journal* 52: 217–22.

Schmoller, H. 1974. The Paperback Revolution. In *Essays in the History of Publishing,* ed. Asa Briggs, 297–8. London: Longman.

Scholes, Robert. 1982. *Stillborn Literature.* Lincoln: University of Nebraska Press.

Schumer, Charles E. 2002. Schumer: New Federal Budget Cuts Endanger NYC Hospitals' Ability to Deal with Future Terror Attacks. Dec. 4. http://www.schumer.senate.gov/newsroom/press-releases.

Schwartz, Delmore. 1952. Masterpieces as Cartoons. *Partisan Review* 19(4): 461–71.

Schwartz, Lawrence D. 1988. *Creating Faulkner's Reputation: The Politics of Modern Literary Criticism.* Knoxville: University of Tennessee Press.

Seabrook, John. 2000. *Nobrow.* New York: Knopf.

Shafer, Ingrid. 1989. Non-Adversarial Criticism, Cross-Cultural Conversation, and Popular Literature. *Proteus* 6(Spring): 6–15.

Shelden, Michael. 1991. *Orwell: The Authorized Biography.* London: Minerva.

Shepard, Richard F. 1971. The Mafia Is Dying Out, Talese Concludes. *The New York Times* 22 November 22: 52.

Sherrill, John B. 1987. *Sanctuary* as Tragedy. *Arizona Quarterly* 43: 119–32.

Shiels, Maggie. 2010. Google Enters Digital Books War with Launch of Editions. *BBC News* 5 May. http://www.bbc.com/news/10098111.

Shriver, Lionel. 2013. How to Succeed as an Author: Give up on Writing. *The New Republic,* 24 October. http://www.newrepublic.com/article/115016/publishing-back-so-long-successful-authors-give-writing.

Shusterman, Richard. 1992. *Pragmatic Aesthetics: Living Beauty, Rethinking Art.* Oxford: Blackwell.

Shusterman, Richard. 1993. Too Legit to Quit? Popular Art and Legitimation. *Iyyun, The Jerusalem Philosophical Quarterly* 42 January: 215–24.

Shusterman, Richard. 1994–95. Popular Art and Education. *Studies in Philosophical Education* 13: 203–12.

Sjöwall, Maj, and Per Wahlöö. 1968. *The Laughing Policeman.* New York: Pantheon Books.

Sjöwall, Maj, and Per Wahlöö. 1972. *The Locked Room.* New York: Pantheon Books.

Skenazy, Paul. 1982. *The New Wild West: The Urban Mysteries of Dashiell Hammett and Raymond Chandler.* Boise: Boise State University.

Skenazy, Paul. 1997. Introduction. In *Raymond Chandler Speaking,* ed. Dorothy Gardiner and Kathrine Sorley Walker, 1–7. Berkeley: University of California Press.

Sklar, Robert. 1994. *Movie-Made America: A Cultural History of American Movies.* New York: Vintage.

Skvorecky, Josef. 1988. *Sins for Father Knox.* Toronto: Lester and Orpen Dennys. Trans. Kaca Polackova Henley.

Slote, Michael A. 1971. The Objectivity of Aesthetic Value Judgements. *Journal of Philosophy* 68: 821–39.

Snell, Susan. 1984. Phil Stone and William Faulkner: The Lawyer and 'The Poet'. *Mississippi College Law Review* 4: 169–92.

Sodeman, Melissa. 2015. *Sentimental Memorials: Women and the Novel in Literary History.* Stanford: Stanford University Press.

Soltysik Monnet, Agnieszka. 2010. *The Poetics and Politics of the American Gothic: Gender and Slavery in Nineteenth-Century American Literature.* Burlington, VT: Ashgate.

Sorensen, Alan, Jonah Berger, and Scott Rasmussen. 2010. Positive Effects of Negative Publicity: Can Negative Reviews Increase Sales? *Marketing Science* 29: 815–27. http://web.archive.org/web/20101008170304/http://www.stanford.edu/~asorense/papers/Negative_Publicity2.pdf.

Speir, Jerry. 1981. *Raymond Chandler.* New York: Ungar.

Spradley, James. 1976. The Revitalization of American Culture: An Anthropological Perspective. In *Qualities of Life. Critical Choices for Americans.* Vol. 7. Lexington, MA: Lexington Books.

Statistical Abstract of the United States. The National Data Book. 1999. 119th ed. Washington: US Census Bureau.

Steinberg, S.H. 1996. *Five Hundred Years of Printing. Revised edition,* ed. John Trevitt. London: The British Library and Oak Knoll Press.

Stephen, Knight. 2010. *Crime Fiction since 1800: Detection, Death, Diversity.* New York: Palgrave Macmillan.

Stossel, Scott. 2001. Elitism for Everyone. *The Atlantic,* 29 November. http://www.theatlantic.com/past/unbound/polipro/pp2001-11-29.htm.

Stowe, Harriet B. 1999. *Uncle Tom's Cabin.* New York: Chelsea House Publishers. (Orig. 1852).

Stowe, William W. 1986. Popular Fiction as Liberal Art. *College English* 48 November: 646–63.

Striphas, Ted. 2011. *The Late Age of Print: Everyday Book Culture from Consumerism to Control.* New York: Columbia University Press.

Strobel, Lee Patrick. 1980. *Ford's Pinto Trial: Reckless Homicide?* Indiana: South Bend.

Strong, Amy Lovell. 1993. Machines and Machinations: Controlling Desires in Faulkner's *Sanctuary. The Faulkner Journal* 9: 69–81.

Stuckey, William Joseph. 1981. *The Pulitzer Prize Novels: A Critical Backward Look,* 2nd ed. Norman: University of Oklahoma Press.

Sturm, Terry. 1991. *Popular Fiction.* Auckland: Oxford University Press.

Summers, Anthony, and Robbyn Swan. 2006. *Sinatra: The Life.* New York: Vintage.

Sundquist, Eric J. 1995. *Sanctuary:* An American Gothic. In *Douze lectures de Sanctuaire,* ed. Bleikasten Andre and Nicole Moulinoux, 83–101. Rennes: Presses Universitaires de Rennes.

Sutherland, John. 1981. *Bestsellers: Popular Fiction of the 1970s.* London: Routledge and Kegan Paul.

Swirski, Peter. 2005. *From Lowbrow to Nobrow.* Montreal, London: McGill-Queen's University Press.

Swirski, Peter. 2007a. A is for American, B is for Bad, C is for City: From Police to Urban Procedurals. In *All Roads Lead to the American City,* ed. Peter Swirski. Hong Kong: Hong Kong University Press.

Swirski, Peter. 2007b. *Of Literature and Knowledge: Explorations in Narrative Thought Experiments, Evolution, and Game Theory.* London, New York: Routledge.

Swirski, Peter. 2010a. *Ars Americana, Ars Politica: Partisan Expression and Nobrow American Culture.* Montreal, London: McGill-Queen's University Press.

Swirski, Peter. 2010b. *Literature, Analytically Speaking: Explorations in the Theory of Interpretation, Analytic Aesthetics, and Evolution.* Austin: University of Texas Press.

Swirski, Peter. 2011. *American Utopia and Social Engineering in Literature, Social Thought, and Political History.* New York: Routledge.

Swirski, Peter. 2013a. Literature and Culture in the Age of the New Media: Dynamics of Evolution and Change. In *Blackwell Companion to New Media Dynamics,* ed. John Hartley, Jean Burgess, and Axel Bruns. Oxford: Wiley-Blackwell.

Swirski, Peter. 2013b. *From Literature to Biterature: Lem, Turing, Darwin, and Explorations in Computer Literature, Philosophy of Mind, and Cultural Evolution.* Montreal, London: McGill-Queen's University Press.

Swirski, Peter. 2015. *American Political Fictions: War on Errorism in Contemporary American Literature, Culture, and Politics.* New York: Palgrave Macmillan.

Swirski, Peter. 2015. The Zettabyte Problem, or the End of Cultural History As We Know It. *The Montreal Review* August. http://www.themontrealreview.com/2009/The-Zettabyte-Problem.php.

Swirski, Peter. 2017. Nobrow, American Style. *In When Highbrow Meets Lowbrow: Popular Culture and the Rise of Nobrow,* eds. Swirski, Peter, and Tero Elias Vanhanen. New York: Palgrave Macmillan.

Swirski, Peter, and Faye Wong. 2006. Briefcases for Hire: American Hardboiled to Legal Fiction. *Journal of American Culture* 29(3): 307–20.

Swirski, Peter, and Tero Elias Vanhanen (eds.). 2017. *When Highbrow Meets Lowbrow: Popular Culture and the Rise of Nobrow.* New York: Palgrave Macmillan.

Symons, Julian. 1972. *Mortal Consequences: A History—From the Detective Story to the Crime Novel.* New York: Harper and Row.

Tanaka, Takako. 1994. What Horace Benbow Sees: Voyeurism, Narcissism, and Misogyny from *Flags in the Dust* to *Sanctuary. Faulkner Studies* 2. 27–41.

Tatarkiewicz, Władysław. 1974. *History of Aesthetics.* Trans. Adam and Ann Czerniawski, R.M. Montgomery, Chester Kisiel, and John F. Besemeres. The Hague: Mouton.

Tate, Allen. 1968. Faulkner's *Sanctuary* and the Southern Myth. *Virginia Quarterly Review: A National Journal of Literature and Discussion* 44: 418–27.

Tate, J.O. 1993. Double Talk, Double Play: Rewinding Raymond Chandler's *Playback. Clues* 14(1): 105–34.

Tebbel, John. 1995. The History of Book Publishing in the United States. In *International Book Publishing: An Encyclopedia*, ed. Philip G. Altbach and Edith S. Hoshino, 147–55. New York and London: Garland.

The Economist. 2015a. Dark Days. 25 April, 32.

The Economist. 2015b. Fixing America's Inner Cities. 9 May: 8.

The Telegraph. 2007. Revealed: ten commandments of the mafia. 7 November: http://www.telegraph.co.uk/news/worldnews/1568645/Revealed-Ten-Commandments-of-the-Mafia.html.

Thompson, George J. 2007. *Hammett's Moral Vision.* San Francisco: Vince Emery Productions.

Todd, Richard. 1996. *Consuming Fictions: The Booker Prize and Fiction in Britain Today.* London: Bloomsbury.

Todorov, Tzvetan. 1990. In *Genres in Discourse*, ed. Catherine Porter. Cambridge, MA: Cambridge University Press.

Toles, George. 1982. The Space Between: A Study of Faulkner's *Sanctuary*. In *Twentieth Century Interpretations of* Sanctuary: *A Collection of Critical Essays*, ed. John Douglas Canfield, 120–128. Englewood Cliffs: Prentice-Hall.

Tötösy de Zepetnek, Steven, and Philip Kreisel. 1992. Urban English-Speaking Canadian Literary Readership: Results of a Pilot Study. *Poetics* 21: 211–38.

Trevelyan, Laura. 2006. Double lives of New York's 'Mafia' cops. BBC News 7 April. http://news.bbc.co.uk/2/hi/americas/4889984.stm.

Troubridge, Laura. 1966. *Life Amongst the Troubridges.* London: Murray.

Tuchman, Barbara W. 1980. *The Book.* Washington, DC: Center for the Book, Library of Congress.

Turnbul, Andrew. 1962. *Scott Fitzgerald.* New York: Charles Scnbner's Sons.

Twain, Mark. 1940. *Mark Twain's Travels with Mr. Brown: Being Heretofore the Uncollected Sketches of Mark Twain Written for the Alta California.* Ed. Frankline Walker and G. Ezra Dane. New York: Knopf.

U.S. Department of Justice. 2004. Law Enforcement Statistics. 7 Sept. https://web.archive.org/web/20091208082354/http://www.ojp.usdoj.gov/bjs/lawenf.htm#LEMAS.

UNESCO. 2002. Book Production: Number of Titles by UDC Classes. *Statistics Yearbook 1999 46ed (Annuaire Statistique).* New York: United Nations Reproduction Section. *UNESCO Institute for Statistics* 4–6. https://web.archive.org/web/20040328192933/http://www.uis.unesco.org/TEMPLATE/html/CultAndCom/Table_IV_5_America.html.

University of Virginia. 1957. Faulkner at Virginia: Law School Wives. 16 May. http://faulkner.lib.virginia.edu/display/wfaudio15.

Urgo, Joseph. 1983. Temple Drake's Truthful Perjury: Rethinking Faulkner's *Sanctuary. American Literature* 55: 435–44.

Uspensky, Gleb, and Peter B. Kaufman. 1992. Fifty Million Agatha Christies Can Be Wrong. *Publishers Weekly* 9 November: 60–2.

Van den Haag, Ernest. 1957. Notes on American Popular Culture. *Diogenes* 17(Spring): 56–73.

Van den Haag, Ernest. 1971. A Dissent from the Consensual Society. In *Mass Culture Revisited*, eds. Bernard Rosenberg and David Manning White, 85–92. New York: Van Nostrand Reinhold.

Van, Dover, and J. Kenneth. 1995. *The Critical Response to Raymond Chandler*. Westport, CT: Greenwood Press.

Vanderbilt II, Arthur T. 1999. *The Making of a Bestseller*. Jefferson, NC: MacFarland.

Végső, Roland K. 2007. Faulkner in the Fifties: The Making of the Faulkner Canon. *Arizona Quarterly* 63(2): 81–107.

Vickery, Olga W. 1959. *The Novels of William Faulkner: A Critical Interpretation*. Baton Rouge: Louisiana State University Press.

Vivien, Miller, and Helen Oakley (eds.). 2012. *Cross-Cultural Connections in Crime Fictions*. New York: Palgrave Macmillan.

Waites, Bernard, Tony Bennett, and Graham Martin (eds.). 1982. *Popular Culture: Past and Present*. London: Croom Helm.

Walker, Tom. 2000. Tracking a terrorist DeMille adds to illustrious list. *Denver Post* 7 January. http://extras.denverpost.com/books/lion0109.htm.

Walling, George Washington. 1887. *Recollections of a New York Chief of Police: An Official Record of Thirty-Eight Years as a Patrolman, Detective, Captain, Inspector and Chief of the New York Police*. New York: Caxton Book Concern, Limited.

Walton, Priscilla L., and Manina Jones. 1999. *Detective Agency: Women Rewriting the Hard-Boiled Tradition*. Berkeley: University of California Press.

Warren, Robert Penn (ed.). 1966. *Faulkner: A Collection of Critical Essays*. Englewood Cliffs, NJ: Prentice-Hall.

Watermann, Stanley. 1998. Carnivals for Elites? The Cultural Politics of Arts Festivals. *Progress in Human Geography* 22(1): 54–74.

Watson, Jay. 1990. The Failure of Forensic Storytelling in *Sanctuary*. *The Faulkner Journal* 6: 47–66.

Watson, Jay. 1993. *Forensic Fictions: The Lawyer Figure in Faulkner*. Athens, GA: University of Georgia Press.

West, James L.W. 2o05). *The Cambridge Edition of the Works of F. Scott Fitzgerald*. Cambridge: Cambridge University Press.

Westlake, Donald E. 1996. *What's the Worst That Could Happen?* New York: Mysterious Press.

Whalen, Bernard, and John Whalen. 2014. *The NYPD's First Fifty Years: Politicians, Police Commissioners, and Patrolmen*. Nebrasca: University of Nebrasca/Potomac Books.

Whitaker's Books in Print 2000. 2000. Whitaker and Sons: London.

White, David Manning. 1957. Mass Culture in America: Another Point of View. In *Mass Culture: The Popular Arts in America*, eds. Bernard Rosenberg and David Manning White. Glenco, IL: Free Press.

White, David Manning. 1971. Mass Culture Revisited 2. In *Mass Culture Revisited*, eds. Bernard Rosenberg and David Manning White. New York: Van Nostrand Reinhold.

Whitehurst Stone, Emily. 1965. Faulkner Gets Started. *The Texas Quarterly* 8: 142–8.

Whiteside, Thomas. 1980. Onward and upward with the Arts: The Blockbuster Complex. *New Yorker,* 29 September: 48–101; 6 October: 63–146; 13 October: 52–143.

Whiteside, Thomas. 1981. *The Blockbuster Complex: Conglomerates, Show Business, and Book Publishing.* Middletown, CT: Wesleyan University Press.

Williams, Tom. 2012. *A Mysterious Something in the Light: The Life of Raymond Chandler.* Chicago: Chicago Review Press.

Wilson, Andrew J. 1994. The Corruption in Looking: William Faulkner's *Sanctuary* as a Detective Novel. *Mississippi Quarterly* 47: 441–60.

Wolfe, Peter. 1985. *Something More Than Night: The Case of Raymond Chandler.* Bowling Green: Popular Press.

Wolfe, Thomas. 1986. *The Web and the Rock.* New York: Harper and Row. (Orig. 1939).

Woolf, Virginia. 1942. Middlebrow. In *The Death of the Moth*, 113–9. London: Hogarth Press.

Wright, David. 2012. Literary Taste and List Culture in a Time of 'Endless Choice'. In *From Codex to Hypertext: Reading at the Turn of the Twenty-First Century*, ed. Anouk Lang, 108–23. Amherst: University of Massachusetts Press.

Wuensche, Robert. 2002. Hot Topic Enron: The Pride and the Fall. *Houston Chronicle* 20 October. http://www.chron.com/cs/CDA/story.hts/special/enron/1624822.

Zalesky, Jeff. 1998. The Big Bad City. *Publishers Weekly* 245 (49) 7 Dec: 54.

Zeliger, Daniel. 2013. The Boston Book Festival Returns for Fifth Year. *ArtsEditor,* 11 October. http://www.artseditor.com/html/newsitems/1013_bookfest.shtml.

Zuidervaart, Lambert, and Henry Luttikhuizen (eds.). 2000. *The Arts, Community, and Cultural Democracy.* New York: St. Martin's.

INDEX

Note: Page number followed by 'n' refers to end notes.

© The Editor(s) (if applicable) and The Author(s) 2016
P. Swirski, *American Crime Fiction*,
DOI 10.1007/978-3-319-30108-2